Invention: The Art of Liberal Arts

First published by Respondeo Books in 2020
www.respondeobooks.com

Respondeo Books
P.O. Box 5648
Santa Fe, NM 87502
United States

　　Publisher's Cataloging-in-Publication Data
　　Names: Lee, J. Scott, 1948-, author.
　　Title: Invention: The art of liberal arts / J. Scott Lee
　　Description: Includes bibliographical references. | Santa Fe, NM: Respondeo
　　　　Books, 2020.
　　Identifiers: LCCN: 2020938959 | ISBN: 978-0-9993059-5-9
　　Subjects: LCSH Education, Humanistic. | Education, Higher--United States. |
　　　　Education, Higher--Curricula--United States. | Education--Philosophy. |
　　　　Critical thinking. | BISAC EDUCATION / Higher | LANGUAGE ARTS
　　　　& DISCIPLINES / Rhetoric
　　Classification: LCC LA227.3 .L44 2020 | DDC 378.73--dc23

Book design by Adam Robinson

INVENTION

THE ART OF
LIBERAL ARTS

J. SCOTT LEE

Respondeo Books
Santa Fe, NM

For Bruce Kimball from whom I learned much.

"For there was a time when human beings wandered at large in the fields like animals and lived on wild fare; they did nothing by the guidance of reason, but relied chiefly on physical strength. There was yet no ordered system of religious worship or social duties. No one had seen legitimate marriage nor had anyone looked upon children whom they knew to be their own. Nor had they learned the advantages of an equitable code of law.

At this juncture a man—great and wise I am sure—became aware of the power latent in man and the wide field offered by the mind for great achievement if one could develop this power and improve it by instruction... To me, at least, it does not seem possible that a mute and voiceless wisdom could have turned humans suddenly from their habits and introduced them to different patterns of life...

This is the way eloquence came into being..."

—Cicero, *De Inventione* I, 2-3

Table of Contents

Section II
Making Liberal Arts Education

Augustine's Confessions, Pygmalion, *and some research on general education lead to appreciating a small liberal arts college's achievement.*

From the student's standpoint, Bernard Shaw's Pygmalion *offers a comic view of higher education and independence. Also, it issues a warning—to students and faculty—about programs designed to shape character.*

Visits with faculty in Colombia and Taiwan explore the Torah and the Bible, the Phaedrus, *the* Analects, *and* Don Quixote: *liberal arts, four educational ideas, and selecting core texts in a global context.*

The defenses of liberal education are ecologically thin. Seeing invention and technē as chief sources of transformation and change might help faculty to open students and their programs to the world of innovation.

Section III
Curricula as Objects of Art

Research indicates that faculty across the country have been engaged in innovation within institutions in general education and core text curricula. Young faculty might consider the choice of Odysseus *in the* Republic.

The inclination to rectify the past with building in the present contests with acting in the present to build an unknown future. Dido and Aeneas share art, experience, but not education which makes a difference to their futures.

Section IV
Poetic Coda

Aristotle's Poetics *can lead us to build curricula of core texts that aim at a loving joy in inventive learning for its own sake, shared by a community that takes freedom and invention as its greatest good.*

Appendices

Additional Material at RESPONDEOBOOKS.COM

AN AFFIRMATION IN A CRISIS

As we were finishing the editing of this book, coronavirus swept the world with contagion, death, and fear. Governments clamped down on congregations of people. Many businesses simply stopped operation. Others laid off workers. Social clubs and eating at restaurants with friends gave way to drive-by pick-ups. Shelves in groceries were bare of essentials. People around the world began to self-isolate. Some have already been irretrievably lost. More will be. Health effects and the economic dislocations will last for months, possibly years.

Was this, is this a time for a book proclaiming that art, invention and the liberal arts are priceless? Is liberal arts education, the many inventions in the arts and sciences of ordinary human beings, something to pay attention to now? Is art what we need – yes, need – in a world-wide disaster and in the future as we recover?

Absolutely and unequivocally.

When Leningrad faced the Nazi threat, surrounded, with over a million inhabitants starved to death within its barricades, Shostakovich's Symphony 7 played by the remaining musicians of the city and broadcast both to its inhabitants and the Russian people turned the tide. Germans could hear the broadcast and as one former soldier outside the gates said, "we knew we would lose the war."

Olga Berggolts stepped to the microphone of the radio of Leningrad to read her poems, written under bombardment, to her fellow citizens. Night after night the radio broadcast speeches, poetry, and music to lift people spiritually, in part by reminding them that life was normal, that is, precious and creative. This is what human beings do in a crisis and in better times: they invent.

No less is true now. People are using inventions and the arts to break their isolation, to offer cheer and hope, even to build plans for the future. In the worst-struck country of Europe, Maurizio Marchini sings opera from his balcony in Florence. Italians are literally hanging out windows singing to each other their national anthem and popular songs.

They sing because they know the power of the musical art and its inventions to free them to be themselves as a people. They sing because they learned it in their education. Having been taught to sing, they take joy in singing to each other.

Without that teaching and learning, without the inventions of arts and sciences, none of this joy in the human spirit would have been possible.

The art of humanistic liberal arts education gives us the inventive power and freedom to act with courage and hope. STEM professionals, economists, business people, and politicians matter, and they will invent vaccines, economic rescue plans, and policies to help people around the world. Underlying recovery, more than anything, is the education of a people, the freedom and invention of the arts, the power of speeches, written words, images, music, communicating--in other words, the power of the liberal arts to invent the possibilities we need and yearn for. These possibilities bind people together to build a better world.

To the victims, heroes, and peoples of the coronavirus pandemic, we join you in song. With confidence for a better future, we inscribe this book.

J. Scott Lee, author
Philip Lecuyer, publisher
Martha C. Franks, editor

FOREWORD

I n what is perhaps his most widely-read text, *The Vocation Lectures*, Max Weber articulates something most of us already have some awareness of: taking up science or politics as a *vocation* and not simply an occupation is something quite out of the ordinary. That person *lives for* his pursuit; he does not simply *live from* it. They are "all in", as the expression goes. Scott Lee long ago found his vocation in promoting the cause of liberal arts education in America and across the globe. Like the liberal arts themselves, Scott's vocation bridges the gap between science, art, or scholarship, on the one hand, and politics on the other. For one must understand the liberal arts in order to properly defend them.

Each of the essays in this volume is interesting in its own right; together, they constitute a kind of roadmap of the path Scott has taken in pursuing this vocation. They thus stand as a monument to decades of work he put into the defense of liberal arts education and the promotion of core texts programs. They explore the nature of, and the best ways to defend, the liberal arts. Most importantly, the book is not simply a collection. It is structured to make an argument about the nature and purpose of the liberal arts, and how those arts might be best deployed in the modern world.

I first met Scott in the early years of the existence of the Association for Core Texts and Courses (ACTC). Any one of the thousands of people who have attended an ACTC conference in the past 25 years will have met Scott Lee. He leaves an indelible impression as someone both artfully and passionately committed to the promotion of the liberal arts. No one could fail to be impressed by the driving energy that has gone into the making of ACTC. Nor could they fail to be even more impressed by the artful manner of his labors. ACTC is thus exemplary: it is a successful invention of the liberal arts.

This book consists of papers and speeches Scott has given over the course of his work as one of the founders and the long-time Executive Director of ACTC. Readers of all political stripes and interpretive camps will find them of interest. For, like ACTC itself, Scott's thinking defies easy slotting into one of the conventional categories so often used to discuss great books, core texts, the tension between teaching and research, educational reform, defending the humanities, and the future of the liberal arts. There are many good books on these matters. This unique volume of speeches and essays deserves reading by anyone seriously interested in thinking about the liberal arts.

Several distinctive themes are explored in this volume. I would draw your attention to three. To begin, the book calls our attention to, and entices us to think about, the fact that discussions of liberal arts education typically focus on the meaning of "liberal" as opposed to the meaning of "art." It thus poses the following question: can we come to understand more deeply the liberal arts by understanding what an art is? One of the most important themes of the book is that we can learn something valuable about the liberal arts by way of thinking about the *arts* of liberal arts education. Indeed, the question of art structures the entire book.

A second distinctive theme of this work is how those who would preserve and promote the liberal arts typically defend their cause. What is their rhetorical strategy and how successful is it proving? The book moves from exploring the idea of art and *technē* of liberal arts education to "enriching the ecology" of arguments for the liberal arts. While it is true that the liberal arts can be defended by establishing their value in better educating citizens in a democracy, by teaching critical thinking skills, by making us life-long learners, and so on, these are but the latent functions of the liberal arts and not their primary one. Instead we need to grasp the central argument for the liberal arts which is derived from their manifest function in educating us to freedom.

A third distinctive theme is the articulation of the idea of core texts, and how they are used to constitute courses and programs. The idea of a core text moves away from the narrower idea of a great book in two obvious ways. Texts are a wider class of things than books, including seminal science papers and experiments, film, dramas, musical productions, and the plastic arts—all of which are significant products of human ingenuity. Moreover, a text may be a "core text" without being a "great" or "classic" work. It may not be "canonical"; it may be too new or little known to be classic. Furthermore, it may be a Western or non-Western text, for core texts are universal texts. They speak to what is universally human and not simply to what is culturally particular. This argument is well stated in the following way: "especially with regard to questions of students working across disciplines or inventing arguments … a more capacious view of what counts as a classical work would reward our students."

A key argument made here is that one discovers something essential about the liberal arts by way of reflecting upon the activity of *invention* of core texts and programs. This *making* is done by liberal artists, so to speak. For those of us involved in teaching liberal arts, we can come to understand something about ourselves by such reflection. We thus ask the question: who are we? We also ask the question of how we come to the *inventio* of core texts. Is this *inventio* based on criteria we create or ones we discover? Perhaps, as is argued here, it is a combination of both.

Core text courses and programs allow us to counter some of the harmful consequences of the specialization and resulting "silo effect" that is now characteristic of modern higher education. We must, as a matter of necessity, train people for various technical pursuits. We need experts, scholars, and scientists. This need dictates specialization. And yet, at the same time we are now all too aware of the risks we run, and the resulting dangers we may confront, from producing "voluptuaries without heart and specialists without vision." We are inescapably broad-minded. So, we are here reminded in this book of something essentially important about liberal education. "The proper use of education, and particularly the liberal arts, is to render students capable of making available to themselves the world's cultural resources in order to construct a future." What kind of education could be more important than this?

Dr. Patrick Malcolmson
Professor Emeritus
St. Thomas University
Canada

INTRODUCTION

Invention is the heart of the liberal arts, and the liberal arts are themselves the road to the arts, sciences, and a better life for all of us. Invention is the future and we owe what we are to invention. The liberal arts not only offer hope for the future and explain the tragedies and triumphs of the past—in civilizations around the globe as well as in the West—but they form the very ground of change, ancient to modern. This means nothing less than that they are the basis of intellectual and productive freedom. Though our political rights afford us a kind of guarantee that we may practice such freedoms, and though humans had to work hard to start civilizations that materially supported intellectual and productive freedom, historically and epistemically invention and the liberal arts come before the political and economic *rights* we exercise. As such, if properly taught and offered, either in conjunction with majors or taught separately as a degree, liberal arts send baccalaureate graduates into the world prepared to change it for the better, to invent a new world—just as those who came before them did.

The key to invention is art—*technē* in the broadest, Greek sense of the word. As such, art roams in the domain of the sciences, forms, uses, and helps to advance them. It produces works across the arts and sciences of incalculable value to women and men, around the globe, for shaping a better future. Art shapes our world through *technology,* and there is a realm of technology of the liberal arts that is at best neglected and fractured in our undergraduate curricula. Change that fracturing and neglect and we change undergraduate education.

There are three areas of neglect. The first is what our students in North America and around the world read—together—as a part of a shared curriculum. Some institutions, some faculty and administrators do provide opportunities to read shared 'world classics'—core texts of major cultural and epistemic significance. Such institutions are named and discussed in this volume, but these opportunities are not widely required, provided or, even, available in institutions offering the B.A. or the B.S., in short, by institutions with arts/humanities and science majors and departments.

The second area of neglect is exemplified by the common practice of supposing rhetoric to be adequately taught by a writing requirement, focusing on basic imitations of academic writing and research, along with a math requirement that is taught as a baseline out of what students knew in high school. None of this is an exploration of the liberal arts or an exemplification of their historical foundations and range extending into modernity. Too frequently a range of student performances and products depending on the liberal arts and easily displayed in public is ignored, at least as a common requirement for graduation. These problems and their consequences are explored in this volume. The greatest consequence of this neglect is that students have only a very restricted sense of the possibilities and intellectual freedom open to them when they graduate.

The third area of neglect is ineffective outreach and conveyance by the humanities and higher education institutions of past achievements and of possibilities for the future of freedom that liberal arts education teaches its students. I mean that, despite efforts to reverse the low regard by the public of humanistic liberal education, especially after the Great Recession of 2008, defensive arguments apparently have not been effective because they ignore persuasives inherent in the liberal arts. All three areas of neglect are intertwined, but in my career they manifested themselves somewhat sequentially over time.

The orientation of our colleges and universities towards and

the constant stream of statistics about employment and salary prospects, particularly for humanities graduates, does real and extensive harm to education for freedom. True, this emphasis has been part of college recruitment from almost the very first and in recent years the data suggest that, in particular, humanities graduates do well enough in employment issues.[1] Yes, the argument that you ought to 'get what you pay for' in the form of a job or career, and the argument that humanities and liberal arts majors are facing costs of education that are too high for the reward, do seem like powerful arguments. Sadly, years of economic statistics showing reasonable salaries, employability well beyond being a 'barista,' high job satisfaction, and compensation closure between humanities graduates and engineers has done nothing to improve recruitment in the humanities and liberal arts or, seemingly, to prevent program reductions, while throwing public attention off what the humanities and liberal arts education accomplish.[2]

---

1   Frederick Rudolph, *Curriculum: A History of the American Undergraduate Course of Study since 1636*. San Francisco: Josey-Bass Publishers, 1987, p. 14. "As Christopher Jencks and David Reisman put it: 'The question always has been *how* an institution mixed the academic with the vocational, not *whether* it did so." Rudolph notes that "the [American] course of study had always to some degree—except perhaps at St. John's since the 1930's and for a time at the University of Chicago—been relevant to the practical affairs of men, intentionally oriented towards social utility."

2   Studies have repeatedly shown that the graduates of liberal arts and humanities fare well, especially over time: HTTPS://WWW.AACU.ORG/ NCHEMS-REPORT (2014). The problem of public perception when liberal education is cast as employment training appears to be two-fold; first is the cost issue of college in relation to the average humanities major's compensation after graduation which is $ 52,000, "less than the median for all graduates ($60,000) and much less than those in engineering ($ 82,000.)" Scott Jaschik, "Shocker: Humanities Grads Gainfully Employed and Happy: Data Suggests STEM majors are not the only route to success." WWW.INSIDEHIGHERED.COM, February 7, 2018. See, also, the summary of college costs HTTPS://WWW.USNEWS. COM/EDUCATION/BEST-COLLEGES/PAYING-FOR-COLLEGE/ARTICLES/ PAYING-FOR-COLLEGE-INFOGRAPHIC which is based on several federal

Alternatively, we can organize these persuasive efforts around freedom. Freedom—the world available at your call, *and* the ability to speak and write in public, analyze mathematically what a company needs, bring people of different backgrounds and knowledge to work on a problem, know how to advance the cause of a non-profit, see or craft an innovation to solve a problem or bring light to an issue—in short, the ability to think about what you want to think about and craft a way to do it? Priceless. And if that's not enough, do a little accounting about future prospects: what is a student's intellectual freedom worth to her or him one, five, ten years or a lifetime out?

We are talking about freedom of thought, *a joy of learning* brought on by learning to know the world's inventions through the arts and sciences that produced them. The path offered in this book is particular, and it will not appeal to all faculty, administrators or students. Also, frankly, there are other paths to freedom in liberal educations. For example, there is a kind of liberal education that relies on close contact with students. I was principal investigator of a U.S. DOE, Fund for Improvement of Post-Secondary

---

government surveys. The second problem appears to be that the public is not convinced of post-graduation employability, perhaps because there is no such thing as a "humanities" job (save in education) as there is an "engineering" job. In the face of this public resistance, William Adams argues we need to double-down on locating humanities skills within the workplace. (See Jaschik, above.) Yet, humanities majors have just as much success in entering medical school as do their physical science or social science competitors. HTTP://WWW.SAVVYPREMED.COM/ SAVVY-PRE-MED/2014/9/23/WHICH-MAJOR-IS-MOST-LIKELY-TO-GET-INTO-MEDICAL-SCHOOL, (data provided by the Association of American Medical Colleges.) Despite all this effort, cuts and fear of them in liberal arts/humanities programs roll on: HTTPS://WWW.INSIDEHIGHERED. COM/NEWS/2019/06/06/CUTS-LEAVE-CONCERNS-LIBERAL-ARTS-TULSA. (Jaschik, Inside Higher Education), June 9, 2019. In short, no amount of statistical persuasion has worked since the Recession.

This footnote was written before the economic havoc wrought by COVID-19. If 2008 is any parallel for post-2020, the persuasive inadequacy of market arguments will only be reinforced.

Education (FIPSE) supported, "Assessing Trends in the Liberal Arts Core," (*Trends*) project composed of data collection and campus interviews with students, faculty, and administrators, involving the general education developments and causes for change between 1978 and 1998 in 66 colleges and universities across the United States (later expanded to 81 institutions, extended to 2002). As I note in Chapter 8:

> Faculty cooperation is the truly amazing story of *Trends*. Faculty from every discipline worked together to develop new general education curricula, and, then, focused student recruitment, orientation, housing, alignment of courses into learning communities, co-operative faculty learning teams, and the development of supplemental instruction, especially for at-risk students, on the general education curriculum. I said earlier that we were looking in the pool of general education to find liberal education. Though often not liberal-arted in the curriculum, the cooperation I just outlined was, nevertheless, motivated by concerns for the students that were very much like the traditions of the liberal arts, particularly in core curricula where common courses and readings are found.

Also there is the "Oxford" model in which a student crafts her own 'general education' and 'major' with the help of faculty advisors. Finally, there is the "liberal-free" ideal, typologized and documented by Bruce Kimball, characterized by required categories of multiple choices of courses within general education and, of course, choice of major; this general degree structure is centered around the faculty's freedom to do research and to teach what they want, a freedom derived from the German university and transferred to American institutions. Each of these are forms of freedom found in liberal education programs and institutions.

That said, none of these roads offer the sweep across the foundations of disciplines and, also, the corresponding inventions of the liberal arts, qua arts, that produced the works of knowledge—epistemic, political, poetic, and technical—that are not only relied upon in the West, but are found in other civilizations as well. Sweep and invention across time and world characterize the road to freedom of core text programs in liberal arts education. It takes a special kind of student and a special kind of faculty to aspire to such an education.

Some Enlightenment thinkers were concerned with freedom in nature. Rousseau tells us that "humans are born free and are everywhere in chains." Locke argued the ground of intellectual freedom was in made things—property—which were to be contrasted to the productions of nature. By reversing the Aristotelian account of the production of art, Locke argued that through labor humans extracted and appropriated from nature property: "Before the appropriation of land, he who gathered as much of the wild fruit [etc.,] as he could; he that so employed his pains about any of the spontaneous products of nature… by placing his labor on them did thereby acquire a property in them."[3] The rise of land property and its agriculture prior to government and, thus, prior to relations of state to state[4] brings with them the problem of preservation of value. The invention of money, particularly the acceptance of gold, is the solution, since it does not devalue (at least through wastage) over time, while money permits enlargement of an estate.[5] The construction of money and its consensual acceptance created an entirely new situation in human history, "as degrees of industry were apt to give men possessions in different proportions, so this invention of money gave them the opportunity to continue and enlarge them."[6] Locke is a philosopher of ideas; the unstated import of his argument is the making of intellectual freedom, for the invention and durability of money allowed human beings to *plan, to look ahead* to something other than the immediate use of

---

3   John Locke. *The Second Treatise of Government*. Edited by Thomas P. Pearson. NY: Macmillan Publishing Company (1690), 1952, 23.

4   Ibid., 27.

5   Ibid. 23, 27, 29.

6   Ibid., 28. Alexis de Tocqueville's *Democracy in America* invokes a number of the points above about the relation between wealth and cultivation, Volume 2, Part I, Chapter 9 and 10.

what was given them through their labor, and *to experiment or invent* to increase their productivity. To put this starkly, *the invention of money freed the mind.*

There were, of course, other inventions that contributed equally to the construction of intellectual freedom. The most obvious of these were the invention of writing apparently through some form of accounting.[7] Following close on were the schooling of scribes and the invention of a phonetic alphabet, uniting speech and writing.

What matters about these inventions is that they were the making of positive conditions for freedom. As is argued in this book, before rights were recognized, there were positive accounts of the development of artistic freedom. Locke's argument was not about virtues and vices, but about the development of human power, arts and freedom. Landed gentry or professionals of the American revolution certainly thought, in constructing the American Constitution, that they were "securing the blessings of liberty to ourselves and our posterity." More centrally for the argument of these essays, the soft, imperfect parallel of the rise of American education to the prohibition of state support of religion has been an act of freedom. To state a premise of this work: though American higher education institutions were originally constructed as quasi-religious/state enterprises with many colleges having clerical boards of directors, they were serving secular purposes as well, and shortly after Independence began a move out of state and sometimes out of religious control.[8] This is to say that both transmission and creation of knowledge were originally independent of direct government and, often, formal religious control. This is not to say that religious and democratic sensibilities did not inform early institutions.[9] Most early developments of the

---

7   Andrew Robinson, *The Story of Writing: Alphabets, Hieroglyphs, and Pictograms.* London, Thames and Hudson, 1995, p. 62.

8   Rudolph, Ibid, pp. 7-8

9   Albert Delbanco, *College: What It Was, Is, and Should Be*, Princeton University Press, 2012, speaks to origins, 39-40. Samuel Schuman in

American college were constructed by clergy and scholars, not by government agencies, and the concern with professions and career training, not to mention providing an engine of knowledge for economic production, are well documented. That independence of American institutions, that 'start-up' quality, has had a profound and enduring effect on the pluralistic inventiveness of American higher education, particularly at the undergraduate level.

In the United States it is hard to appreciate just how precious such freedom within higher education institutions is. As part of my work with the Association for Core Texts and Courses (ACTC), a team of ACTC members traveled to Kazakhstan, Kyrgyzstan, and Tajikistan in 2001 to help in a curricular core text project organized by the Aga Khan Humanities Project (AKHP). At the end of the project, representatives from all six AKHP institutions met in Dushanbe for a summary meeting about progress. At the dinner afterward, I sat with a member of the AKHP team, with a faculty-party 'minder' from Almaty University, and with the Minister of Education of Tajikistan. The Almaty faculty member argued that his brother, who studied in St. Louis, rarely saw students in the library; for that Almaty faculty member, students had to be in the classroom to be studying. The Minister of Education argued that he needed to control the nascent Tajik institutions because they all needed to be developing in the same way. I rejoined that at least in the U.S., American institutions trusted and guided

---

Seeing the Light argues, correctly, that all early American colleges were religiously founded, but that "all initially served religious and secular purposes, and all the [original colonial] colleges have evolved into religiously unaffiliated institutions today." More importantly, "in 1816…the legislature of the state of New Hampshire attempted to assert its control over Dartmouth College…In 1819, the Supreme Court sided with the college…In effect, the Dartmouth case marks the point at which the colonial system of higher education as a kind of joint enterprise of the church and state bifurcates," pp. 30-31. Neither are we ignoring the establishment of land-grant colleges (1862) nor the vast growth of state supported institutions. To varying degrees, the autonomy of boards, hiring of qualified presidents, and independence of faculty have been a constant theme of American higher education.

their students to study independently, while faculty developed an enormous range of programs, particularly in liberal education. My (female) colleague and team leader of the AKHP tried, in front of this table, to explain how students were blossoming with the texts they were reading and the pedagogical projects that they were undertaking. Alas, it all fell on deaf ears, not simply because of gender, ideology, or power, but because these men themselves had no education that would allow them to possess the concepts we indicated. Neither of these men *could conceive of* 'independence,' 'investment' (students actually studying at home or with other students), 'invention', or 'competition' amongst institutions.[10]

I have given some indication of the scope of the *Trends* project. The AKHP project gives some indication that the arguments, evidence, and conclusions which this book offers apply in wider contexts than might at first appear. From the first ACTC was international in the sense that it was a North American association and it never advocated one model or endorsed any given program. Whatever echoes its 1996 mission statement contained of Matthew Arnold's "best that has been thought and said," ACTC was committed from the first to curricula drawing upon "Western and other traditions" and attracting faculty and administrators from those traditions. At its conferences and in its proceedings one would find representatives from such institutions as Beijing Institute of Technology, Boya College of Sun Yat-sen University, The Chinese University of Hong Kong, Singapore University of Technology and Design, Taiwan's National Chiao Tung University, Universidad de Navarra, University of Amsterdam, University of Winchester, Universidad Francisco Marroquin (in Guatemala), Universidad de Tecnológica de Bolivar (Columbia), and Zayed University. Attendees from those countries presented their curricular developments, emphasizing core texts from those regions. The late Ted de Bary and Rachel Cheung at Columbia University

---

10   J. Scott Lee. *Report to the Mellon Foundation on the Aga Khan Humanities Project* elaborates the AKHP achievements and the particular dinner discussed above. See the RESPONDEOBOOKS.COM website.

introduced me to many colleagues from China. A number of the European institutions mentioned above organized conferences with my encouragement on core texts in Europe which drew attendees from the States and Asia as well as Europe. Additionally, I traveled to Qatar for work on what core text education might contribute in the fight against terrorism.

Not surprisingly the principles of innovation and tradition are adaptable anywhere. Institutions around the world look to U.S. higher education and in particular the traditions of 'great books' or core texts to build new programs, but this is not hegemony. All work with institutions was pluralistic and inductive. As programs are differentially developed through institutional traditions, linguistic and scientific materials are selectively employed by faculty of those institutions. Abroad, these are united—in ways rarely possible in the U.S.—to new forms of curricula employing Western, Eastern, and/or Moslem traditions. Domestically, no less is true of the Cherokee, HBCU's, and colleges of various religious and secular traditions that ACTC worked with. The influence of these traditions on my own thinking appears in this book, particularly in the chapters on "Globalizing Undergraduate Education Using Core Texts," "Enriching Liberal Education's Defense," and the appendix on "The Concept of Core Texts," but the influence is far wider and deeper than represented in this volume.[11]

---

11   Not illustrated is the NEH-funded project "Wiping Away the Tears" offered with the extensive cooperation by the Cherokee Nation, involving Mary Ellen Meredith with the cooperation of Chief Chad Smith (HTTPS://WWW.CORETEXTS.ORG/INSTITUTE/PROJECTS-AND-GRANTS/ NEH-LANDMARKS-OF-AMERICAN-HISTORY-GRANT/). Some work with particular institutions is represented, but not included were papers delivered at HBCU institutions, including Kentucky State University, Lincoln University, and Norfolk State University. Also not included was work with Brent Cedja, community colleges, and the National Council of Instructional Administrators. Recently, Temple University worked with ACTC's Liberal Arts Institute on a special topic conference on "Women and Core Texts" organized by Genevieve Amaral and Douglas Greenfield while Chinese University of Hong Kong, Concordia University of Irvine, New York University, Pepperdine University, with

This book celebrates the inventiveness of administrators and professors of disciplines and departments who have over the last century constructed curricula which span disciplines, eras, and civilizations. These educators come from the sciences, the arts, and the humanities and they have reached out to colleagues to build together in selected institutions better educations for their students.

In pursuit of invention, this book straddles theory, practice, and products of core text, liberal *arts* education. Its rhetoric is based on original research data gathering and 'ethnographies' of the evolution of general, liberal education programs in a wide cross-section of American and overseas institutions; the titles, abstracts and content of 24 years of ACTC Annual Conferences papers and panels; ACTC's summer seminars and site-visits to institutions around the globe; data, evaluations, and reports of its projects to five national agencies and foundations; and, finally, the research I conducted into the bibliography of liberal arts education. Any mistakes in the research or interpretations are mine, but the course of my work both at the American Academy for Liberal Education (as the *Trends* principal investigator) and at ACTC provided the basis and opportunities to develop the views on invention and the liberal arts found in this book.

In using the term "liberal arts," we begin, historically and espistemologically, in the *septem artes*, containing the sciences of the quadrivium and the arts of the trivium found in organized

---

help from the Lilly Fellows, organized a conference on "Global General Education and Core Texts: What Should Students Read?" ACTC also engaged in more 'traditional' special topic conferences, as well. We inaugurated ACTC Student Conferences with the help of Timothy Fuller of Colorado College. These have become bi-annual and international affairs. At Saint Mary's College of California in 2006, we held the "Trends in the Liberal Arts Core: Cooperative Integration Between the Humanities and the Sciences" special topic conference. In 2013, at Notre Dame, with Phillip Sloan's help, we held the "Research University and the Liberal Arts College" conference. And in 2014, with the help of Dan Cullen and Jane Rodeheffer, we held a conference at Rhodes College on "Religion and Secular Cores."

curricula or found as formulated and used outside of universities. The meaning of the term is expanded by four considerations in this book: the invention of modern sciences with the seven liberal arts as an important part of their origins; the science of poetics particularly as conceived by Aristotle; the continued development of the 'trivium' and the 'quadrivium' through works of the Renaissance in Alberti's *On Painting* and Botticelli's *Adoration* paintings and more modern textual developments of the trivium found in an Appendix syllabus on "Rejuvenating and Reinventing the Liberal Arts"; finally, these arts receive extension through their products which are discussed throughout the book. (There are parallels to liberal arts in other cultures: e.g., calligraphy.) A discussion of how art is used in this book appears in Chapter 1. Discussions of the range and function of invention appear in Chapters, 2, 7, and 10. How the liberal arts and invention result in curricula, student experience, and assessment are found in Chapters 2, 3, 4, 5, 8, and 10. Chapters 1, 6, 7, 9, and 10 discuss the use (and non-use) of core texts in liberal arts curricula. Two appendices address the concept of core texts and how our persuasive efforts must turn us towards demonstrating our activities before the public, also discussed in Chapter 1. Textually-based papers representing, classroom liberal arts approaches to artistic invention, gender, student judgment, and assessment have been placed on the website at RESPONDEOBOOKS.COM.

Yet, for all the inventiveness—recognized or not—in liberal arts education, the liberal arts and their close partners, the humanities, are taking it on the chin. In a recent *Wall Street Journal* Review, "Stop Worrying about the 'Death' of the Humanities" (that echoes some of the arguments in Chapter 1 of this book), Adam Kirsch implies, somewhat inadvertently, an insight for the direction toward which academic humanities, at least in its teaching function, might turn. The basic assertion is that

> the real action [of humanistic culture] takes place outside the classroom, in theatres, concert halls, art galleries and libraries, or simply in living rooms where people read and think. Being a successful literature or history or art major requires

different skills than the ones needed to make these things part of one's inner life.

If that last statement is true, a couple of consequences would seem to be true, as well. First, the departments of institutions which house the humanities are generally (not always) cut off from the surrounding cultural institutions which are of enormous concern to them, the productions of which are their natural staff of life. More importantly it would appear that graduates of colleges and universities are 'acting' spontaneously or habitually in discussing "humanistic culture." Are they acting artfully? Might they intend more, see more, talk more, and support more if their discussions were artful? These are not ancillary questions: the liberal arts are universal arts that relate not only different subjects but *human beings to each other* across knowledge, action, and production. These arts are really the *primes inter pares* of shared knowledge for connecting one person to another and different groups to each other, including academics to the public.

Kirsch never mentions the liberal arts, but if the humanities want support for their activities, they might turn in a fulsome way to cultivating the liberal arts which *everyone* can carry out to 'where the action is.' Also, Kirsch is writing *publicly* about "the things that humanists cherish: free thought and free expression, the quest for beauty and truth." It might be worthwhile to the academy and to the public to see that 'liberal-arted' public and tête-à-tête conversations about 'humanistic culture' are a vote of confidence in 'our' culture (in all its diversity) and in ourselves.[12]

---

12   April 26, 2019 print edition of the *WSJ*. Much of the debate about the state of the humanities, so often reflected by discussions about English degrees, is, rightly, about whether the humanities have cut themselves off from the public. Kirsch says that "For reasons good and bad, the humanities today are focused on critique rather than celebration." No one doubts that art and culture is discussed in critique, but Andrew Kay set off a firestorm about the future of English as a discipline in a *Chronicle of Higher Education* article, "Academe's Extinction Event: Failure, Whiskey and Professional Collapse at the MLA," 5/10/2019, in part because he

A line of argument in this book is that liberal education, particularly through the humanities, needs intentionally—through

---

centered his article on questions of whether critique had built anything.
Possibly most damning was a paper Kay quoted by Anna Kornbluh, of
the University of Illinois at Chicago:

> Her thesis was unsparing. 'We have rhapsodized demolition as liber-
> ation while literally laying ruin to the university,' she argued, 'a horror
> to be beheld by future historians — in the unlikely event there are
> any.' Literary theorists, by prizing an ethos of destruction in the name
> of freedom, had ironically aligned themselves with the external forces
> — political, administrative — that had for years conspired to obliter-
> ate the institution in which they work.

In a later interview with Kay, Kornbluh continued, "We need to build up
animating stories about how reading, writing, and thinking support human
flourishing." In short, cut off from the culture by 'theory' which destroys
her institution and discipline, Kornbluh seems to be turning to art.

Perceptions of disconnection have surfaced for some time. Louis
Menand, *The Market Place of Ideas* (2010), in a strange lament reflects
upon how the combination of 'theorizing' and professional protection
simply removed him and colleagues from the culture they lived in:

> Academics of my generation grew up in a period—the sixties and
> seventies—when the world of art and ideas was undergoing changes
> that seemed to be coming from way outside the box of received
> [university and disciplinary] ideas and methods. I think that many
> of us hoped to instantiate something like that ad hoc, performative
> mode of pedagogy and inquiry within the university... We believed
> we could shake off the effects of academic socialization in part by
> theorizing about them... Of course, professors in my generation are
> now relatively secure in our domains. But is it possible that we envy a
> little those contributors to the culture who have to do battle with the
> forces of the market and with heteronomy—with reality checks of life
> outside the university? (124).

It is doubtful that Menand's 'performative...pedagogies' means the liberal arts. However, the industry's structural issues which tend to isolate
humanists and those concerned with liberal education activities from the
public and the link of that structure of work to the ineffectiveness of persuading the public on behalf of the humanities and liberal arts education
is broached in the first chapter and taken up in the Appendix, in "Turning
Ourselves Towards the Public for the Sake of Liberal Education."

pedagogy, arts, and new connections to or inventions of cultural artifacts and institutions—to reward *performance* before the public. In some respects liberal education advocates might take a cue from José Ortega y Gasset, in his 1930 work, *The Mission of the University*, who pinned reform of Spanish (and European) universities on a combined, interdisciplinary, use of the liberal arts.[13] He sought to differentiate the university from the more general culture and the public media of the time. Yet now the times seem to call for something of a reversal of the solution he came to. Isolation only hurts the humanities and liberal education, especially in light of the outreach to the public made by the sciences and social sciences.

This book traverses the realms of dialectic, rhetoric, and poetic. In speeches and academic articles over time I explored the possibilities and problems of liberal arts education. Often in my research or administrative capacities I was speaking to audiences which came from different walks of life, many arts and sciences, and many culturally different institutions around the world. Even if the actual or intended audience was only composed of humanists in North America, the audience could hold widely diverse views about liberal education. Over time, I came to see that liberal education was disconnecting from the wider world that it hoped to be a part of. So, my efforts came to aim at an intellectual, productive emphasis on the liberal arts, especially in their public and inventive capacities. For these reasons, some chapters retain the marks of addresses to an audience. Other chapters retain their 'academic' character. All have been revised, some to greater extent than others. The chapters are not in chronological order of delivery or publication but are arranged to develop the grounds of freedom and invention in liberal arts education. The book's structure takes its basic form from the capacity of artists, the activity of making

---

13   See my paper from the Building Universities' Reputation conference, 2017, at the Universidad de Navarra, "On Educating the Whole Person or Learning to be a Knower: Rebuilding the reputation of the humanities," available at RESPONDEOBOOKS.COM.

educations, and, finally, a poetics of education. From beginning to end its concern is with the constant invention, striking accomplishments, and freedom of the liberal arts. Through that emphasis on freedom and invention, this book has come to addresses the question, "why liberal arts?"

I have tried through the dedication, footnotes, and recognitions found in chapters to acknowledge so many people who have helped to build and show me the glories of liberal arts, core text education. If I had the good fortune to work with you and I haven't acknowledged you, *mea culpa*, but I am conscious of my debts to so many. In particular, for the publication of this volume, I want to thank Phil Lecuyer and Martha Franks, publisher and editor of Respondeo Books and tutors at St. John's College Santa Fe, who believed I had something to say about a subject dear to us all. Their work in helping to bring this volume to fruition was essential. I am very grateful. Also many thanks to Patrick Malcolmson, emeritus professor of political science at St. Thomas University, Fredericton, whose conversations with me over a number of years about some of the articles that appear in this book instilled in me a confidence that I was 'on to something.' Any author knows how such faith in one's writing from colleagues instills confidence.

At this point in history the book's title may puzzle readers initially, since invention is often associated with sciences. But invention is deeply rooted in the history and theory of liberal arts and is responsible for the making of the liberal arts and its history of innovations, including inventing the sciences. The arts, *technē*, are connected to the sciences partly through their theoretical grounding and partly through the central concern with making. The liberal arts not only share many of the characteristics of all arts, but are responsible for an education which produces a joy in learning, an intellectual freedom shared with others across disciplines, eras and cultures. This work argues liberal arts, core text educations for undergraduates can, and in many cases should, be offered to the world's students so that they are artfully free. It's really that simple.

SECTION I

Invention, Possibilities, and
Student Capacities

CHAPTER 1

Invention: The Art in Liberal Arts

C onferences reflect current opinions on topics of concern to participants. Many recent conferences indicate a "crisis" in humanistic liberal arts education. A call for a conference celebrating St. John's College's 50th anniversary of the Santa Fe campus "recogniz[ed]" that the traditions of education at liberal arts colleges "have been put on the defensive." The call found an "emerging consensus" that "consumerism," "new economic challenges," and "the fragmentation of general studies" caused by specialization were "symptomatic" of "a crisis of uncertainty and disorientation affecting every field of human endeavor." The call asserted that liberal education "can reaffirm its relevance and [humane] purposes" in response to this broad crisis. (Held on October 17, 2017).

St. John's College is not alone in formulating a crisis that liberal education faces, nor in asserting that a crisis is really an opportunity for humane education. Phi Beta Kappa (PBK), the American Council of Academic Deans (ACAD), and the Working Group of the Faculty of Arts and Sciences of Harvard University have supported extensive and eloquent discussions about the stress our liberal arts colleges face, as well as the contribution such colleges have made, particularly as they reinforce democracy.[1]

---

1 See, below, the Phi Beta Kappa/American Council of Deans 2013 call for that year's conference. Also, the Working Group of the Harvard University Faculty of Arts and Sciences on "The Teaching of the Arts and Humanities at Harvard College." HTTP://ARTSANDHUMANITIES.FAS.

The purported crisis in liberal education can be approached in a way not usually developed at any length in current discussions: we could speak of an education in liberal *arts*. I think that there are advantages to such a view, because almost all of the terms of discussion of the crisis imply principles of orientation, organization, and response that are derived externally: from the economy, technology, political culture, and, frankly, university education.[2] In those terms, liberal arts education is always secondary, a servant to some other larger concern, a sufferer, not an agent. The arts, on the other hand, have a history not only of adaptation, but invention that weaves together knowledge, culture, economics, and politics. They have been at the heart of liberal education discussions for as long, and since 1200 CE they have formed a strong foundation for higher education out of which developed the modern liberal arts college and the university.

During that long development, it became almost a certainty that, in order to teach in a liberal education program, one had to be trained in one of the disciplines of the humanities or sciences at a graduate university. Correlatively, with a very few exceptions such as St. John's College, the functioning of undergraduate liberal education has largely come to reflect the organization of graduate institutions by discipline and department. Given the humane purposes of liberal education and its *de facto* location within the

---

HARVARD.EDU/FILES/HUMANITIES/FILES/MAPPING_THE_FUTURE_31_MAY_2013.PDF

2   For example, the PBK/ACAD conference call was hardly less sweeping than the SJC call, stating that higher education is "undergoing ... transformations" of economic necessity, and that education is being "driven by technology" or by demographic stresses on class rigidity for millions of families who aspire for a better life. The call seemed to say that the transformations have put the "structure and character of higher education" along with the entire democratic premises of American society at risk, and that these transformations not only have subjected higher education to the winds and change of fortune, but that more than any other branch of higher education, liberal arts and sciences are suffering "scrutiny."

humanities, it is not untoward to speak of "humanistic liberal education." Overall, then, the issues are whether considerations of the arts can address a crisis, its purported causes and solutions, and the key role the humanities can have in building a liberal education.

I'll begin with why we might want to discuss art, and how I'm using the term. Then I'll look at a cluster of institutions that employ the arts: these include orchestras, museums, churches, humanistic liberal arts education, and the theatre. We will examine some of the troubles four of these institutions currently face, and we will see that theatre offers a model of cooperative, public arts which humanistic liberal arts education might carefully consider in addressing its current problems. Finally, I'll propose a possible renewal of the liberal arts which might both address current problems in colleges and help to change public perceptions of liberal arts education.

Forty to fifty years ago when one went to college, one chose to get a B.A. or a B.S. Notwithstanding a plethora of alternatives, the same choice is still available and nobody doubts that students graduating, today, with a B.S. possess a science. I've been wondering, what art or arts do those graduating with a B.A. possess?

The word, "art," like the word "science," has many associations and, therefore, implies the question, "what is art?" The range of Aristotle's discussion of art provides, I think, a suitable scope for viewing the problems of humanistic liberal education, because that range can help us think about answers to the two questions I just asked. For Aristotle *art means the capacity to make, the activity of making, and the object made that is separated from a maker.* The generic term, "art," comprehends these three specific, correlative relations. For Aristotle art runs from the intellectual virtue of *technē*, (N.E. VI, iv) which is the etymological root of our modern terms, 'technique' and 'technology,' through formulations of specific arts as capacities or powers (*dynamis*) we humans exercise—particularly in those concerned with thought, for example, the arts of dialectic and rhetoric (Rhet I, 2 1355b), to the objects of human production (*dynamis:* Poetics 1, 1447a*).*[3] These objects include lyrics, comedies, tragedies or epics, instrumental music, choirs, painting, sculpture, architecture, mechanical arts, medicinal treatment, <u>indeed, almost *any* made thing</u> that usually happens and is not spontaneous, a product of chance or of nature (Phys II, 5). Thus, for Aristotle, art is a cause of things coming into being in this world that, otherwise, would not exist without active human agency (N.E., VI, 4). It touches our deepest natures and desires, and it exercises our minds and passions to a degree of inventiveness that our imaginations struggle to keep up with, incorporates almost anything that the universe has to offer, and

---

3   An important set of terms and argument connects *technē* to the equally important and differential term, *mimesis*, and thus power and poetics. "... a bed or a coat and anything else of that sort, *qua* receiving these designations—i.e. in so far as they are products of art—have no innate impulse to change" (Phys. II 1, 192b 18) And, "Where a series has a completion, all the preceding steps are for the sake of that...and generally art partly completes what nature cannot bring to a finish, and partly imitates her" (8, 199a 15). Imitation differentiates the arts, particularly as products, but in the steps an artist takes toward the products, as well. This implies both spectra of arts and imitation. The scope of imitation is confined to the arts in Aristotle (unlike Plato). See R. P. McKeon, "The Concept of Imitation in Antiquity," in R.S. Crane, Critics and Criticism, U. Chicago Press, 1952. The article, in respect of Aristotle, has long informed this writer's thinking, but its purpose was, perhaps, shaped by a concern, at the time, to differentiate the modern study of literature (and art) from historical and concurrent studies of the same in terms of ethics, religion, civilizations. In the section of McKeon's article on Aristotle's concept of *mimesis*, questions of particular form(s) and matter(s) become important. The net effect of the section on Aristotle is to differentiate him from Plato by showing two things: how relatively restricted the concept of imitation was, in comparison to Plato's use, essentially to things made by humans, and how Aristotelian distinctions actually made considerations of the arts, qua arts, something that Plato could not do. Changes in critical and cultural fashion have turned the appreciative situation on its head; now, in order not to reduce art (and liberal arts education) to some other more important function, it becomes desirable to think of the *range and scope* of Aristotelian arts and artistic terms as a way to expand what liberal arts education can do and can articulate.

results in a changed world that, without art, would be barren or, at best, no more than a garden of Eden. Art partakes of the characteristics of our modern disciplines; knowledge is an important mark of the arts for Aristotle (N.E. II, 4, 1105a 24-27, 35-b2). Indeed, at points where knowledge of arts converges with experience, Aristotle's view on art begins to approach the modern view in which knowledge must be empirical (Meta I i). For Aristotle, the teaching of art, as a sign of the possession of knowledge, refers not only to the ordering of experience but to the causes of what exists and how it is produced—again, a position not that distant from modernity (Meta I i).

Aristotle repeatedly identifies arts as origins of invention and as often ties these origins to the development of knowledge as well as the invention of new products and capacities (Soph Encl end, Poetics 4, Meta I i). Indeed, the arts lay the foundation for the *purely* speculative sciences because they may involve a component associated with the speculative sciences—contemplation (Rhet, def). Moreover, art, faculties, and thought are all described by Aristotle (Meta VII, 7) as producers of makings. When a faculty or thought itself becomes subject to reflection or theorizing about the causes of thought in respect of specific ends, it is possible to speak of an art which contemplates and artistically produces thought. This is precisely what happens in the definition of rhetoric.[4] The thoughts reflected on are *pistoi*, persuasives, and Aristotle writes extensively in the introduction to his *Rhetoric* that Dialectic and Rhetoric, as arts, are counterparts and share many, though not

---

4   This contemplation of thought in the Rhetoric seems to partake of the wider possibilities of the soul reflecting on its own thought that appears in the De Anima: III, 4 (430a2–9): "Thought is itself thinkable in exactly the same way as its objects are. For in the case of objects which involve no matter, what thinks and what is thought are identical; for speculative knowledge and its object are identical." Cited in "University Education, the Unity of Knowledge—and (Natural) Theology: John Henry Newman's Provocative Vision" by Reinhard Hütter. In *Nova et Vetera*, 11, 4, 2013; 1050.

all, of the same concerns with inference: enthymemes and examples in rhetoric and demonstrations and induction in dialectic.

The prefatory matter of the *Topics* is much more restricted, but dialectic concerns the opinions, *doxa*—of all or the majority or the wise—and it aims at methodical conversations and the examination of reasonings about the bases of the sciences and problems susceptible of address by opinion (I. 1, 100a 18-25). In their critical and poetic functions, the arts frequently stand outside the normative conventions of disciplinary thought while retaining an artistic character (Parts of Animals I, 1, 639 and Poetics 25 1460a 14-1461a8). The combination of criticism, poetic production, and technological development wrought by art means that art, in Aristotle, is foundational to invention and freedom; we make, for ourselves, the possibilities that we experience. Thus, artistic invention and freedom pervasively concern not only persons but institutions. Aristotle's thinking on art can be adapted in order to conduct something like thought experiments about institutions, not only about liberal arts education, but about our public debate and critical evaluation of the arts and sciences, as well as the audience for them. All of these artistic concerns deeply affect humanistic liberal education, for they situate in a *paideia* the four concerns of the humanities: *transmission, interpretation, judgment, and invention.*

Not only liberal education, but many other older cultural institutions are facing uncertain, perhaps disoriented, futures, as newer technologies and fashionable art forms *seem* to be supplanting them. *The New Republic* has noted unsuccessful attempts by orchestras, seeking to maintain support, to substitute social outreach programs, audience participation, and adoptions of more popular music forms in place of the studied appreciation of the classical repertory, an appreciation acquired more or less over a lifetime. *The New York Times* recently noted the decline of space allotted to contemplation within museums in favor of installations offering "experience."[5] Establishment and fundamentalist

---

5   Judith H. Dobrznski, "High Culture Goes Hands-On," *New York*

churches, a third great cultural institution, have suffered increasing disaffections of attendance regardless of denomination.[6]

Times, August 10, 2013. This particular article included the 'installation' of a slide between floors of a museum. Obviously, some installations, whether contemplative or not, are serious works of art. See for example, Darby English, *How to See a Work of Art in Total Darkness*. Philip Kennicott's article title, "America's Orchestras are in Crisis: How an effort to popularize classical music threatens to undermine what makes orchestras great" epitomizes displacement angst. *New Republic*, August 25, 2013. Kennicott's position was rebutted in an August 30th reply by Jesse Rosen, but for purposes of this article, what mattered was the apparent agreement by these two authors that artistic works were central to recovery. Roxanna Popescu, "Letter from San Diego: Endangered Opera." *Paris Review,* May 12, 2014. This article laments the closing of opera—that hybrid of theatre and orchestra—in San Diego, Orange County, Baltimore, Cleveland and New York City and makes some of the linkages between the failure of the arts and the failure of the humanities made in this paper.

6   Laurie Goldstein, "Francis Has Changed American Catholic's Attitudes, but Not Their Behavior, a Poll Finds." *NYTimes*, 3/6/2014. Even when "American Catholics [are] saying they were 'more excited' about their faith ... the poll showed that church attendance had not shifted in the past year, with 40 percent saying they had attended Mass at least weekly"; Ross Douthat, "Can Liberal Christianity Be Saved?" *NYTimes*, 7/14/2012. "Yet instead of attracting a younger more open-minded demographic..., the Episcopal Church's dying has proceeded apace... In the last decade, average Sunday attendance dropped 23 percent, and not a single Episcopal diocese in the country saw a churchgoing increase"; John S. Dickerson, "The Decline of Evangelical America." *NYTimes*, 12/15/2012, "In 2011 the Pew Forum on Religion and Public Life polled church leaders from around the world. Evangelical ministers from the United States reported a greater loss of influence than church leaders from any other country... Studies from established evangelical polling organizations—LifeWay Research,... and the Barna Group— have found that a majority of young people raised as evangelicals are quitting the church, and often the faith, entirely." Self-reported attendance probably masks further disaffection: Michael Paulson, "Americans Claim to Attend Church Much More Than They Do." *NYTimes*, 5/17/2014. Different polling methods, designed to detect 'social desirability bias,' suggest that as much as 43 percent of people "acknowledged

Humanistic, liberal arts university and college programs, since the recession, are widely reported to be suffering cutbacks, much lower student application and humanities major rates, as well as loss of financial private giving.[7] In other words, a cluster of some of our most important cultural institutions appear unmoored from their traditional grounds of acceptance and support.

The one exception is the theatre. To cut a long story short, on

---

rare attendance" at church, a higher percentage than is usually suggested by customary self-reporting methods.

7   Reported drops in humanities majors (see the Harvard report, cited above) at prominent universities, cut backs of programs at public universities, steep declines in giving to baccalaureate private institutions, and long-term declines in the number of private liberal arts colleges (see Kimball, below), have produced a question about the health of humanistic liberal arts education in the last three to four years. What might be at stake in questioning that health is the subject of this paper. Jinjoo Lee, "Concerns About Job Market Lead Students to STEM Majors," The Cornell Daily Sun, 2/25/2014, reports that in 2011 "the percentage of students with a humanities major" dropped 10% and has only recovered 1% point since then. Gordon Hutner and Feisal G. Mohamed, "The Real Humanities Crisis Is Happening at Public Universities." The New Republic, 9/6/2013. This article analyzes the new models of education, whether found in universities or in the federal government, that work against sustaining the humanities: "Under this new business model, humanities programs suffer in general and small departments, like classics and philosophy, find themselves perpetually under threat, no matter what their historical significance to higher learning." Though St. John's later successfully reversed its application totals, the economic crises saw a decline in applications "from 460 in 2008 to 357 in 2010." Daniel de Vise, Washington Post, 5/ 13/2011, "At St. John's, a Defender of the Liberal Arts." Declines in giving to private colleges were the most severe, except for community colleges (which derive a much higher percentage of their income from governments). "John Lippincott, president of the Council for Advancement and Support of Education, said he wasn't surprised that the numbers were down, but that the depth of the decline was a surprise. 'We're in unprecedented territory,' he said, both because of the severity of the economic difficulties and the volatility of campus conditions." Scott Jaschik, "Contributions to Colleges Drop 12%." Inside Higher Ed, 2/3/2010.

the whole its audiences are not disaffected. Its non-profit theatres recovered well and quickly from the 2008 recession, its audience attendance is much better than comparative trends in cinema, and it is filled with playwrights' works that might be considered 'disorienting.' Even so, the theatre knows and goes about a relatively successful business. Why is that, and what lessons are there for the humanities and liberal arts?

Granted that the theatre has experimented broadly with "happenings" and "audience experiences" for the last forty to fifty years, still its mainstay—one that draws audiences—remains "classic works" or works that, at least, seem aware of the potentials of the dramatic and theatrical inheritance. The theatre is simply filled with people who are immersed in these two complementary traditions. Also, theatre people know that they are "live." In Hume's terms, they are vivacious. The audience, because it is assembled, is live; the actors have voices and gestures whose timbre and sweep are, by and large, authentic and inescapable. The theatre can assemble its considerable range of artists, its stage, with its focus of audience attention, and its vivid here and now-ness to achieve—what? It is, of course, true to think that theatre is entertainment. But to "entertain" is to consider and, potentially, when you go to a theatre, you could be asked to use your heart and mind for a wide range of forms stretching over the spectacle of props and choreography, the music of an orchestra to the whistle of a lonely character exiting the stage, the language of the streets or Shakespeare, arguments ranging from physics and philosophy to race, class, and gender. You'll consider the persuasions of a lover, human character choices and suffering that make a difference to how we feel, and you'll be asked to think about actional or conceptual frameworks with a mini-system, mini-world or mini-verse before us.

Theatre people seem, by and large, not to conceive of accessibility to this range as a dumbing down or as too plebian to warrant attention. The theatrical problem is not Shakespeare's because he was great in his Elizabethan vocabulary and iambs or complex in his plots, nor the audience's because it simply isn't expert enough or intellectually rigorous enough to appreciate technical nuance, but the production company's: how will they make the language convey what Shakespeare was using it for? Presentation in the theatre isn't a matter of democracy—it is a matter of availability. Presentation is a matter of welcoming in a controlled, focused manner so that those who are drawn to theatre (or any other art form) are helped to partake of what it has to offer. Availability, then, is the use of the theatrical arts to make affectively intelligible the dramas presented.

There's an attractive orientation in theatre that perhaps churches, museums, orchestras and the humanities could all take a lesson from, and the orientation's attractive power rests in *art*. Art and artistic structure is the phenomenon that is shared by museums, orchestras, to some degree churches, and certainly the humanities. We recognize this phenomenon in two different ways: obviously, so-called fine arts products and activities are central, but equally important and just as nuanced are the argumentative and symbolic arts, exemplified by the liberal arts, that are used to apprehend and appreciate the fine arts. For the humanities, whatever completion the historical draw of politics and culture (as a substitute for politics) may offer, the fact is that art is quintessential, since the humanities would cease to exist and would have no history whatsoever if art did not exist. And the same is true of liberal education; liberal education without art is simply not liberal education, for, then, its "freedom" has little room for invention, its examinations of disciplines will then be confined to stock rehearsals of accepted postulates, and, as is happening, it will lose a position, largely aesthetic, from which to criticize current political debate of any stripe. Put differently, for the humanities what is at stake is what constitutes the fields of the humanities; for liberal education the claim that colleges offer a liberal *arts* education is at stake.

The vivacity of the theatre can be captured in the humanistic classroom, but not through technological gee-whiz nor some sort of 'theatrical' staging effects. Nor is it likely to be captured in lectures. Notwithstanding the times all academics have marveled in remembering the lecture a professor gave, lectures are not "made to be performed" in the way dramas are. Put differently, if a professor cannot figure out how to "perform" an idea, then she or he will have to resort to other means.

The seeming absence of performance instruction has important implications for focusing the thought of humanities students through pedagogy. The arts of grammar, rhetoric and logic, dialectic, interrogation and conversation, arts of interpretation, of meaning, and of a specific artistic appreciation (e.g. knowing scales in music, perspective in the visual arts, prosody in literature, specific forms of arts)—these take on enormous importance. Such arts suggest a partnership of artists in the classroom, not unlike that of playwright and performers in the theatre. Not only must the professors generally employ these arts in the (relative) absence of stage props, choreography, performed musical scores, oral interpretation, and, especially, acting, but the students themselves *will have to learn to employ them* because there is little or no staging provided to them.

Some canaries in the cage of higher education are chirping loudly that no arts like these, that I am advocating for, are any longer being learned on today's campuses. Verlyn Klinkeborg, member of the editorial board of the New York Times, has taught at many top flight colleges and universities. In an essay on the "Decline and Fall of the English Major," he notes that the "kind of writing—clear, direct, humane—and the reading on which it is based are the very root of the humanities," but that students, today, cannot produce clear writing. He adds, brutally, "the humanities do a bad job of teaching the humanities" largely because "writing well <u>used</u> to be a fundamental principle of the humanities…" [my emphasis] Of course, the problems of the humanities are more general than problems of the English major. And here is where the shoe really begins to pinch. Arum and Roksa's *Academically Adrift* found in national samplings that "three semesters of college education … have a barely noticeable impact on students' skills in critical thinking, complex reasoning, and writing."[8] Statistically

---

8   Richard Arum and Josipa Roksa, *Academically Adrift: Limited*

controlling for socio-economic background doesn't improve the picture. Worse, Blaich and Pascarella found in a national study of 11 liberal arts colleges and 6 universities where the kind of practices that tend to be recommended to improve scores are employed—e.g., discussion groups, peer groups, working across disciplines, imagining an argument from someone else's point of view—the capacities of students for moral reasoning and critical thinking on average "increased only a small amount" over four years.[9] Positive attitude toward literacy declined in 53% of all students. Two-thirds of students during four years reported declines in academic motivation, and interest in "contribut[ing]" to both the arts and sciences declined for twice as many students as those that experienced growth in interest. One might think that college can only affect such measures marginally, but, no, it turns out that practically the same measures indicated large advances by undergraduate students in the 1980s. As Arum and Roksa put it, "low gains…are…not simply an artifact of our measurement strategy, but a disconcerting reality."[10]

Let's be clear. The data doesn't say that no students improve significantly in moral and critical reasoning or writing ability. Some do, but not nearly enough. Apparently, fewer students want to make contributions to the arts and sciences, but some do. Some are still academically motivated. Still, the data does say that by our own lights there is both a problem and an opportunity for the humanities and liberal arts education. Arum and Roksa make it very clear that, generally, time on the task of studying, and

---

Learning on College Campuses. University of Chicago Press, 2011, 35. The situation did not seem to change through 2014; see Arum and Roksa in a 9/2/2014 You Tube: *Lack of Academic Rigor in College Often Means Trouble Later for Students,* a *Chronicle of Higher Education* interview.

9   Charles Blaich and Ernest Pascarella. HTTP://WWW.LIBERALARTS. WABASH.EDU/STORAGE/4-YEAR-CHANGE-SUMMARY-WEBSITE.PDF, p. 3. These are 2006 results but the authors seem to find a continuum between Arum and Roska's 2011 work and their original study.

10   Ibid. p. 37.

specifically far more reading and writing than is the usual practice in our colleges and universities, improves student learning.[11]

So, what might students take time to read or artfully produce? As Executive Director of the Association for Core Texts and Courses (ACTC), I am a strong proponent of using classical works, but I have come to believe, especially with regard to questions of students working across disciplines or inventing arguments, that a more capacious view of what counts as a classical work would reward our students. After reviewing more than 50 general education programs, including many core text, great books programs, and after having approved over 2000 paper proposals for our ACTC conferences over 20 years, I find it disturbing that philosophical or theoretical—in the Greek sense—discussions of art and appreciation of some of the technical development therein entailed have virtually disappeared from coherent general education curricula and discussions at ACTC. Plato's *Republic* and, occasionally, the *Phaedrus* appeared often enough, but little or no *Cratylus* or *Gorgias*. The *Nicomachean Ethics* and *Politics*, but little of the *Topics, Rhetoric,* or *Poetics* from Aristotle. *On Friendship* from Cicero, but little or no *De Inventione* or *De Oratore*. The *Confessions* or *City of God*, but no *On Christian Doctrine*. I can extend this list to the present through all the inventions that these liberal arts have produced, including works by Vitruvius, de Pisan, Alberti, Bruni, Petrarch, Erasmus, Reynolds, Saussure, Kenneth Burke, McLuhan, Sontag, and Smullyan, just to name a few. Sure, there are courses with these texts and authors, and there are professors who teach these arts in isolated courses, but we don't teach *across the curriculum these liberal arts texts* that contain the questions and techniques that would make the liberal arts truly available to all.

Enduring, Great, or Big Questions may be asked in general education programs, but I can assure you that "What is Art?" is rarely among these in any systematic way.[12] Since we offer bache-

---

11   Ibid. p. 131 and 132.

12   We are dealing in generalities. Yale's Directed Studies program has an explicit (fine) arts program; Concordia University—Irvine's new core

lor-of-arts degrees, the chance of losing touch with this question seems particularly disturbing because it comprehends other fascinating questions that the liberal arts raise and that scholarship has pointed out. Questions of perception, aesthetics, imitation, elements of speech, separations and relations of language to the physical, psychological and conventional worlds, available modes of interpretation, the relations of the origin of language to the divine and civilizational origins of our humanity, not to mention questions of equity, justice, the nature of truth and the determination or freedom of thought are not only pointed out by scholars, but directly observable in such liberal arts texts by our undergraduate students.[13] Indeed, taken very seriously, the liberal arts question, "what is art," will lead to examinations and reformulations of whole disciplines, as Henry Adams illustrated in *The Education of Henry Adams*.[14] But we don't teach *across the curricu-*

---

program does raise the question with students, "What is art?"

13   E.g., Richard P. McKeon, "Criticism and the Liberal Arts: The Chicago School of Criticism," *Profession,* 1982, 1-17. Howard Bloch, *Etymologies and Genealogies,* 1983. Kathy Eden, *Hermeneutics and the Rhetorical Tradition: Chapters in the Ancient Legacy and Its Humanist Reception.* 1997. Appended to this volume is a syllabus for a summer seminar for faculty that ACTC held in 2019 on "Rejuvenating and Reinventing the Liberal Arts." The seminar contains works, ancient to modern, that trace the questions suggested above, while seeking to inculcate in students a working familiarity with the techniques and distinctions of these arts.

14   On Adams: see particularly the chapters of the book which begin after 1890. It is important to note that a disguised comic reversal in Adams' intellectual interest appears earlier in the book, when he discusses his work for his father in England during the Civil War. The period was one of great tension and it appeared as if Great Britain would side with the South. Adams discovers the real motives of Great Britain's government in publications around 1890, and this changes his view of what history is. His first step (after the reversal) is to begin to consider the new technologies of science in relation to the figure of the Virgin Mary in the 12th Century. In a real liberal arts "move," he begins to think of her as a symbol drawing human "energy" toward her. The story of his own development, then, becomes the culmination of his "Education," a

lum the liberal arts texts that I indicated that contain the questions and techniques that would make the liberal arts truly available to all.[15] Again, I repeat, in isolated courses all of the arts, questions and texts can be found. In some isolated institutions, the bachelor-of-arts degree is more artistic. But, comprehensively, in the current structural situation of the university and collegiate education, the humanities are probably our chief source of hope for an education in the arts which reaches all students systematically. The question is whether a humanistic liberal *arts* education is desirable.

I think it is. Teaching distinguishable liberal arts are to the vivacity of human achievements as the arts of the stage are to the liveliness and intelligibility of drama. What arts are used and the proportions of their use, *the recognition that art in its largest sense is the object of study*, are central to focusing the mind of students

---

liberal arts reconsideration of history. The discussion of Adams is treated in a context of the development of core text program purposes vis-à-vis the liberal arts in Chapter 7.

15   Thus, most of the texts mentioned above are great, or at least, important; their conceptions and operations of art are essential to any understanding of the works, *including those of science*, that are read in liberal arts education or, frankly, an understanding of the way the world really operates. Yet, the smaller the liberal arts, core text program, the more direct discussion of liberal arts and their formulations are forced out, and the curricular situation resembles that described by Aristotle at the end of *On Sophistical Refutations*: "For the training given by paid professors...was like the treatment of the matter by Gorgias. For they used to hand out speeches to be learned by heart...supposing that [the] arguments on either side generally fell among them." Thus, fine art works, in liberal arts programs, become not examples of art, but vehicles to questions and issues while it is supposed that students learn to read and write in this way.

There is a quasi-exception to the statement above excluding teaching of liberal arts to all students. Concordia University—Irvine has a Core Philosophy I course in which "elementary statement logic" is taught. Unpublished manuscript, "The Core Logic Unit: An Imaginative Approach to Reasoning," Susan Buchanan. ACTC 20th Annual Conference, April 11, 2014.

in the humanities. Conversely, the proper production by students from the humanistic point of view is conversation with fellow students and teachers, the essay, formal speeches and debates, video, audio, and web productions, musical and stage performances, oral interpretations, original translations, poems, stories, and conversational defenses or explanations of one's work— guaranteed through a curriculum. And these artful productions suggest that the term "undergraduate research" does not necessarily point to, inculcate, require or comprehend the pedagogy or use of any of these other arts.

At stake in the classroom interaction between books, essays, works of fine arts and the corresponding liberal arts that students employ is the realization of the possibilities, the intellectual freedom, which humans make for themselves, not only in the past but for a future. That is, we can no more know the truth about human existence or beyond without examining the possibilities found in products and performances of art, than we can know the possibilities of human existence or beyond simply by possessing the truth. We must work out both and get better or worse in doing so.

The argument above seems to preclude the scholarly nature of book and article publishing in the humanities—the artifact of research that many humanists hold most dear. But not really. Literate audiences were small in ancient times. As literacy has spread, generally, products of art, such as playscripts and their cinematic versions, became widely distributed—think of the motivation for the publication of Shakespeare's folio—whereas humanistic publication has shrunk and sunk into academic libraries and tiny, specialized audiences. This is a mistake we are paying for. We need, instead, a vigorous public scholarship.

If time permitted, I would elaborate three examples of public scholarship. Here, I'll simply allude to the specifics they offer. They involve transmission, interpretation, criticism, and invention— four functions basic to humanistic liberal arts efforts which make freedom possible.

Our first example is a recent article in the *New Republic* by

Helen Vendler.[16] She argues that the recent digitalization of Emily Dickenson manuscripts has revealed that "perhaps, for Dickinson, the principal unit of thought in poetic composition was sometimes not the stanza, not even the line, but the individual word." Her liberal-arted, scholarly defense of Dickenson's poetry within the traditions of grammar has real consequences, because she raises for our students the pedagogical question, "can you think of a better word, here?" She makes clear the intellectual, emotive and formal advantages of such an education in artistic making, but we can add that such repeated exercises would move in the direction of building precision in vocabulary and perception, as well as a sense of reasoned choice, while appreciatively reading a great core text author. That's a lot of bang for your buck.

The second example belongs to Roland Barthes. He originally published "The World of Wrestling" in 1957 in *Espirit*, a literary magazine founded in the 30's.[17] In "Wrestling" Barthes invokes a knowledge of Greek philosophy and drama, as well as French classical theatre. Still, this comic, ironic essay is intelligible to any student, at present, because the modern, media-promoted versions of American wrestling have enough in common with the French wrestling hall of 1957 to allow for understanding that, ultimately, reaches back to earlier art forms. Barthes' careful extraction of devices of meaning via the staging of matches—devices such as the utterly catastrophic "forearm smash" against the chest of the oppo-nent—indicates how the audience is led to experience a match, a "spectacle of Suffering, Defeat, and Justice," as a "Natur[al]... understanding of things," rather than the constructed under-standing it is. Given sufficient examples in a curriculum of liberal arts texts, students would see that mark of humanistic liberal

---

16   Helen Vendler, "Vision and Revision: How Emily Dickinson Actually Wrote Her Poems." *New Republic*, March 24, 2014, p. 48. For a skeptical view on the value of the digital collection, see Angie Mlinko, "Infamy or Urn?" The Nation, Jan. 27, 2014, 31-32.

17   Collected into his 1957 publication, *Mythologies*. New York, Noonday Press, pp. 15-25.

arts—recurrent use—and, thereby a range of intellectual choices open to them. The analytic construction and deconstruction of art by critics of the 20ᵗʰ Century recovered that movement of Greek arts between the development of a poetics of whole works and the rhetorical handbooks of separable topics, extracted from works, designed to lead to future compositions.

Finally, J. L. Austin delivered, at university and on BBC radio, lectures which became the work, *How To Do Things with Words.*[18] Born out of philosophical work with descriptive sentences which could be subjected to scrutiny on questions of truth or falsity as logical statements, Austin's concern is to distinguish and elaborate a class of utterances which are performative, not descriptive,[19] where we can say accurately and truthfully that someone is "doing...an action."[20] I will not state the analysis of his six conditions for recognizing performative statements that leads me to the conclusion that in his own terms to perform a play, to read a poem or any literate text is "doing an action."[21] But I would point out that play scripts are instructions for performance to a director, actor, and the entire company. If those artists don't act as fully as they can with their own arts, you know that production has failed. In this sense, Austin's work is germane to knowing, perhaps even assessing, when we are acting in a liberal-arted fashion, for the theatrical point is generalizable to all works of art: each of them are potentially instructions on how to read a work. Perhaps, the unusually gifted may read a work well without actualizing liberal arts to guide them, but this is no more likely than if one is likely

---

18   Second edition. J. O. Urmson and Marina Sbisà, editors. Cambridge MA: Harvard University Press, 1962, 1975.

19   Or, better, "constative."

20   Ibid., pp. 1-2, 5-7, 13.

21   The six conditions: (a) use of conventional procedures; (b) appropriate of persons and circumstances for invoking the procedure; (c and d) correct and complete execution of the procedure; (e) the corresponding feelings and thoughts that the convention invokes, intentionally used in the conduct indicated by the utterance; and (f) the appropriate conduct.

to sing or project well on stage without having had phonetic and interpretive voice training. That is, in choosing to examine and use, or not use, the liberal arts, we choose performatively to read a work well, artfully, habitually, spontaneously, or badly.

If our students do well, artfully, what then would persons who hold a bachelor-of-arts look like—independently from a major? First, they would have the character of an artist, a free, liberal one at that. They would think about art and be able to manifest such thought by exercising a capacity for generating works of the mind and imagination which captured their own and others' souls. They would know how to listen, look and read with an attention and respect for the work and voices of others. They would properly believe, because the belief belonged to their experience, that contributing to and making artistic productions would involve cooperation, planning, foresight, reasoned choice, and their own plain, disciplined hard work with others. They would have at their command a ready technology of production, appeals, reasoning and expression which could be put at the service of themselves, their families, corporations, non-profits and associations, governments, and international organizations. They would also possess a technology of the mind which they could summon to think about ideas and ideals, now and in the future. They would be immune to disenabling criticism, while not losing a thoughtful skepticism. They would have the experience of their own immediate culture and the reasoned possession of traditions of the West and other major cultures over a range of disciplines and formed works, and their experience and possession of tradition would be a resource for them to draw upon in almost any contingency. They would have ways to analyze, translate, communicate, analogize, question, and invent experience for themselves and others. They would be able to examine science, art, politics, business and economic affairs, religion, culture, communities, neighborhoods, families and friends with an eye to human passions and the confidence, charity, faith and hope that belongs to those who hold the future. They would be able to discriminate when to make, to act, and to contemplate, and when each was best and when it was not. Finally, they would know how to look out upon the achievements of humanity to discover, with wonder and appreciation, not only how to bring their vision of a liberal arts education to a wider public, but what a precious thing our humanity is. No one discipline can build either such a character or offer such a degree, but a humanistic liberal arts education can.[22]

The humanities have one primary job: to make available, by focusing the mind of students in and out of the university, works of art and intellect that a crafted, intellectual heritage of the West and other traditions of the world have transmitted. The liberal arts are the most substantive way by which to make these inheritances available for inquiry and examination. Philosophy, religion, politics, economics, culture, and everything else follows, sometimes simultaneously, *after* that. A core text core which includes examination of the liberal arts as such does all this. If the humanities really pay attention to art, then they will look to the artistic reasons why theatre is not failing in a world where cultural institutions seem on the verge of crumbling. If they do, not only the humanities, but liberal arts education will be better off.

(Rev. Originally delivered 2014 to 2015 in different versions at Transylvania University, St. John's College, Santa Fe, and Oglethorpe University.)

---

22   There is a correlative outcome to this kind of character, especially for those who are already engaged in educating others. As I said at the beginning, the arts have a history of being woven into the fabric of liberal education for over 2400 years, in both the West and the East. One of the marks of arts, particularly rhetoric, for both Plato and Aristotle was that it should be able to give an account of itself, to offer systematic reasons for its operations, both how and why they work. (Gorgias, 465d, 504d, Rhetoric 1. I, 1354. 10). An added, serious account of a liberal arts education, as an arts education, as well as a political or quasi-spiritual education, would enrich our own accounts to ourselves and to the outside world of what it is we know, do and make.

CHAPTER 2

ACTC, Liberal Arts and Invention.
Botticelli's *Adoration* (1475)

I am surrounded by friends and colleagues, here, and I am thankful and grateful for every one of you, including those new to ACTC. In past years, at this podium, I've tried to capture and acknowledge the unique contributions that so many individuals have made in building this association. So, without going through a nearly endless list of people to whom I owe gratitude, I do want to mention six people, specifically. The first is my wife, Geri Mooney, without whom none of my career would have happened. I was fortunate to be a co-founder of ACTC with Steve Zelnick. He had the original idea for the Association and asked me if I wanted to join him in this nascent effort. I was similarly fortunate to work with three Presidents—Phil Sloan, Rick Kamber, and Jane Rodeheffer—all of whom shared a vision of a pluralistic, international association dedicated to the best in liberal arts core text education, and unfailingly provided cooperation and advice in the growth of ACTC and its various endeavors. I want to thank Kathleen Burk for ably assuming, as this conference demonstrates, the Executive Directorship of ACTC. To the Board, my hat is off in salute for all the moral and material support you provided to develop ACTC through many diverse projects. And to those who for many years sought institutional support for ACTC—thank you. Finally, I've had the privilege of working with so many of you who have given so much to grow this association for 24 years. I am extraordinarily grateful for your work in making ACTC a living intellectual community. With all my soul, I thank you.

It is intellectual life that binds us all together. Of course, the intellectual life I am speaking of shapes something as grand as the world's many histories, an exploration of learning what it is to know, and, finally, the links among the world's arts and sciences. Further, many of ACTC's programs and members describe their purpose as inquiry into Western or global civilization, as well into what it means to be human. That's quite a scope for the intelligence in this association to range over.

ACTC's mission statement carefully marks out what makes ACTC different as a professional association: "The Association for Core Texts and Courses (ACTC) is an international, professional, liberal arts organization dedicated to fostering the use of core texts (world classics and other texts of major cultural significance), in undergraduate education and the development of required or widely taken core programs steeped in such texts." The words "liberal arts" mean something akin to the wide access to knowledge once achieved through the arts of the trivium and quadrivium. Moreover, the presence of core texts of the arts and sciences in our programs and at our conferences echoes the ambitions of ancient education and is a potent ground for growth of the intellects of our students and ourselves.

In this talk I'll set the cultural and academic scene for why such an attractive kind of education seems neglected. I'll trace what makes ACTC a different kind of professional organization and why the potential of invention within core texts of the liberal arts might address that neglect. Finally, I'll illustrate the intellectual freedom that comes through undergraduate programs like ours when emphasizing the arts and invention by centering the inquiry on Alberti's *On Painting* and Botticelli's "Uffizi" *Adoration of the Magi*. I have no silver bullet or new media initiative for our problems, but I think we can take positive steps in the right direction to make liberal arts matter.

As a liberal arts association, we are inextricably bound to the arts. Unfortunately, we find ourselves in a world which has largely discarded liberal arts education in favor of technological and economic education, and that, often, in a contentious way. In a kind of fulfillment of Bacon's promise and in a conviction that old truths are still true, Stephen Pinker's recent *Enlightenment Now* vigorously defends science, data gathering, progress, and reason against mavens of C. P. Snow's "Second Culture, the worldview of many literary intellectuals and cultural critics" who "express a disdain for science... Their methodology for seeking truth consists not in framing hypotheses and citing evidence but in issuing pronouncements that draw on their breadth of erudition and lifetime habits of reading."[1] Specifically, Pinker finds such mavens in general liberal education programs, organized religions, humanists, and prominent artists of the 20th and 21st Centuries.[2] What positive overall view of arts and religion he has might be reductively captured in the following passage: "Religious organizations can provide a sense of solidarity and mutual support, together with art, ritual, and architecture of great beauty and historical resonance, thanks to their millennia-long head start. I partake of these myself, with much enjoyment."[3] In short, these don't count for much. More illustratively damning of what it is to be tied to the arts are the Organization of Economic Co-operation and Development (OECD) "Regional Development Reports." OECD represents and connects the policy-makers of foreign affairs and economic ministries of the first world nations with major university research arms. Its "Regional Development Reports" periodically measure the world's best locales for "well-being" through nine categories of compiled statistics. Given publicity through such media outlets as the *New York Times*, OECD's 2014 report does not measure arts, religion, and sports as components of well-being, though these three categories of human activities and products are nearly universal yet tend to rely on local or home-grown institutions around the world.[4]

---

1   NY: Random House, 2018, pp, 5 and 33-34.

2   Ibid. pp. 400-401, 420-441, 446-447.

3   Ibid. p. 432.

4   HTTPS://READ.OECD-ILIBRARY.ORG/URBAN-RURAL-AND-RE-GIONAL-DEVELOPMENT/HOW-S-LIFE-IN-YOUR-REGION/SUMMARY/ENGLISH_9CI2BI55-EN#PAGEI (Summary, p. 1).

On the wrong side of a science-versus-the-world argument and with its concerns with arts and local institutions ignored by governments and policy researchers, core text liberal arts education has two major strikes against persuading the public and educational institutions that it matters. And to be honest, Bruce Kimball has shown, persuasively, that within academia there is a long tradition, extending at least as far back as the rise of the German University, of competing concepts of liberal education, including attacks on the *artes liberales*, which occasionally make their way into the media.[5] Today, perhaps the best we can say is core text liberal arts education is as much ignored as it is attacked.

Yet, I do not recall anyone in ACTC being against reason. Years of panels discussing fundamental core texts of the sciences indicates where ACTC stands. Our discussions of religious texts are probing and reasonable. True, we don't have many policy-makers and few economists, but thoughtful political scientists abound in ACTC, and Adam Smith, Marx and, occasionally, even Milton Friedman make their appearances in our panels. Globally, international use and exchange of core texts has been an ACTC policy objective. Humanists in our ACTC Qualitative Narrative Assessment programs formulate hypotheses and gather data. While most of our programs are not fervidly revolutionary, skeptical, or nihilistic, they have diversified far beyond their historical progenitors. Our recent sponsorship of a special topic conference at Temple University on "Women in the Core" exemplifies this, as does our special topic upcoming conference on "Global General Education and Asian Texts." Ancients and post-modernists, epics and film, discussions about social media and ancient texts all appear in our panels. Our conferences encourage a civil discourse, frequently aimed at promoting a democratic character. Why, data even suggests that given time, liberal education graduates,

---

5 Bruce Kimball. *Orators and Philosophers: A History of the Idea of Liberal Education.* Expanded edition. New York: College Entrance Examination Board, 1995. For an extensive discussion of Kimball, see Chapter 7, "Enriching the Defense of Liberal Arts Education."

including our own students, fare well enough in the market of money and jobs.

What's missing? What can we do to change this situation of neglect and attacks, while we remain local in programs, committed to core texts, dedicated as faculty and institutions to knowledge, including its advancement, and democratic in our intentions? What we can do starts from within, and what we might do can be approached through what we are.

While ACTC mirrors the colleges and universities which are essential to its existence, there are very specific reasons for thinking it is not a conventional professional association, whatever its interests are in advancing careers of people dedicated to teaching core texts. In our first decade of existence, repeatedly, professors came to ACTC saying to me and to others, "I was so lonely, I didn't know you existed. What a relief." Or, "I've given up going to my disciplinary conferences; this is the only conference I go to now." At the origins of ACTC were faculty and administrators who had no associational, institutional, or collegial alternative— no community—to share their ideals, ambitions, hopes, and implementations of a classical liberal education.

During the early years of ACTC, I was the principal investigator in a very large-scale DOE Fund for Improvement of Post-Secondary Education (FIPSE) project which traced— through thousands of data points and hundreds of campus interviews with faculty, administrators and students—the causes of change in general liberal education.[6] The more an institution sought, through its general education, to characterize itself through a structured liberal education which involved the historical and current affiliations of the institution, as well as its students' intellectual preparation, the more distinctive and unique an institution's education became. Such structuring usually happened

6   "Assessing Trends in the Liberal Arts Core: A Vision for the 21ˢᵗ Century.' Final Report," by George Lucas and J. Scott Lee. The three-year project was originally conceived and developed by the American Academy for Liberal Education. It was privately continued by ACTC. The Final Report can be found on RESPONDEOBOOKS.COM.

when faculty members worked together across disciplines in general education and, especially, in programs commonly teaching core texts. Put otherwise, if you asked early attendees of ACTC what they wanted to do, the general answer was "I want to work with my campus colleagues to construct programs for students." In short, these attendees were educational inventors.

For 24 years, ACTC has worked with faculty in conferences and summer seminars to help bring into existence or improve programs dedicated to core texts, their teaching and curricula. Of those programs, about half have gone out of existence. This reflects a hard truth of institutional rejection, as well as acceptance, of our core text liberal arts programs.

Core text liberal education is an institutional phenomenon, which partly through the characteristics of different civilizational threads, partly through the intellectual history of liberal arts, partly through the histories of each institution of higher learning and, most especially, through dedicated faculty and administrators—still has an existence, however tentative, in our institutional life. Liberal education is not a disciplinary matter in the sense of professional organizations which form to regulate and judge the production of a particular body of knowledge. Further, considering the pluralism of programs and works of the arts and sciences within a curriculum of liberal education, no one discipline has an uncontested claim to it.[7] There is no discipline of liberal education. ACTC reflects all this, but to say that there is no single discipline of liberal education is a far cry from saying that such education has no coherence, modes of inquiry and research, structured history and development, or knowledge to teach. The peculiarity of

---

7   Certainly, three majors at St. Olaf College, my time at and degrees from the University of Chicago, and teaching at Temple University's Intellectual Heritage where the commonly taught syllabus stretched from ancient to modern times across the sciences and humanities—all tended to confirm the sense that there is no single discipline of liberal education. Whether education as a discipline makes a claim, other disciplines and the history of liberal arts education's construction at colleges and universities leave such claims in dispute.

this educational phenomenon has real consequences for ACTC, its members, and for institutions that strive to produce a liberal education.

Ask students or professors what degrees they took or offer and the answer comes back in terms of a specific disciplinary major: "I got a degree in physics; we offer a degree in English and in Secondary Education. My degree was in the history of art, not studio art." The federal government classifies degrees in this way. Yet, in the U.S., in a college or university we say that we offer a bachelor of science or a bachelor of arts degree and, depending on the institution, between 25% and 50% of the credits will not belong to a major. In a few programs or institutions there are no majors, save the liberal education itself. In Europe or Asia, licentiates function in the same way to obscure nascent and growing liberal education programs.

This matter of degrees is important. Needless to say, the acronym, STEM, captures a two-fold situation. It would seem as if the acronym in so neatly summarizing such majors, like a digital billboard, draws attention to what it is advertising, leaving out what it is not—a noticeable portion of the humanities degrees in institutions. No one doubts that if a student has acquired a bachelor-of-science that she or he is competently familiar with a science—with its subjects, its methods, and its techniques in the long run aimed at discovery. But, on the other hand, if I ask, "what arts does a student of a bachelor-of-arts possess?", I am very hard-pressed to say. I will say one thing: characterizing humanistic or liberal education as a possession of skills is a very weak answer to the question, "what arts does a bachelor of arts possess?"

Both to address the question of coherence and to restore the importance of liberal education, many current defenses of humanistic liberal education tend to characterize it as intrinsically ethical, political, or, occasionally, religiously-metaphysical education. Kronman, Nussbaum, Delbanco, Deneen, and Hütter come to mind.[8] Many of ACTC's programs argue such a defense and I

---

8   For a characterization of the defense of liberal education by these

do not wish to quarrel with it. But as a pluralist, I must comment that the defense is ecologically thin. First, it often leaves us in a secondary position. As in Aristotle's *Politics* or Plato's *Republic*, we are, then, directly or indirectly, in the service of other more important concerns.[9] Second, for those outside the academy, there are other institutions which compete with such liberal education claims: media, political organizations, church, and family all come to mind. Such defenses have truths within them, but they hardly exhaust the interests of students or parents whose intellectual and career interests extend well beyond ethical, political or religious considerations. As will be clear towards the end of this talk, I am not saying we should abandon these appeals or that ethics, politics and religion are not central concerns of liberal education, but to enrich the ecology of our public defense, we might begin to focus on the question I raised a moment ago, "what arts do our bachelor of arts students possess?"

In thinking seriously about that question, I came to think about our own panels and programs. My interests were in the characteristic intersection of liberal education with disciplines, because conversations at ACTC so frequently replicate or involve the situation of educated people talking across disciplines to illuminate an idea which without a conversation could not be expressed or, often, thought. Characteristically, this involves great human achievements, texts or works of the arts and sciences so diverse yet core to educating ourselves in who we are or might be that were we to remove them, liberal education as we practice

---

writers see Chapter 7.

9   When, in related fashion, we argue our utility—we are good for business, for international relations, for civilizational intersections, for becoming a lawyer—we are again secondary. In Greek political treatises, laws (constitutions) or education serve human happiness or flourishing, in so far as a community can provide for those, with contemplation or learning as an activity in accord with virtue. But there are alternatives to political ends: one is to pursue knowledge for its own sake, or, an artistic alternative is to pursue knowing the means of communication for the sake of empowering people with arts and sciences.

it would disappear. Because of their accessibility to the public, I focused upon the internal characteristics of imitative arts, widely conceived, that made our conversations possible and, yet, so unlike other professional conversations.

But after a number of years more, I came to see that a certain class of texts was missing from our conversations and our programs, which was curious, since we claim, usually, that we are liberal arts programs. I conducted a survey, based on our conference proposals from 2003 to 2014 of the core texts of the liberal arts which appeared in our panels. I refer, here, to works on grammar, rhetoric, dialectic and in other areas which stake a claim to the liberal arts or sciences. I found that works that actually formulate these arts from ancient to modern times were rarely discussed at ACTC's conference.[10] In essence, we had liberal education without liberal arts.

Was there a consequence? Yes. In this situation we find ourselves on the horns of a dilemma. Either we fall back on our disparate disciplinary training to provide method, or we rely on patterned habitual modes of conversation which are successful in generating trans-disciplinary insights that we all keenly feel as the strengths of our programs. But neither explores common *technē* of the liberal arts for our students nor gives an account of one of the chief characteristics of our programs. We all say that our works are signs of the human spirit because they are significant human achievements. In short, they are profound inventions, but, too often, we don't include works that would account for and illuminate what invention is.[11] I readily admit almost any course of

---

10   A sample list of "missing" works and authors concerned with the liberal arts can be found in Chapter 1, but these works range from Plato to Sontag and include many I did not list, there. See the "Rejuvenating and Reinventing the Liberal Arts" syllabus in the appendix.

11   For example, as a rough range for what invention is or entails, we can survey Cicero, Bacon, and Alberti, which correspond, roughly to "the discovery or devising of things, arguments or signs, to render a case probable or true. (*De Inventione*, I, vi, 9)," "the invention of knowledge… [which] penetrate[s and] overcome[s] nature in action [and] seek[s]…

core works could be taught as exemplification of invention, but my experience in core programs indicates they usually are not. Also, in scattered courses,—sometimes aligned to core curricula— logic, rhetoric, and composition are encountered, and the diverse methods of the disciplines yield real insights to works of art. But, speaking generally, we neither programmatically read the core texts of the liberal arts, nor cultivate the *technē* of the liberal arts embedded in these texts. In terms of inculcating in our students a technical capacity to write and speak for the public, or for our programs to make a just claim that liberal arts education is and continues to be inventive, we are missing an opportunity here.

After having presented these considerations to colleagues of the ACTC Liberal Arts Institute and interested parties in the general membership, I am happy to announce that ACTC has been invited by the Bradley Foundation to submit a grant application for a summer 2019 seminar of reading on core texts which invented and developed the liberal arts. Kathleen Burk, Ben Desmidt of Carthage and Joshua Parens the University of Dallas will lead the seminar, if funded. The aim of the seminar is theoretically, practically, and productively to introduce core texts of the liberal arts into core text programs, and to cultivate the *technē* of these arts in ourselves and our students so that the public may, ultimately, understand the important application of the liberal arts in our communal life.[12]

In the time remaining, I would like to illustrate what a focus

---

certain and demonstrable knowledge" or "directions for new works" (Novum Organum, aphorisms 8 & 90) and, extrapolating from Alberti, the production of beautiful, varietal, abundant, and pleasurable works which, particularly, go beyond nature III, par. 53-60. This applies not only to painting and sculpture, but to poetry, and, sometimes, the ugly as well.

12   ACTC subsequently was awarded a grant by Bradley, which in conjunction with the ACTC Liberal Arts Institute support led to the summer seminar faculty and curriculum development project, entitled "Rejuvenating and Reinventing the Liberal Arts," held at Carthage College in 2019. The seminar's syllabus can be found in Appendix 3 of this book.

on invention, works of significant achievement, and an examination of the explicit use of liberal arts might achieve for students.
So, let us explore a work of Leon Battista Alberti and a painting of
Sandro Botticelli's as our illustration of this powerful pedagogical
combination.[13]

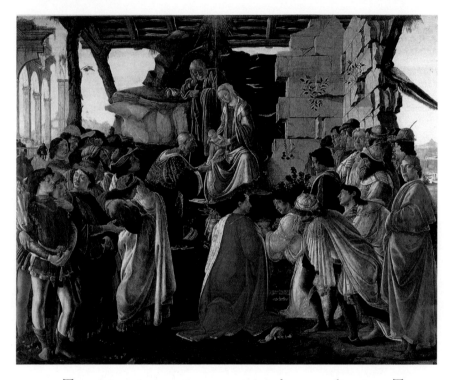

The picture in question was painted as an altarpiece. The

---

13   The poetic but not rhetorical portions of the following discussion of Botticelli were published in *Core Texts, Community, and Culture:
working together in liberal education.* "Art, Integrating Disciplines, and
Liberal Education: Imagining the Possible with Botticelli" Eds., Ronald
J. Weber et al. (10th Annual Conference of the Association for Core Texts
and Courses, April 15-18, 2004. Dallas.), University Press of America,
Lanham, MD, 2010, pp. 113-122. Also, the discussion was contextualized by an analysis of Joshua Reynolds' passages in *Discourses on Art* of
painting as a liberal art. No discussion of Alberti or invention appeared
in that chapter.

arrangement of the entire painting and your eye's tracking of it are a direct consequence of Botticelli's use of perspective—an original invention born of the liberal arts, specifically designed for painters by Leon Battista Alberti in his 1435 work, *De Pictura* or *On Painting*.

In Giotto's *Adoration* of 1305, before Alberti, we see what perspective in painting looked like. Alberti's success in shaping the art of painting through the liberal arts begins in geometry:

In Botticelli's *Adoration*, (1475) you can see some of the chief features of perspective's deployment. The perspectival centric point of the painting is next to the Christ-child's foot. The star's ray marks what might be called an inverted centric line, cutting the painting into two equal parts on the left and right. The geometric height of the *horizon* is determined by the human figure on the far right, who, if you put his feet on the bottom of the painting would have the top of his head mark the beginning of a horizon line running across the top of the ferns on the wall to the place where the Christ's foot is held, through the centric point. Above that line things are made to seem above us, the spectators. So, to the left of Mary's elbow and shoulder (our right) the undersurface of the blocks shows. Below her elbow no undersurfaces of blocks can be seen. Conversely, on the far lower left, you look down on the top of the lining of boots.

The figures that fan out to the right and left imply what would amount to a foreshortened tile pavement of geometric squares receding toward the centric point, dependent for their angles on the *braccia*—or approximately one-third body proportion of the figure to the right—which would mark out geometric points at the foot of the painting and determine the proportions of figures. The two angular blue lines that meet at a lower point on the 'centric' line represent a second focal point that determines how the figures stand and 'recede upstage' towards the Christ child and Mary. These lines not only place the human figures, but they are the foundation on which the outlines and surfaces of the painting appear.[14]

For Alberti, "the great work of the painter is the 'historia'," the scene of human movement, which is what we see in the Botticelli painting.[15] To achieve the "historia," Alberti "want(s) the painter… to be learned in the liberal arts." The first art to learn is geometry. The second are those of the poets and orators, for they "will be of great assistance in preparing the composition of the 'historia,' and the great virtue of this consists primarily in invention."[16] To illustrate invention, Alberti invokes the description that Lucian gives of Calumny painted by Apelles in which verbals abound: figures "approach," a face is "cunning," a hand is "holding," another hand is "dragging," a youth begs "with outstretched arms," a man is "leading," other figures are "attendant" or "arranging dress," a figure is "clad in mourning," "rending" her hair, and so forth. Despite this admirable variety[17], Alberti argued that, "Everything

---

14   The relevant passages and drawings for perspective appear in Bruni, *On Painting* (1435), translation Cecil Grayson introduction by Martin Kemp. London: Penguin, 1991, 2004, pp. 54-58, and 68-70.

15   Ibid., pp. 67-68.

16   Ibid. p. 88.

17   "Though variety is pleasing in any 'historia', a picture in which the attitudes and the movements of the bodies differ very much among themselves, is most pleasing of all." And he would "praise any great variety, provided it is appropriate to what is going on in the picture." Pp. 75 and 76.

the people in a painting do among themselves, or perform in relation to the spectators, must fit together to represent and explain the 'historia.'"[18] Alberti's argument focusses on what is going on in the painting, not on the mythological, historical, or Biblical background or aftermath of the 'historia.' 'Historia' are praised for invention in actions of a moment, not for their indications of past narratives from which the painter might draw, though there can be little doubt that Alberti as well as Botticelli, knew those narratives.

"Composition," Alberti's analogue to literary composition found in Quintilian, brings together the painting of geometry, perspective, bodily proportion and the historia.[19] For example:

> Now follows the composition of bodies, in which all the skill and merit of the painter lies... all the bodies in the 'historia' must conform in function and size... It would be a great fault if at the same distance some men were a great deal bigger than others, or dogs the same size as horses ... [20]

---

18   Ibid., p. 78.

19   Michael Baxandall, *Giotto and the Orators: Humanist observers of painting in Italy and the discovery of pictorial compostion,* Oxford, Clarendon Press, 1971, 1988, pp. 130-132, links painting to rhetorical grammar of Cicero and Quintilian, via Isadore of Saville, *Etymologiae* ii, 18. See Copella and Sluiter p. 245 for a translation that displays the structure discussed, here. Baxandall carefully expounds the analogy. Briefly, composition united the parts of the painting—surfaces or planes, members of body, and figures—into the whole historia. Surfaces or planes stood in Alberti's mind as the word does in a sentence, and etc. for the other parts. Compounded through the plane, member, body, to the whole picture—that is, the 'statement' (Baxandall uses "narrative" and "period" for statement) of the picture. To extend the analogy further: it seems that if the composition of the parts are the painting's statement, then that statement's syntactical reference is to the historia; or the 'syntax' of the painting stands in relation to Homer's verses, as the historia stands in relation to the plot of the *Iliad.*

20   Alberti, Ibid., pp. 74-75.

Why does Alberti persistently link perspective or geometry to the historia?

The simple answer lies in realistic, imitative likeness: "we do expect a painting that appears markedly in relief and similar to the objects presented"[21], and, as in the passage above, Alberti notes countless mistakes by painters in such efforts. The more complex answer arises from the fact that an historia in a painting cannot be the 'whole' story drawn from some source—in Botticelli's case the arrival of Magi—because painting is 'instantaneous'—this moment of the historia is selected.[22] For Alberti, proper perspective introduced unity into the 'historia' by making the eye dwell on figures as part of an almost inexorable movement towards the focal point.[23] Perspective used in historia arranges the parts of it and orders their appearance into a simpler or more complex size to be taken in by the eye—that is, to be perceived. In sum, we are dealing with potential magnitude of action through concerted alignment, proportion and gestures of the figures in an instantaneous moment.[24] We can trace Botticelli's use of this magnitude by re-entering this painting's human movement, for, ultimately, the picture's ability to focus our attention calls forth from an audience its recognition of what is in the scene.

---

21   Ibid., p. 67.

22   In one sense, this would mostly be true of any painting. Even if a painting depicts eternity through the arrangement of heavenly saints leading to God, it is still a moment frozen in the painting. In another sense, paintings are a bit like lyrical haiku, depicting a single momentary impression. Even so, a number of Botticelli 's *Adorations* and those by other artists seek to circumvent this limitation through processionals leading to the Christ Child.

23   "A 'historia' you can justifiably praise and admire will be one that reveals itself to be so charming and attractive as to hold the eye of the learned and unlearned spectator for a long while with a certain sense of pleasure and emotion." Ibid., p. 75.

24   What we are calling 'magnitude' was to Alberti close to 'harmony': "I believe that all the bodies should move in accordance with the action," p. 77.

Ruined Roman columns stand off to the left, but Botticelli's
scene is framed by a broken down squared-stone wall, now surrounded and covered by a crude "lean-to" of stakes and thatch. On
a rise above the foreground, perhaps a "rock" which many would
associate with the Church, this "parapet" frames Joseph and the
Virgin Mary, whose gesture offers the baby Jesus. As the star of
Bethlehem casts its rays through the framework of roof stakes
upon the Holy Family, the principals of the picture fan downward
in an arrangement of all who attend the Savior. Within the frame
of such ruins the eye descends to work its way through an "historical" scene with a strangely modern cast.

One of the most prominent modern figures is the first Magi
who, with his gift of gold in front of him, kneels to kiss the Savior's
foot. The likeness is of Cosimo d'Medici, grandfather of a clan
of Medici's, all present in this picture, and the founding patron
of the school of painters of which Botticelli was one. Lower to

the right, the two other Magi kneel looking to each other, as they await their turn with their gifts. These are Cosimo's sons. All three were deceased at the time this altar piece was painted. To the left, standing dressed in an extraordinary white toga is Cosimo's grandson, Lorenzo, "Il Magnifico." To the right across the picture and in front of a crowd, stands his younger brother, dressed in a black jerkin, Giovanni. "Up stage" on the stone wall is the peacock, adumbrating the resurrection. Against one part of the stone wall among many who are looking upon the scene is one figure who points to himself and looks out to the audience of the painting. This is Guasparre del Lama who, having had an entrepreneurial career ascending from the ranks of the laboring class to become a money changer—paralleling in some respects Botticelli's own rise in fortune—commissioned this altarpiece and may have requested that Botticelli feature his patrons, the Medici, in its arrangement. To the lower right, mirroring the direction of the gaze if not the countenance of del Lama most critics believe is the young, 25-year old Botticelli, who would have had motive enough to include the Medici.[25]

The entire effect of the ensemble is precisely the same effect produced by any proper arrangement of figures on a raked, proscenium stage so that the audience may see the action. Cosimo's sons look at each other as if to say "who is next after father?" Lorenzo gazes upward at his grandfather, Giovanni reflects with eyes cast down, and some witnesses of the scene direct their gaze and gestures toward the older and younger Medicis, as if wondering and learning how to kneel from masters. Others on left and right contemplate or adore the Christ and Holy Family. The three figures on the lower left seem to be remarking on the postures of Cosimo's sons. In turn, the humble figures of the Holy Family, centered upon Mary's silent gesture with her child, sit atop a pyramid of representatives of the masculine modern social order amidst the

---

25   Up to this point, the description of the figures and its Biblical scene is largely owed to Rose-Marie and Rainer Hagen in their *What Great Paintings Say*, volume 2, Koln: Taschen, 2003, 76-81.

ruins of an older culture, the heroic virtues clearly subordinate to the virtue of humility.

The painting's magnitude—its steady inexorable call to adoration—asks us whether art is changing the way people think, feel, and see. Modern figures entering historical scenes happened frequently enough in Renaissance painting so that we wish to make no claim that Botticelli was the first to make this sort of theatrical collapse of history and modernity.[26] That said, the action of the painting would be historical, that is, accepted by the audience of this picture as true. And, of course, so would the Christian virtue it exhibits, at least in so far as it was aligned with the historical story of the three Magi. Yet, despite any Florentine familiarity with paintings replete with interpretations of Biblically historical events set into contemporaneous surroundings, there is no reason to think, when we are being asked, that the Florentines and we cannot perceive the collapse of the distinction between the past and the present, between history and art.[27]

---

26   For example, Jean Fouquet painted the mistress of Charles VII as the Virgin Mary. Fra Lippi, Botticelli's mentor, painted "the Coronation of the Virgin." A group of bystanders depicted at the funeral includes a self-portrait of Filipino Lippi, together with his son Filippino and his helpers, FRA DIAMANTE and PIER MATTEO D'AMELIA." HTTPS:// EN.WIKIPEDIA.ORG/WIKI/FILIPPO_LIPPI. And, later, Raphael painted Leonardo as Plato, Michelangelo as Heraclitus, and Bramante as Euclid in the *School of Athens*.

27   Jan Van Eyck's portraits of historical bourgeois managers of the rising Burgundian state or church officials in piety before the figures of the Virgin Mary and Christ Child are innovative but in a different sense. Craig Harrison notes that despite the apparent realism (carried out by amazing technical proficiency in creating not only stone, cloth, and marble textures, reflections in mirrors and light through glass, but by assembling scenes which look as if they had been built by gothic masons and architects) of Van Eyck's paintings, the portraits neither imitate [copy] known physical scenes nor known historical biblical events. Here, known contemporary figures are placed (as they wish to be seen) in pious, reverential scenes. Like the Medici, the magnificence of their wealth or the dignity of their office is incorporated into the painting, but the collapse is not between history and modernity, but between modern office

Still, one is tempted to say that through the painting the variety of contemporaneous figures are all "playing their parts" upon the stage and are "assuming their roles" for the sake of the honor of being observed by the public in association with the Epiphany. And, indeed, the Medici played an active role in the *Compagnia de' Magi*, the brotherhood which, a bit like krewes planning the New Orleans Mardi Gras, met to plan and execute the Feast of the Epiphany.[28] At the very least, then, certain groups within the Florentine culture seem to "paint" the painting, long before Botticelli picks up his brush, co-opting a Biblical scene for their own aggrandizement. As has been observed by two critics, in a scene of "Christian piety" the picture "reflects the destinies and dependent relations of people in the Renaissance city where the ruling bankers [in an ostensibly republican city] were pleased to don the attire of the three kings."[29] Still, such criticisms and even

---

and godhead. These portraits, unlike Botticelli's Magi, are private scenes more or less privately shown for some time. Since they were privately shown, their function is less an imitation of what is devoutly to be wished about the august, than a private assurance, apparently insufficiently conveyed by church ritual, of the piety of the well-heeled. Art is making possible a private assurance—through the manner of its techniques and staging—that wealth, office, and religious cults may be received by Godhead through the proper piety of individuals. Again, these were not for public display, so it is entirely possible that in a nascent way, a way foreshadowing but not formulative of Protestant doctrine, the real figures were seeking to have an individual audience with God, sometimes unmediated by a priestly figure. Only in art, not in the Church, could this be so. Again, this is a foreshadowing of private communion with God, a loosening of a mental space about the relations between humans and God, made all the more likely both by the persuasive realism and by the obscure iconography of the paintings which, Craig Harrison in *Jan van Eyck: The Play of Realism*, second revised edition, London: Reaktion Books Ltd, 2012, notes, cannot be readily identified with Church doctrine.

28   Which, at one point in its history, decked out all of Florence to look like Jerusalem. Rob Hatfield, *Botticelli's Uffizi Adoration: A Study in Pictorial Content*. Princeton Essay on the Arts, 1976, p. 115.

29   Hagen & Hagen, Ibid., p. 81

the presence of a detailed contract, which we have in other cases of Botticelli's work, cannot explain the power of the painting.

For when we ask, "is this what the Medici would have done were the Baby Jesus available to them?", we have entered the world of possibility. We now have a problem of credibility; simply painting figures into a Biblical scene does not make it so any more than enactment in a play or festival does. Moreover, the painting fixes the image in a way that a stage spectacle or festival, given their dependence on continuous, yet ephemeral performance, cannot. We are now "permanently" asked by Botticelli's painting, could this be so?

Again, undeniably, the painting synthesizes elements of Biblical and Roman history and contemporary leadership through religious veneration, destroying the distinction between the past and the present. But so, in fact, would the Festival of the Epiphany—another *artistic* event. What difference does it make to the collapse of this distinction between past and present that these are works of art? [30] Certainly, whether we look at the production of the single artist or the collective production of the *Campagnia*, in order for the collapse to take place, to exist, these productions *must be separated* from their material, living authors. Put differently, they must be "completed." Botticelli laid upon his altarpiece his pigments, handed the altarpiece over to del Lama, and went on to paint different pictures in different homes of the well-heeled. The leaders of the city planned and executed their festival, handed it over to the public, and went on to concern themselves with the governing of cities, armies, and banks. And this means that the syntheses of past and present, made by festival or painting, are utterly dependent on art for their coming into being and, in the case of the painting, their continuation. This is what a painted "instantaneous moment" can be.

The synthesis of past and present, of banker, Christ, and observing artist, would not have existed except for the art. The

---

30   In the picture the collapse is reinforced even with the Roman ruins, for these would not have been ruins in the time of Jesus, any more than this scene took place in the time of the Medici.

moment of this painting never happened in this particularity and as such, to have re-presented "the Medici" in such an a-historical setting is not only to honor them, but literally to place the figures of them before and beneath God. Without the separate production of such works, this bowing and adoration by the Medici before any person would not have been *seen* and few would have *contemplated or felt the emotions attendant upon the scene* in any activity of the living participants.[31] True, we might say that the Christian culture with its exaltation of humility prepared the way for this painting. Indeed, quite probably, without textual artifacts separated from

---

31   Almost anyone in Florence could have seen this work. "Historical information: The painting was commissioned from Sandro Botticelli by Guaspare di Zanobi Del Lama for his own chapel situated on the inner facade of the church of Santa Maria Novella. The chapel was in fact dedicated to the Magi, probably because the name of Del Lama (or Lami) was the same as that traditionally attributed to one of the Magi (Gaspar). The commissioner, a broker belonging to the bankers' guild, the Arte del Cambio, and an open supporter of the Medici, must have ordered the painting before 30 January 1476, when he fell into disgrace and was condemned by the consuls of the Guild for illicit dealings." HTTP://WWW. PALAZZO-MEDICI.IT/MEDIATECA/EN/SCHEDE.PHP?ID_SCHEDA=318.   It was later removed from the church, passed into private collections of the Medici family, and emerged for public viewing in the Uffizi in 1796. Earlier, the Uffizi had been designated by the last surviving member of the Medici family as a home for the Medici collection and a shared public good: "The Family Pact, signed by Anna Maria Luisa de' Medici, the last of the Medici dynasty, ensured that all the Medici's art and treasures collected over nearly three centuries of political ascendancy remained in Florence. She bequeathed most of it to the Tuscan State upon her death in 1743 so that 'they would remain as decoration for the State, for the utility of the Public and to attract the curiosity of Foreigners', and it all had to stay in place and not leave Florence or Tuscany. In particular, she declared that the Uffizi Gallery was a 'inalienable public good', paving the way for its great wealth of art to be shared with all.

Sixteen years after her death, the Uffizi, built by Cosimo the Great, the founder of the Grand Duchy, was made open to public viewing and still contains a large portion of works commissioned and collected by the Medici." http://www.uffizi.org/museum/history/

the authors who wrote the early Christian gospels, preserving the notion that the kingly[32] are worshipful in an act of adoration, we would be unable to identify Christian culture in this aspect or with this content. Yet without art no one sees this inversion of humility and pride, and it is nearly unimaginable. Hence, only if the entire male society from artisan, to money-changer, to patriarch had had the opportunity and the wisdom to adore the Christ, and only if his mother extended that opportunity to them, only then would it be so. And only in art is it so.

The consequence is that art—not religion, politics or, even, culture—is providing not only the expressive vehicle but the substantive invention by which we may finally join with the audience of the Medici, to whom the painter's image looks out, to see this scene for what it is.

In this picture, we see what it would take to make our leaders and society—in all their majesty, richness, vanity, encultured clubiness, and dependent relations—bring themselves to the bar of humility. It would take something like Godhead, something that all could recognize as supremely more important than the state or power. It would take a divinely human innocence, grace, and blessedness, of mother and child, father and family. It would take a supreme leader. Even those who were in *his* family would have trouble bending their knees. To be truly at the bar, the politically connected would all have to be present; it would not do to have the "three kings" bow in a private meeting.[33] Among the ranks of those aspiring to be noticed and elevated, a leading act of humility would have to ripple through society. Though some witnesses might be so pre-occupied with themselves for having made such a scene possible that they might look out to see its effects on others, not only the connected of society would need to learn from their leaders, but so might any witnessing audience whose eyes are focused by the scene's arrangement, personages, and action.

---

32   Or, following the idea that the original, not the Medici, magi are astrologers—the knowledgeable.

33   As they seem to in the "historical" gospel (Matthew 2.11).

This is a conception of equality devoutly to be wished, an emotion moving away from envy or indignation toward benevolent hope, which arts in the widest sense of the term—as made things—have slowly worked into our culture over succeeding generations. It is an affective conception which is simply inconceivable without art.

I have tried to trace the parts of the image and their synthesis which leads us toward a recognition of freedom. In tracing the seven-hundred-year development of "equality of conditions" in America and Europe, before the institutional rise of democracy, de Tocqueville remarks, "little by little enlightenment spreads. One sees a taste for literature and the arts awaken; the mind becomes an element in success; science is a means of government; intelligence a social force; the lettered take a place in affairs."[34] Aristotle long before de Tocqueville remarks early on in the *Poetics* that what matters in artistic developments is less the formal intention artists take to a project, but the recognition of what they have achieved once they produce, say, a tragedy or a comedy. Here, these statements are two sides of the same coin.

When artists view their own works with the end of contemplating what they have wrought, they are no different than any other audience of art.[35] Botticelli may well have had no intention when he began this work of insinuating what de Tocqueville called the leveling of conditions, but by the time he was finished

---

34   Alexis de Tocqueville, *Democracy in America*. Translator, George Lawrence. NY: Perennial Classics Edition, Harper Collins. 2000, p. 9-10.

35   Aristotle, *Poetics*, 4. As a prefatory to an argument which distinguishes the historical differentiation of poets and poetry along formal lines of imitation, particularly of tragedy and comedy, epic and mock-epic, Aristotle remarks the spectators of imitations recognize that "this is that," i.e., that this art work is a tragedy, comedy and so forth. In *Learning to Look*, Joshua Taylor makes much the same comment at the onset of his analysis of differential treatments in paintings of 'the same' subject matter: "Perugino…has made us feel in a particular way about the Crucifixion, in a way we may not before have considered… the painting becomes, then, the basis for a new experience." Indeed, Perugino could conceivably belong to "we," p. 52. For more on the *Poetics* and history see Chapter 10.

he looked up and out from his painting to see those inside and out of the picture who gazed upon a sacred space that declared all humbly equal before God. Here, intellectual freedom and equality in image merge.

Yet, perhaps, if both the Florentines and we can read intellectual freedom through an image of equality, there is still one more step to take. For Marshall McLuhan, Renaissance painting as a medium used perspective to impose a cultural "point of view" that was partial, sequential, and specialized, one that created 'content' and could not, per force, offer an integrated, simultaneous view or world. Yet, the choric figure of Botticelli looking to the audience offers the very opposite in McLuhan's own terms: an integral, simultaneous *perception* of the freedom that comes when one possesses a medium or arts.[36] Through a medium that all might access, the figure of Botticelli and the entire painting challenge the unaware to become aware, the passive to become active, and observers to become artists, precisely because of the possibilities arts possess.

I think Botticelli took the notion of invention across the arts to heart. Frank Zöllner, a sensitive scholarly critic, has argued that Botticelli was specifically familiar with Alberti's argument, quoted above, that a painter should be "learned in all the liberal arts... [especially] the art[s] of geometry [and of] poets and orators... who ... will be of great assistance in preparing the composition of an 'historia', and the great virtue of this consists primarily in invention."[37] Interestingly but, perhaps, not convincingly, Zöllner

---

36   *Understanding Media: the Extensions of Man.* New American Library, 1964, 1966, pp. 27-29. Alberti "like[d] there to be someone" in the picture to guide the thinking and emotions of the spectators, pp. 77-78. Baxandall, *Painting & Experience,* notes this common practice but finds that secular gestures were more difficult to pin down and changed with fashion, apparently including Botticelli (67-70).

37   Alberti continues: "Indeed, *invention is such that even by itself and without pictorial representation it can give pleasure*" [my italics]. Alberti offers "the description that Lucian gives of the *Calumny of Apelles*" by the Greek artist, Zeuxis, as evidence that the 'imagination' is seized "only by

argues that Botticelli would have rejected invention as theoretically primary to his own painting. Almost without fail, Botticelli produced only unique works when he produced his novel Greek, mythical paintings. When he produced Biblically—or religiously-grounded paintings, the case was very different. There are 18 *Virgin and Childs*, 11 *Madonnas*, five *Annunciations*, four *St. Augustines*, two *Lamentations*, and there once were six or seven *Adorations* by Botticelli, five of which still exist. Botticelli kept producing his

the description in words," Ibid. p. 89. Botticelli's placement of a relief of Centaurs in his own *Calumny*—a reference to Zeuxis' ancient painting—leads Zöllner to argue that Alberti's notion of invention is a "thoroughly modern notion of the primacy of the concept" which Botticelli would reject, that Botticelli would not have accepted "the theoretical primacy of *inventio*." Why not? Zöllner notes that Zeuxis' depiction of Centaurs were highly praised by many in ancient Greece, but Zeuxis rejected the praise because "these gentlemen...place no value on the execution, to which any artist aspires...'" (167-168). Notwithstanding that Alberti cannot convey the invention of the Calumny without, at least using words, Zöllner's argument is that Botticelli paints his argument with Alberti against invention through a finished painting. Zöllner's chief concern is centered upon the intelligence with which Botticelli painted. Here, I offer an alternative about Botticelli's concerns with invention that shares Zöllner's conviction of the intelligence and artistry of Botticelli.

religious paintings across his career, which included along the way major style shifts and major shifts in his political surroundings. The *Adorations*, too, span his entire career from Lippi's workshop to near his retirement. The existing five differ markedly. Each is an invention in its own right.

Those knowing Aristotle, Cicero, or Quintilian will be familiar with the centrality and extensive elaboration of *topoi* (Greek) or *loci* (Latin) in dialectical and rhetorical arts. *Topoi* are commonplaces which a person employs to think. *Topoi* are like variables in math; they can be adapted to almost any matter or situation. Through the use of *topoi*, a rhetorician invents, while a dialectician discovers the principles for inquiries. Botticelli's situation is closest, perhaps, to Cicero, who treated the artistic products of Roman

life as *topoi* for speeches.[38] I suggest that Botticelli, knowing what
he did about the liberal arts and their intersections with painting,
through conjuring up, time-and-again, the *topoi* of Christianity,
created over his lifetime, along with his fellow painters, a painted
"art of rhetoric." Whatever commissions Botticelli was offered,
whatever influence he sought, his work is almost certainly systematic and developmental, since he not only returns to these *topoi* to
incarnate his stylistic changes, but the Christian *topoi* might be
arranged in narratives, themselves, of what he thought painting
could embody in permanent moments. In other words, *topoi* of
Christianity's intersection with its own past, the arts and sciences
of his day, and the culture of his times indicate the centrality of
invention to Botticelli's work.[39]

---

38   Cicero. *Cicero in Twenty Eight Volumes. IV. De Oratore.* Book II
and III. Trans. H. Rackham. Cambridge MA: Harvard University Press,
1942, 1968, II, par. 166-169, 172, p. 317-321, III, par. 26-28, p. 21-23.
Alberti signals a story in Cicero's De Inventione, II, 1-3 in which Zeuxis
chooses five women from which to model his paintings, the point being
that the overview of all women allowed a selection for composition. But
Cicero employs the story to illustrate how he has constructed his inquiry
into the art of rhetoric by consulting many sources. It seems likely that
Botticelli would know of the reference. Vasari is at pains to indicate
that early in life Botticelli "found it easy to learn" but that he was not
"contented with any form of learning, whether reading, writing or arithmetic," and so his father wearied of "the vagaries of his [son's] brain."
This characteristic of Botticelli's mind structures Vasari's whole life of
Botticelli which, after training in painting with Lippi, leads to an abun-
dance of inventions and beauties in painting and drawing. Vasari depicts
the mature Botticelli as "being a man of inquiring mind" and illustrates
his wit through three passed-down stories of practical jokes on his students and a neighbor. Giorgio Vasari, *Lives of the Painters, Sculptors, and
Architects,* Translator, Gaston du C. de Vere, I, Alfred A. Knopf: 1927,
1996 pp. 535-542.

39   I am, of course, aware that many of our programs are reaching out
to Eastern civilizations to construct East/West dialogues. Since there
is no ancient to modern historical narrative of Eastern and Western
civilizational interaction to construct, in this effort, what we see is the
spontaneous use of core texts of multiple traditions as *topoi*—places where

What's important for a core text, liberal arts education is that Botticelli is only one instance—in more than a two thousand-year history—of individuals acquiring, using, and extending the liberal arts as *technē*, while producing world changing art in the meantime. Some authors, such as Virginia Woolf in her *Letter to a Young Poet* and in *A Room of One's Own*, develop a *technē* of art, while explicitly imagining a future freedom, in this case, for women, men, and art. If the past is any indication, the future of the kind of education we espouse may well rest on whether we more explicitly explore and develop those works that formulate and inculcate the *technē*, scope, and invention of the liberal arts. Botticelli had no idea of the global future that he was painting for. Garnering reputation in Rome and Italy was about as much as he could hope for, though his life and art show he desired change in his time. In short, he was as local as could be. Yet, the significance of invention offered by his and others' synthesis of fine and liberal arts was an intellectual freedom, not only which all can appreciate, but everyone can achieve. Moreover, the liberal arts are responsible for innovations found in Bacon's, Newton's, and Henry Adams' developments of disciplines, while the founders of the American republic and the emancipators of American history—Lincoln, Douglass, Stanton, Anthony, Julia Ward Howe,[40] Dubois, and King—all employed the liberal arts to invent freedoms we cherish.

We can take a lesson from all this. David Brooks has been interviewing students at universities where our programs happen to reside. What he found is that they don't trust national institutions:

---

we go to think about questions such as "What is Nature?" or "What is Humanity?", perhaps even, "What is Art?" Systematically, habitually, or spontaneously, rhetoric's inventions and dialectic's questions occupy the ground they always have—the intersection of disciplines, civilizations, and, especially the sciences and arts.

40   Thanks to Mary Townsend for a paper on Julia Ward Howe's late 1880's address on behalf of suffrage which uses an explanation of Plato's treatment of women in the *Republic* to make the case for equality and the franchise.

I asked the students what agents of change they had faith in. They almost always mentioned somebody local, decentralized and on the ground—teachers, community organizers...I came away from these conversations thinking that one big challenge for this generation is determining how to take the good things that are happening on the local level and translate them to the national level, where the problems are.[41]

Whatever our nationalities, we are local, unique, authentic and that's where we can step in if we begin to teach the liberal arts and their technical as well as conceptual capacity for invention. That's what can give hope. There's a battle going on in the younger generation between those who, in pain, want to silence speech and tradition, and those who want to speak about what and how to take what has been rendered and remake it for the future. They don't know it, but the arts, liberal and fine, are the path to that future. We can help them to imagine the possibilities.

And, in fact, such imagining of possibilities happens time and again at ACTC. ACTC is an on-going invention about inventions, and in speeches, papers, panels, and conversations, highly educated people work with avid attention to listen to and speak about the inventions they bring and the inventions that the world has created. We meet for the sake of the future, but it is a future practiced in the moment, an intellectual freedom or autonomy we try to give to our students and to each other. It has been my pleasure to work in and serve such a community of artists and scholars for twenty-four years. Again, I thank you with my whole soul.

(Rev. Delivered at the ACTC Annual Conference in plenary session: 4/20/2018.)

---

41   *New York Times*, "A Generation Emerging from the Wreckage." 2/26/18.

CHAPTER 3

Rethinking Universities, College, and Hutchins

Faculty and Student Resistance to Core Text Curricula

I was asked by Albert Fernandez whether I would wish to give a talk in the annual lecture series here at Shimer. I suggested a talk on Hutchins' *Higher Learning in America* which I had been working on as part of a series of papers inquiring into possible core texts on education that might be appropriate for undergraduate great books or core text curricula in colleges and universities. I travel to many colleges and universities in my capacity as the Executive Director of the Association for Core Texts and Courses, and I have had the pleasure of being on this campus before. I have worked with and grown to respect and appreciate over many years the Shimer community as a significant gem in higher education, with genealogical roots to Robert Maynard Hutchins. So, I readily accepted Albert's gracious invitation.

A speech should "be able to cut up each kind according to its species along its natural joints" —Plato, *Phaedrus*, 265e.

Writing an article in 1995 defending a Dewey-based program of liberal education, Louis Menand was, then, a graduate faculty member of CUNY resistant to core text curricula.[1] Menand notes

---

1 Louis Menand, "Re-Imagining Liberal Education," in *Education and Democracy: Re-imagining Liberal Learning in America*. Ed. Robert Orrill. The College Board, 1997, pp. 1-20.

that postmodern notions have undermined the use of core texts because the "sort of texts" typically taught in such curricula are theoretically deconstructable in relation to disciplines and hegemonic in papering over the wide differences amongst various populations. Exhibit A of the core program is Hutchins *The Higher Learning in America,* Exhibit B the Harvard *Red Book.* Since Menand contributes to the Dewey-Hutchins debate, Menand's topics from the cultivation of virtue and culture to the reorganization of universities frequently reflect Hutchins' arguments. This suggests a question, "have we missed anything in Hutchins?"

Generally, liberal arts, core text programs are viewed as an education into the complex world of adults and, thus, an aid in maturing judgment. Part of that complex world is the adjustment that adults make to the institutions they come to participate in, including universities and colleges. Notwithstanding even a thorough examination of *The Republic,* programmatic attempts to have students reflect upon works about undergraduate, liberal arts education and their books are few and far between. The absence of these texts has left core text faculty proponents relatively inarticulate in class about such programs, and in the students' case, nearly "clueless," as to why core text, liberal arts education ought to be included in their undergraduate curricula.[2] It is as if we expected an education in books, particularly of the pre-moderns, to be obvious, *prima facie* in its necessities, excellence, and function.[3]

Hutchins is often read by faculty, but rarely by students,

---

2   Of course, these remarks do not apply to the initiated body of Shimer students before me, but, rather, to many faculty and students found at other institutions. Still, because this particular audience specifically takes a program in great books designated as a Hutchins program, it perhaps has a sensitivity to the need to reflect upon why core texts ought to be part of a liberal education.

3   Yet from the ancients to moderns such works exist. From Plato's *Phaedrus* and *Republic,* to Augustine's and Rousseau's *Confessions,* to Newman's and Henry Adam's reflections on institutions, disciplines, and educations, such works are available to our students to read and ought to be included in some measure in core text programs.

particularly chapters II and III, "The Dilemmas of the Higher Education" and "General Education." Hutchins' argument foresaw dilemmas for university organization and learning, within and without the academy, that have become manifest since he wrote. So, to place the book in a core course would be to engage students and professors in a conversation about texts, curricula, colleges and graduate programs of universities, student and faculty life, disciplines and interdisciplinarity, the past and present, as well as the cultural movements that actually shape lives. Menand's imagined liberal education and university is as like democratic-vocational life as is possible[4]; Hutchins' program prepares for, enhances and participates in democratic and vocational life by carefully distinguishing what a university and liberal education can uniquely add to them. The book argues that the royal road to reforming professional and graduate education lies through liberal, general education based in great books spanning ancient to modern life. Surprisingly, a careful reading of Hutchins' chapters reveals argumentative joints, alternatives within the dilemmas of university programs, teaching and scholarship, whether he would approve of these or not, which can still shape our judgment about colleges, universities, their organization, and their curricula.

Hutchins believed both that American culture and much of institutional academic culture was largely anti-intellectual, and that the acquisition and growth of professional, vocational schools within universities, as constituted when he wrote, was ineffective and useless, even for the end that "a professional school['s...] graduates shall get jobs."[5] Hutchins proposed a radical reorganization of the

---

4   Dewey "conceived of the educational process as itself democratic... You can only teach a virtue by calling upon people to exercise it. People... learn...by doing. Dewey believed that the classroom was a laboratory in which to experiment with the business of participating in the associated [social] life." Ibid. pp. 12 and 17.

5   Robert Maynard Hutchins, *Higher Learning in America*. Intro. Harry S. Ashmore. New Brunswick, Transaction Publishers, 1936, 1995, p. 55.

university, by centering that university on what we, today, call its mission or intentionalities.

According to Hutchins, universities should not be an organ promoting "material prosperity [or] adjustment to the [social] environment," but rather be a "haven where the search for the truth may go on unhampered by utility or pressure for 'results'."[6] This "search for the truth" would be centered on "research," which Hutchins characterizes as "creative thought," as opposed to the elaboration of practical experience or "tricks of the trade" in vocationalized professional schools.[7] What, then, might be "creative thought" as research?"

Medical schools are Hutchins' example of appropriate professional, vocational training in line with a university's mission because they "were made part of universities in order to secure for them the benefits of any thinking that might be going into them." The centerpiece of the infusion of thought was the "laboratories," because by these means "a connection was sought not with large hospitals but with strong departments in the basic sciences." Thinking was focused, in laboratories, "on the intellectual problems of the profession," which, more broadly, could be designated as "each profession's theory." Hutchins characterizes a theory as the "general principles, the fundamental propositions, ...of any *discipline*."[8] Thus, creative research elaborates or probes these propositions, which are neither necessarily few nor many in number.

---

6   Ibid., pp. 43 and 62 Of course, there are two arguments that the search for truth is not what concerns a university. The first is the positivistic argument that what is sought is not truth (or meaning) but predictive explanation. The second is the postmodernist argument that either the truth is unattainable or that institutions and individuals seek power, masquerading ideology as truth. While Hutchins would deny these propositions, his notion of "creative research" could accommodate them. There is, besides, a neglected argument about technology within Hutchins' argument, treated below, which provides further accommodation.

7   Ibid., pp. 44 and 47.

8   Discussions of "theory" in the humanities, today, tend to argue that there is only one, general, theoretical position composed of Sausserean

One might think that to illustrate disciplines, Hutchins might directly refer, as he does in Chapter 4, to divisions of knowledge embodied by standard departments. However, the "professionalization" of "vocations" into disciplines actually widens the consideration by Hutchins of what might count as principles.

For Hutchins principles were not necessarily grounded in science. Rather, each discipline's theory has its "intellectual problems," which require a discipline to locate its appropriate principles and to solve problems both of knowledge and practical outcomes[9]: thus, if a professor at a law school taught his students to "underst[and] the principles, if any, of pleading, [the students] could, then, have worked out for themselves the rationales of the rules of any jurisdiction."[10] We reach, here, a real joint in the argument, for Hutchins was not recommending the "scientification" of law, business or journalism, or indifference to applications of knowledge, but rather the focus of learning upon the foundations of disciplines.[11] It is possible foundations of disciplines which really concern Hutchins.

---

semantics, Freudian psychology, and Marxian economics which is, then, applied repetitively to an infinity of contemporary and historical situations. In one sense, discussions of theory are endless because infinitely applicable; in another, theory is dead because no one is really examining the prevailing fundamental theoretical positions. In this post-modern theoretical sense, Hutchins whole scheme of education becomes accidentally doable, but essentially useless, for we could read all the great works, but why bother when we have the right theoretical principles and we can apply our principles to contemporary problems, literature or to literatures and problems outside the scope of conversation of any canon?

9   Ibid., pp 46 and 52.

10   Ibid. p. 49.

11   Here, again, modern theory challenges Hutchins, for the former assumes that there is one comprehensive theory to explain almost any disciplinary, historical development. No one doubts that disciplines do train people differently, but not in light of principles, only techniques of specialized application to given situations. Thus, expertise is not a matter of fundamental differences, but simply specialized application. You may as readily apply modern theory to the development of modern history

The disciplinary approach is not something easily given up by Hutchins in working on his problem of the nature of universities, for it supplies the characteristics of graduates, professionals, intellectual "training," and institutional ends that can distinguish a university education from vocational training. Further, it is "intellectual content," that is, theory, by which learning the subject matter of a discipline is distinguished from learning the rules of the trade.[12] Through these common characteristics Hutchins collapses distinctions between professions and disciplines into the term "learned profession." And, by this collapse, Hutchins' argument outlines that *each learned profession* has "a great intellectual heritage which should be the prime object of the attention of professional schools."[13]

The theory and discipline argument is a joint in the argument and presents several problems for students and faculty to ponder. The distinction between laboratory work and inquiry into the principles of pleading, leads to quite different directions not only of subject matter, but, as it were, the "raw materials" of investigation—the latter of which, Hutchins hints, extends through libraries, not laboratories, back to the ancient world in an historical body of legal, political, and philosophical writings.[14] We might

---

of science (Fuller) as to analysis of performance (Barthe) as to analysis of removed cultures of South America. This is basically what Menand means when he thinks post-modernism has deconstructed the idea of disciplines.

12   Ibid. Again, "All that can be learned in any university is the general principles, the fundamental propositions, the theory of any discipline," p. 48. "An educated man knows what he is doing and why.... The subject matter of a learned profession is intellectual [which can] generally be mastered only in a university.... To the extent to which attention of the student is directed to vocational interests and away from intellectual content of the discipline, the university fails to do the thing it might do", p. 52. "A professional discipline, to be a professional discipline, must have intellectual content," p. 56.

13   Ibid., p. 57.

14   For example, "The *Republic* of Plato is basic to an understanding

ask if the learned profession of law obviously appeals to a great intellectual heritage, in what sense could Hutchins use a laboratory to arrive at a "great intellectual heritage"?

The issue of laboratories as pathways to principles and inclusion of medical schools in universities brings up a similar problem for those students interested in arts. Later, Hutchins advocates the use of the liberal arts in general education upon "classics," some of which he sees as exemplary of the "arts of reading, writing, thinking and speaking, together with mathematics." The gerunds, of course, indicate performative doing. Music, however, is notably absent, and elsewhere the Fine Arts receive scant mention. Hutchins discusses the liberal arts as "rules" and "means" by which we determine "how excellence is achieved" in these activities and products. We might ask our students, must, then, this general education include performance? Is analyzing examples of excellence in achievement in the arts the same as "understanding" it? Are "rules" a necessary step towards principles in these arts? Beyond "rules," is performance necessary to understanding theories of arts, or should performance be considered as something outside general education. And, if understanding of the fine arts' theories depends on performance, might that admit so-called schools of the fine arts to a university?

Further, disciplinary divisions, in Hutchins' view, led to mutual unintelligibility amongst the professoriate. Without epistemic sharing, the fundamental condition of a knowledge community would be lost: "unless students and professors...have a common intellectual training...professors cannot talk to one another, not at least about anything important. They cannot understand one another." [15] Crucially, what Hutchins *must* mean by the use of the

---

of law; it is equally as important for an education for what is known as citizenship," Ibid. p. 81.

15   To the extent that post-modern theory is shared by academics, this proposition is denied, of course. But there are theory disagreements between those who tend toward Enlightenment political thought and those who tend toward post-modernity. And, there are obvious theoretical gaps between the humanistic post-modernists and theoretical

words "important" and "understand" is to be able to speak to each other's theories by sharing a means of the search for truth, akin to but not the same as the means of a laboratory or specialized historical bibliography. Here, Hutchins crosses the boundaries of expertise, some would say without a passport. But in Hutchins' view the alternative is that there is not even a diplomatic corps or trading exchange of ideas.

Finally, the reliance on disciplinary investigation carries with it tensions for institutions over what constitutes education, which go beyond the characteristics by which one knows one is dealing with a disciplinary education. For example, in a class with students, professors might ask, do students really want to get an education in an institution where an advisor or trusted professor has no idea what the other professors in the institution are teaching or know?[16] Put differently, in the absence of unitary, shared epistemologies, is there a systematic answer to the problem of relating the divisions in theory, methods, and subjects within institutions by means of education for students?

The choice of means that Hutchins makes to solve his

---

physics—the Sokal hoax pointed this out. See, http://www.physics.nyu. edu/faculty/sokal/lingua_franca_v4/lingua_franca_v4.html. See also, E. O. Wilson, *Consilience: The Unity of Knowledge,* New York: Alfred A. Knopf Publishers: 1998, p. 9, who offers a different comprehensive theoretical position from post-modernity, locates his principles in scientific, particularly biological, discovery. More generally, Gerald Holton, an historian of science, has argued that there is still a "silence between the disciplines" in education and, of course, the specter of C.P. Snow has not been banished from the campuses. During interviews conducted on campuses of institutions participating in the *Assessing Trends in the Liberal Arts Core* project, I have had discussions on campuses with professors of the social sciences who cannot find theoretical agreement, even though they are housed in the same division of the university. For the *Assessing Trends* project's Final Report by George Lucas and J. Scott Lee, see RESPONDEOBOOKS.COM.

16   This is not fanciful. See the Final Report of the ACTC, NEH supported "Bridging the Gap Between the Humanities and Sciences: An Exemplary Education Project," on RESPONDEOBOOKS.COM.

intellectual problems of theory, discipline, and education is surprising: general education. General education is said to aid the mission of universities to provide creative research by instituting the possibility of professors communicating across disciplines. Yet, general education is, by its nature, pre-disciplinary as Hutchins understands it and is, in this sense, literally no part of the university, but, rather, a condition for it: "the scheme I advance is based on the notion that general education is education for everybody, whether he goes to the university or not."[17]

Ultimately, it was books, not the laboratory, in which intellectual heritage was located because then-current educational practices made inquiry into an intellectual heritage impossible:

> we are so impressed with scientific and technological progress that we assume similar progress in every field. We renounce our intellectual heritage, read only the most recent books, discuss only current events, [and] try to keep the schools … ahead of the times.[18]

Hutchins thought that, if specialists were not to be cut off, through ever-increasing divisions of subjects, "from every field but [their] own," then they had to have "the same basic education that other specialists have"[19] which meant "having a common stock of fundamental ideas."[20] All professors would, over time, have this general

---

17   Ibid., p. 62. In Hutchins conception, general education would not correspond, as a schooling, to any institutional arrangement that existed at the time or since, for it was to run from age 16 to 20, that is, from the junior year of high school to the junior year of college. Hutchins did invite 16 -year-olds to the University's College; Leon Botstein, President of Bard College, and Earl Shorris, author of *Riches for the Poor*, who through his book and collaboration with Botstein, established the Clemente Course in the Humanities, are [were] two living examples. [Shorris died in 2012.]

18   Hutchins, Ibid. p. 64.

19   Ibid. p. 59.

20   Ibid. p. 85.

education and, possessing it, would use it to discuss their varying disciplinary pursuits of knowledge.

As Hutchins might have predicted, today the idea that there is an intellectual heritage, much less what it is, seems conservatively outdated, scientifically unimportant, or even simply astonishing to faculty and students alike. But widely accepted solutions and problems in similar areas of heritage and disciplinary cultures might cause all of us to rethink our doubts. For example, the problems of divisions of knowledge within universities leaves Hutchins in a position that would not be that far from either Kuhn's position in 1956 on the structure of scientific revolutions which strongly suggests historical, practical solutions to theoretic problems in the historiography of science, or Snow's 1959 position on two cultures in academe. Like Kuhn, Hutchins characterizes practical phenomena that everyone acknowledges—in Kuhn's case, scientific revolutions, in this case fractured knowledge and vocational training in higher education. Like Kuhn who must turn to historiography to justify his thesis, Hutchins can perform no experiment nor survey which will show that his general education proposal works, and so he must rely, as we will see, on a kind of historical record of interdisciplinary conversation to argue his model. But his problem is more complicated than Kuhn's, too. Initially, Kuhn sought to change practice in the rather small field of scientific historiography—a change which did not require major institutional adjustments.[21] Hutchins must attempt a revolution in the minds of those who represent the entrenched structures of knowledge and vocational training, in all fields, that had spearheaded the creation of modern universities. This is another crucial joint in the argument for it implies that Hutchins is engaged in a form of cultural

---

21   The likenesses can be traced through Hutchins and Thomas Kuhn, "Historical Structure of Scientific Discovery, Science, June 1962, v. 136, 760-764. Kuhn's work was related, according to Steven Fuller, to Harvard's general education. Steve Fuller *Thomas Kuhn: A Philosophical History of our Time.* Chicago: University of Chicago Press, 2000. P. 379

critique and studies, no less thorough in its persuasive implications than any postmodern criticism.[22]

Therefore, Hutchins must have a two-part argument: political and poetic. His ethical/political argument about general education addresses cultivating human capacities, particularly intellectual virtues, with an argument derived from Aquinas based on Aristotle's *Ethics*,[23] and I will, briefly, turn to that argument in a different fashion than did Hutchins. But universities are made, not born. They were *invented* in the 12th Century. So it is both consistent and fruitful for Hutchins' chapter on general education to expend the same effort on books, the liberal arts for accessing them, and an intellectual heritage as a resource for education, that is, on made things, as it does on the capacities of human nature. For Hutchins' ultimate concern is what inventions, including universities and the theories they generate, add to our perception of a common humanity.

Since Hutchins' problems are disunified branches of knowledge, disunified social organization of universities, and disunified undergraduate curricula, he argued that the Truth was identical in

---

22   The first chapter, "External Conditions [of the University]," is a thorough-going examination of the influence of structures of power upon the function of research and education, and, though the word "ideology" is never employed, anyone who reads the chapter without thinking that Hutchins understands the attempts of sources of social power, including deployments of language, to co-opt universities or to exclude others by means of forming specific associations through networks of the prevailing social order would be willfully insisting on a "formal" language and topical use that his arguments can accommodate. There is no discussion of race, gender or ethnicity, but the application of the discussion is perfectly apposite.

23   Ibid., On Aristotle: pp. 62-63, and 68, and Aquinas, pp. 63 and 96-97. Today, as our assessments of learning focus on human behaviors and products, we still speak of cultivating capacities and competencies. (Nussbaum, *Cultivating Humanity* and *Women and Human Development: The Capabilities Approach.*) This is also the basis of Hutchins life-long learning argument because the idea is for graduates to carry their intellectual abilities into the world by staying engaged intellectually.

all times and places, an education "designed for the whole people" would be the same regardless of time or circumstance, and that "in general education we are interested in drawing out the elements of our common human nature...not the accidents of individuals."[24] But the concern with university re-organization and the reliance on classics means that Truth and human nature are interpreted by Hutchins through human achievement as well as through epistemics or politics. Undoubtedly, Louis Menand is partially right when he interprets Hutchins' remark that a "classic is a book that is contemporary in every age" by thinking that Hutchins had in mind enduring truths that could be found in classic works.[25] But it is certain that not only do classics contradict each other, but that statements of truth change and the reasons for these changes can be learned. That is what an intellectual inheritance means, and Hutchins knew that, too.

This is why Hutchins' use of the words, "drawing out," are important.[26] The whole point of his book is to reform institutions of higher learning toward "talk[ing] about things that matter"—i.e., knowledge, theories, and creative thought.[27] A "drawing out" is a specific kind of communication—one that relies on a *conversation*. Within general education, to "draw out" the elements of human nature, means to engage in a discourse about it with works in contradiction and in constant reformulation, using common arts of discourse and math which can negotiate across the private or technical languages of disciplines. Thus, we come to another joint in the argument: for whatever the virtues sought or the heritage employed, there can be no such education without conversation—a drawing out—based in human constructions of books, universities, and, even, laboratories which would necessarily lead not only to positions quite different from Hutchins' apparent

---

24   Hutchins, p. 66.

25   Menand, Ibid., p. 5.

26   Ibid. He uses the phrase twice at crucial passages in the argument, 66, 73.

27   Ibid. p. 59.

position but to works extending well beyond questions of human nature.[28]

Conversationalists in a class would gather the scope of the works and conversation by noting Hutchins' reliance on William Whewell's distinction between progressive and permanent studies. In addition, they would arrive at the most persuasive argument for using an intellectual heritage to sustain a conversation: namely, that in restricting ourselves to relatively recent works in any field— from the Enlightenment on—we necessarily limit our intellectual resources. Put differently, the 'we know more argument' is actually a 'know less' position.

To explain what we could 'know more' about, curiously, Hutchins' begins by approval of a foundational work of modern sciences: "If we read Newton's *Principia*, ... we understand ... the basis of modern science."[29] The book and statement seem to illustrate progressive, not permanent, studies for, "a body in motion tends to stay in motion" capped an intellectual revolution at the time of writing, the book is on the cusp of the Enlightenment, it insists on an experimental, that is, laboratory, connection to its theoretical development of the Motion of Fluids (II, ix, 51, 39, and ff. e.g.), and it advanced scientific progress. Yet, the significance of this selection becomes clear in the approbation Hutchins extends to Nicholas Butler's claim:

> "[that] only the scholar can realize how little that is being said and thought in the modern world is new. It was the colossal triumph of the Greeks and Romans to sound the depths of almost every problem...."[30]

Hutchins approves of opening education up to the works of

---

28   Not only some post-modern positions might be accommodated, here, but also some ancient precursors, not the least of which would be Gorgias and Cicero.

29   Ibid. p. 79.

30   Ibid. Quoted by Hutchins, p. 80.

the Greeks, Romans, and Medievals, but his deployment of the *Principia* shows why and that he would go further than Murray: what is at stake in reading such works may or may not involve our notions of progress, but the readings will give full scope to the intellectual problems out of which thoughtful solutions—ancient or modern—emerged.

And here we arrive at, possibly, the most important joint of all in Hutchins' argument. An education centered on intellectual problems for students would be completely silly if the past and the present were not different. It should come as no surprise that Hutchins, despite an adherence to universals of education, also argued that "the aim of education is to connect man with man, to connect the past with the present, and to advance the thinking of the race."[31] Opening up to the past implies the examination of change. One of the chief values of a book is that it is a made thing, quite separate from its author and, as time passes, its specific culture. Great books, whether belonging to the sciences or the humanities, are art: made things, now present to bring us voices, accomplishments, and cultures of the past. Art, which can be discussed by its Greek cognate, technology, has been one of the chief sources of change in civilizations since their inception. It still is. To produce a book is to invite change, and to produce a great book is to invite great change. In the sense that great books embody change they are, then, a technology of changing our minds. Indeed, if we want to learn both how and why cultures, history, literature, philosophy and science change, we read such books. Conversely, a great books curriculum is, then, a platform exhibiting the variability, development, concerns, and progress of this fundamental technology of cultural change. Such curricula are "natural histories" of books.

Hutchins not only approved Butler but asked him, "Why should this insight [of opening intellectual problems through an intellectual inheritance] be confined to scholars?" In doing so, he is indicating his chief reliance on human nature, taking the side of *students*, and adumbrating a solution to C. P. Snow's cultural

---

31   Ibid. p. 71.

problem: Hutchins is treating his reader here neither as scientist nor scholar, but as learner —that is, intellectually interested *student*—of the problems and ideas that have built disciplines of knowledge.

To do so is to begin an intellectual move that recognizes that the disciplinary framework which originated Hutchins' problem is insufficient to offer adequate solutions. Hutchins centered his argument upon Aristotelian distinctions: general education conduces to practical wisdom, and metaphysics can act as the epistemic unifying field of a university. But the human capacity to learn is, of course, the primary element of human nature that Hutchins relies upon for his program.[32] He, therefore, could have used Aristotle without ultimately appealing to either practical wisdom or the highest knowledge. Selections from Aristotle's *Politics, Ethics*, and *Parts of Animals* stake out a set of ideas relating general education of a liberal character to its students and to its "graduates," which address the increasing capacity of students *to judge* and to learn-by-judging constructs from art, personal statements, and scientific treatises. In the *Ethics*, this activity indicates a maturing, analogous relation between ethical understanding and general learning which is quite different from Plato or the many Enlightenment collapses of judgment into one ostensible logistic or scientific method of learning and knowing. The Aristotelian argument re-visions for us (post)moderns the dichotomous ends which form many liberal education arguments: particularly, wisdom versus expertise, moral development versus research training, and, ultimately, general versus disciplinary learning. Aristotle leads us to consider, not either-or, but complementary, enhancing, indeed, expanding both-and.[33]

---

32   Aristotle. "All men by nature desire to know." Metaphysics, I. 980a 23.

33   The relevant passages, beginning in the *Ethics*, are I, iii, 1094b27-1095b5, and VI, x, 1143a 8-15. These are directly related to Aristotle's discussion of music, where nine points specifying its use in liberal education may be generalized to ask if any subject is so qualified: *Politics*, VIII, v, 1339b11-vi, 1341a9. The discussion in the *Politics* is of early liberal

In other words, instead of facing a dichotomous choice between liberal arts undergraduate education and research-like undergraduate education, is such a thing as a liberal arts undergraduate education backed by a liberal arts research program possible? The answer to the question is that this has been factually done but is little appreciated. Published sources on specific courses, course development in the context of liberal arts and core texts in universities, and descriptions and examples of graduate and post-graduate research programs based in world classics and in the notion of syntopically mapping out and interpreting intellectual problems have been published by like-minded scholars, including R. P. McKeon, Ronald Crane, Mortimer Adler and Mark Van Doren, and Otto Byrd. This body of work appears somewhat dated. But, it should be noted that Ernest Boyer called in 1990 for re-conceiving research scholarship as an *integrative* capacity, focusing not on "what is yet to be found" but on "what do the findings mean?" Initiated through a reference to Mark Van Doren's promotion of integrative views of knowledge, Boyer's call actually fits a program leading from undergraduate education to post-graduate research which would make Hutchins' dream of an interpretive community of scholars—across all disciplines—come

---

education which aims at inculcating judgment. The discussion in The *Parts of Animals*, by aid of the *NE* passages above, stakes out the intellectual capacity of one who is accomplished in such a general (or liberal) education (paideia) as distinguished from an expert, I, i, 639b1-15. These passages may further be linked to discussions of cultural conversations of art (in the Poetics 25, and to the functions and use of dialectic (forms of reasoning and criticism) and rhetoric (judgment) (Topics, I, ii, 100a25-101b4, and Rhetoric I, i, 1354a1-1355b22, and 3 1358a36-b7.) Phillip R. Sloan, in a plenary speech delivered at the Association for Core Texts and Course's 2005 annual conference, argues that a passage in the Metaphysics (IV. iii. 1006a7) links paideia to the acquisition of judgment in knowing when "more learning is required." "Expanding Core Texts Across Borders: A *Paideia* for a World Encounter," in *Contemplation, Crisis, Construct: Appropriating Core Texts in the Curriculum.* University Press of America, 2014, pp. 3-12. Chapters 7 and 10 of this book expand on these connections in the corpus of Aristotle.

alive.[34] Boyer argues that "today, interdisciplinary *and* integrative studies, long on the edges of academic life, are moving toward the center, responding both to new intellectual questions and to pressing human problems." To illustrate this, he quotes at length a passage out of Clifford Geertz's article, "Blurred Genres: The

---

34   The relevant works are R. P. McKeon, *On Knowing—The Natural Sciences*, a complete undergraduate course on great works in physics and the role of interpreting (and differentiating) modes of scientific inquiry, esp., 1-7. _____, "Criticism and the Liberal Arts: The Chicago School of Criticism," in *Profession* (MLA) 72; R. Crane, "The Idea of the Humanities" in *The Idea of the Humanities and other essays critical and historical*, a reformulation of the liberal arts in their humanistic component as four basic modes of inquiry, directly useful for undergraduate education; Mark Van Doren, *Liberal Education*, Boston: Beacon Press, 1959, p. 115; Mortimer Adler and Charles Van Doren, *How to Read a Book*, particularly the chapter, "The Fourth Level of Reading, Syntopical Reading" in which a graduate-level/dissertation reading exercise, in either great books or very important ones, is broadly illustrated on the problem of "progress"; Otto Byrd, in *Seeking a Center: my life as a 'Great Bookie'* in which Byrd traces the pursuit of the idea of justice by students from an undergraduate, interdisciplinary seminar to a professor writing articles—in the syntopical manner—on the controversies surrounding ideas of justice. In his explanation, there are opportunities for special inquiries—for example, into those theories that emphasize freedom and spirit (Hegel and Del Vecchio,)—but the ultimate goal is to "identify the basic theories of justice and to map the controversy as a whole," 82-117. A valuable balance to Crane, is Byrd's *Cultures in Conflict*, an examination of the intellectual heritage of three academic cultures—humanistic, religious, and scientific—and how these might be harmonized. Ernest L. Boyer, *Scholarship Reconsidered*, had great success in sustaining the usual "discovery" research and promoting the "scholarship of teaching," but the possibilities of his "scholarship of integration" (and the "scholarship of application") which best fits the line of undergraduate to professorial activity outlined in this note have received less widespread development, Chapter 2, pp. 15-25. Just as I am arguing that Hutchins can be reconsidered, so Edward Said, though approaching a position similar to Menand, invoked R. S. Crane's definition of humanism in order to describe the project of multi-cultural humanistic critique for the sake of democracy, *Humanism and Democratic Criticism*, NY: Columbia University Press, 2004, pp 15 ff.

Reconfiguration of Social Thought" in which Geertz outlines numerous mixing of genres to indicate new questions, problems, and forms of research. The passage is, of course, unintelligible to one unfamiliar with traditions of books. On the other hand, to one who has or is gaining such familiarity, it suggests both research and *undergraduate* creative work.

So, the books of Hutchins' education would be foundational and innovative: that is, they have the status of being acknowledged as that out of which wide-ranging and fruitful intellectual developments arose and can arise. When Hutchins is summing up the fruits of this education, he returns to his point of origin for it: "… students and professors may acquire through this course of study a common stock of ideas and common methods of dealing with them."[35] The education is to allow professors to speak to each other across boundaries of disciplines that would otherwise preclude conversation. This implies that "basic" and "fundamental" are not confined to any one discipline, for if they were, then no conversation could possibly exist. The same is true for the problems and ideas examined: they are not confined to one discipline. In short, the education Hutchins proposes is inter- or trans-disciplinary. It is, perhaps, not surprising, then, that in many institutions which allow for a core text, liberal arts approach, interdisciplinary courses are often found.

We come, thus, to the last joint in the argument. All of the works, including the above classical references and 20th century developments of integrative research, are to be opposed precisely to the specialization that began Hutchins' concerns, and, instead, to exemplify that foundational ideas—*e.g.,* law, citizenship, motion, change—have vast, what we would call, interdisciplinary implications and relations. And no less is true of the apparently (post)modern topics of race, class, or gender, which many scholars have shown have an intellectual heritage extending back to the ancients. Hutchins is advocating a kind of historical inquiry into documents of thought, for the purpose of locating intellectual

---

35   Hutchins, Ibid. p. 85.

problems which unite and cross over disciplines. This latter point is really the heart of the issue, for upon it depends Hutchins' hope for a "connection of man to man" which contains the notion of a university as a community of scholars—not simply interests—from culture to culture around the world.[36]

Hutchins was addressing disciplinary professors and had more doubts about them than about the students: "the students can do the work if the faculties will let them. Will the faculties let them? I doubt it... Not all [of today's professors] have read all the books they would have to teach. Not all are ready to change the habits of their lives."[37] It's not that the works or curriculum that Hutchins is advocating does not invite disciplinary investigation and contribution; they do. But the direction of each is altered: disciplinarians are invited to examine the foundations of their field and its connections to other fields, rather than simply developments within. This may be seen as either threatening or useless because it doesn't accept the mode of education that lays down principles and moves to specialization—the normal habits of livelihood, status, reward, career development, and production of knowledge within universities.

In short, Hutchins proposal for a new general liberal education was aimed at redefining what research, that is, "creative thought" in a university could be. If an image of specialization might be that of a narrowing cone, standing on a base and then tapering sharply and steeply to the thinnest possible extension, what it appears Hutchins and similarly minded educators had in mind was an hour-glass. Education would begin in world classics with broad fundamental relations to many fields. After acquiring through this examination the passion for a field, a student would acquire the character of those who pursue the field. But, then, because a syntopical, mapping education would open them to the

---

36   Hutchins' book is riven with gendered language. I've chosen to let it stand, relying on modern sensibilities to judge appropriate application of argument and reference, especially in light of the critique of social power in Hutchins' Chapter 1, discussed above in footnote 23.

37   Ibid., p. 86.

renewed examination of their specific fields in relation to broader learning—to their field's intellectual heritage—research would not taper, but broaden. Interestingly, along the way, new Ph.D.'s would be likely to become better leaders of interdisciplinary undergraduate education, precisely because they would have some feel for the possibilities of questions that core texts could take students to. And students would be educated to know more, not less of the world they inherit. This is truly a liberal art—and a humanities—devoutly to be wished. Perhaps, then, if students and teachers read works on education together—like Hutchins' *Higher Learning*—they would be in a position to judge their own education and their own institution far better than is now commonly the case. And, just maybe, as they investigate the joints in such arguments, there might be a little less resistance amongst faculty and students across the globe to a core text education for students.

(Rev. Originally delivered at Shimer College, January 2011. Shimer College has since been incorporated into North Central College.)

SECTION II

Making Liberal Arts Education

CHAPTER 4

History and Imagination in the Core

The Achievement of the Thomas More College of Liberal Arts

I want to thank President Peter Sampo for his kind invitation, extended through Dean Mary Mumbach, to address the President's Council. It is an honor and privilege to speak before those who are entrusted with the well-being of this community. Over the years I have admired from afar what Thomas More College of Liberal Arts has accomplished in liberal education. I have been reading Homer and have been thoughtful of the part hospitality plays, in the *Odyssey*, in constructing the humanity of men and women. I asked myself "what might I bring to this community of learning that would have something of the spirit that accompanied the generous invitation extended to me?"

I am the Executive Director of a professional association of higher education programs that share a conviction of the worth of a liberal arts education and the efficacy of core curriculum and core text programs in developing the mind, spirit, and passion of our young adults. I have done quite a bit of research on liberal arts programs. I thought it might be worthwhile to tell you some of the things I have seen about the fortunes of liberal education in a national context as a way to help you place your own College's achievement. The national context, at least partially, indicates what liberal education might be. And these possibilities in liberal education partake in and even formulate the ideals and history that constitute Western Civilization. There is every reason to believe this: what a college accomplishes in liberal education not only reflects who we are as a culture but helps to make who we become as living communities.

To understand where we are in liberal education and shed some light on what you have achieved, we will look, briefly, at three historical periods which were formative of liberal education today. Then, we'll trace the resurgence of liberal education in the late 70's—a rise which includes the foundation of this college. With the rise as context, we'll focus upon the distinctive and praiseworthy features of Thomas More. After briefly discussing how interdisciplinary courses, particularly your Humanities sequence, prepare us to live democratically and corporately, we'll conclude in speculating on how core text liberal arts curricula might build the imagination of students for the sake of both their own growth and the life of their communities. A long story made short, I will not speak with the beauty that Homer did, nor will my report have his tragic substance. Rather, I am, as one of your College's founding spirits will tell you, a comic by heart. But, as I recall, Louise Cowan placed the *Odyssey* within the realm of the comic; so, perhaps, this tale of liberal education.

At first glance, it might seem that liberal arts, core curriculum education, in the early 70's stood as much chance of rising from the dustbin of history to which it had seemingly been consigned as Liza stood of getting an education from Henry Higgins when she first met him under the portico of the Covent Garden theatre in the musical *My Fair Lady*, or better, in its Shavian original, *Pygmalion*. I don't think we can honestly say exactly why core curricula disappeared from so many campuses. But we know it wasn't just one cause. Yes, student unrest with social arrangements and specific war policies shook many colleges and universities all the way down to their curricular foundations in the mid-60's. But the shrinkage and, in many cases, disappearance of core curricula that occurred after 1965 had been prepared for by higher education and going on for a long time before that. I suspect that the 60's was what in physics is called a phase transition, simply a stone thrown into a pond that brings instantaneous freezing and fracturing. Beneath the still waters there were currents waiting to reshape the surface.

The Liberal Arts at the Time of Augustine, the Medieval Rise of Universities, and the Adoption of the 'German' model in Universities

Surprisingly, perhaps, these currents had been digging channels for the river of liberal education to run in at least as early as antiquity. Bruce Kimball, a fine scholar of liberal arts and education, has argued persuasively that there was no accepted curriculum of seven liberal arts until, at least, the late Roman empire.[1] Kimball credits Augustine with bringing about this achievement of curricular coherence. If so, it is worthwhile examining Augustine's *Confessions* as it sheds some light on the undercurrents affecting liberal education, *before* Augustine re-oriented it.

Augustine complains vociferously about the uselessness of liberal education—from the absurdity of studying literature to the acquisition of learning a foreign language—Greek. Yet, Augustine's complaint is that despite his "literary education"'s manifest inability to address his youthful lusts, his parents and all around him encouraged him in the pursuit of liberal education because it was finely attuned to "satisfy the appetite for wealth and glory" (I, 19, 14).[2] This, of course, puts the liberal arts shoe on

---

1 This is not to say that there were not extensive use and discussions of grammar, rhetoric, logic, arithmetic, geometry, music, and physics—as well as many other arts and sciences—in the schools of the Greeks and Romans. Bruce Kimball, *Orators & Philosophers: A History of the Idea of Liberal Education.* Expanded edition. The College Entrance Examination Board., 1995, 24-28; 29 for a normative, Roman, curriculum. See Chapter 7 of this work, "Enriching the Defense of Liberal Education," for a more extensive discussion of Kimball's book.

2 "My family did not try to extricate me from my headlong course by means of marriage. Their only concern was that I should learn to speak as effectively as possible and carry conviction by my oratory" (I, 19,

a different foot. What Augustine is complaining about is not the uselessness of the liberal arts in developing skills for his culture, but, rather its very utility and centrality in that culture.[3] He argues that the ethical content of the liberal arts was emptied out; indeed, he asserts that when he finally had his own students, all the ethical principles were external to his liberal art, which neither enjoined nor demanded in itself a consideration of ethical training:

> In those years I used to teach the art of rhetoric....I used to sell the eloquence that would overcome an opponent. Nevertheless, Lord, as you know (Ps.68:6), I preferred to have virtuous students. Without any resort to a trick, I taught them the tricks of rhetoric, not that they should use them against the life of an innocent man, but that sometimes they might save the life of a guilty person.[4]

Further, he seems to make the case that though there were models of rhetoric to be imitated in classes, contests for excellent oral interpretation of someone else's work, and reinterpretations of poetic renderings of passionate characters through elevated prose composition, there was little in the way of insight or invention that either teachers or pedagogy brought to his intellectual development.[5] The net result, at least in Augustine's view, is a liberal

---

14), Saint Augustine. *Confessions.* Translator, Henry Chadwick. Oxford World Classics, Oxford University Press. For the general discussion, (II, 4-8), p. 25-28, for the quotation, p.26.

3   In Augustine's *Confessions*, the magnitude of liberal education seems to have shrunk in proportion as the democratic oratory and participation in the Republic had been transformed into either the accoutrements for social advancement or forensic eloquence in capital law cases of the Empire.

4   Ibid., (IV, 2), p. 53.

5   Augustine finds the "most erudite teachers" added nothing to his appreciation of the newly translated *Categories* of Aristotle, (IV 28), Ibid., p. 69. For the earlier contests (I, 28), p. 20.

education that amounts to professional training, and a reduction of art to tricks, modeling, and erudition, without a care to soul.[6]

Of course, Augustine's solution was to reorient his pursuit of knowledge toward God through faith, so that understanding aligns itself properly to truth which abides. (*Confessions* IV. v. 6). While this re-orientation ultimately laid down the purpose of the medieval university's curriculum—turning the soul to preparation for divine things—the re-orientation, nevertheless, took its cue from ancient Greek and early Roman concerns with character, which were, in turn, linked to citizenship. While Augustine's inquiries into liberal education led to curricular coherence, the institutions which were to come to resemble our own educational institutions did not appear until the rise of universities. This rise in the 12th Century transferred students and teachers largely from monasteries to universities, where faculties joined in carefully orchestrated prescriptions of curriculum and pedagogy to allow bachelor scholar-students to learn from masters.[7]

---

6   "Look, Lord God, look with patience as you always do. See the exact care with which the sons of men observe the conventions of letters and syllables received from those who so talked before them. Yet they neglect the eternal contracts of lasting salvation received from you. This has gone to such lengths that if someone who is educated in or is a teacher of the old conventional sounds, pronounces the word 'human' contrary to the school of teaching, without pronouncing the initial aspirate, he is socially censured more than if, contrary to your precepts, he were to hate a human being, his fellow-man....A man enjoying a reputation for eloquence takes his position before a human judge with a crowd of men standing around and attacks his opponent with ferocious animosity. He is extremely vigilant in precautions against some error in language, but is indifferent to the possibility that the emotional force of his mind may bring about a man's execution." Ibid., (29) p, 21.

7   "Robert, cardinal legate, prescribes the mode of lecturing in the arts and in theology, indicates what books the masters of arts should not read, formulates the disciplines of the scholars and the state of the university" of Paris. Lynn Throdike, "University Records and Life in the Middle Ages" NY: Columbia University Press, p. 27. See Kimball, Ibid., Chapter III for a wider discussion.

By the 18th Century the German university had offered a different model from the medieval liberal arts university. The new university curricula prepared the educational ground that would confer the benefits we all enjoy now of scientific, specialized, technological education. This shift in educational endeavor has been succinctly described by Eva Brann:

> ...the whole complex of pedagogical innovations really expressed from its earliest appearance...the abandonment of the unity of an education centered on the rational, speaking human being and the transfer of attention to the inexhaustible multiplicity of an intelligible, exploitable, world. This is what made Jefferson's [proposed] university essentially *modern*.[8]

Eventually, this model was carried across the ocean to Harvard, Johns Hopkins, and Chicago.[9] The model transformed United States bachelor degree-granting institutions from liberal arts colleges into modern research universities and, later, modern research colleges, many with associated professional programs.

The Augustinian reaction to professional liberal arts education and the 18th and 19th Century reaction to theological liberal arts university education were motivated in large part by similar concerns—a perception about liberal education that it was closed, at each time, to invention and discovery, a perception enhanced without question by the rise of Christianity and science in their respective eras.[10] Yet, there were differences between

---

8   Brann, Eva. *Paradoxes of Education in a Republic,* University of Chicago Press, 1979, p. 90. Brann's emphasis.

9   Rudolph, Frederick. *Curriculum: A History of the American Undergraduate Course of Study since 1636.* San Francisco: Jossey-Bass Publishers, 1987 p. 76; on the rapidity with which the "university idea" transformed American higher education institutions, Wegener, Charles, *Liberal Education and the Modern University,* University of Chicago Press, 1978, quoting William Rainey Harper, p. 1.

10   We may notice, further, that Augustine, Galileo, and Bacon all have

the two reactions. Augustine complained that the liberal arts were not effectively attached to character and substituted professional achievement for it; the Enlightenment's complaint was that the attachment was intellectually wrong-headed, paying too little attention to what investigations of nature might reveal, thereby reducing the practitioner's skillful powers.

The shift of education's attention to "the inexhaustibility of things" socially reorganized universities from liberal arts faculties into disciplinarily defined departments. Within universities, the undergraduate curriculum became oriented toward the new departmental, disciplinary, research program.[11] Put differently, the new universities collapsed the distinction with which Cardinal Newman opened *The Idea of a University:* "The view taken of a University in these Discourses is the following: that it is a place of *teaching* universal *knowledge...* To discover and teach are distinct functions."[12] This then is the largely institutional context in which the professoriate and students made their educational choices in the 20th Century.

---

rather similar complaints about "wordy debates" (Galileo) and the general uselessness of the current sciences and logical efforts to assist discovery or invention. They differ on whether this is a matter of reorientation of investigations of words and meaning (Augustine), submission of debates to instrumentalist observations or experiments, and utter abandonment of prior conclusions in favor of whole new beginnings, Bacon. See Chapter 7, "Enriching the Defense of Liberal Education," in this book.

11   Eliot's and Harvard's introduction of the elective system was not simply a willful elimination of an old way of learning or an opportunity to provide seemingly endless choice to undergraduates, it was to maximize the availability of the university as a resource to students in order that they, in turn, could efficiently pursue new areas of intellectual endeavor—namely, a manifold of applied research, economic advances, and manufacturing technologies. Rudolph, Ibid. p. 137.

12   Newman, *The Idea of a University,* New Haven, Yale University Press, 1996, pp. 3-5. Cut out of Newman's theoretical analysis of a liberal education were the arts. See on Respondeo.com "On the Whole Person. Re-building the reputation of the humanities."

Sailing Towards the Modern University

Unattached to a particular university, Henry Higgins, nevertheless, illustrates the output of this educational system. Higgins is a man so advanced in his field, busily converting the study of phonetics into a scientific, methodical pursuit of the advancement of learning, that he has lost sight, professionally, *not personally*, of the sense that education has anything to do with the state of someone's soul. And really, Higgins' determination to make a lady of Liza as a giant joke on society has, at its roots, a conviction that at the very least not only is his education powerful enough to effect a convincing "character" transformation, but that in its technological development of Liza's skills, Liza will be better off, will be able to be a lady in a flower shop, and will even be contributing if somewhat inadvertently, to the undermining of the shallow sort of judgment and meretricious power that allows a class system, set against women in particular, to stifle the human spirit and keep people like her—male or female—in poverty for the rest of their days.

> You see this creature with her kerbstone English: the English that will keep her in the gutter to the end of her days. Well, sir, in three months I could pass her off as a duchess at an ambassador's garden party. I could even get her a position as a lady's maid or a shop assistant which requires better English. That's the thing I do for commercial millionaires. And on the profits of it, I do genuine scientific work in phonetics, and a little as a poet on Miltonic lines.[13] (Act II)

But what if you are Liza? What if you are a student entering the world of undergraduate education—whether in 1912 or the early 1970's—what do you want? You want what Liza wants: a more adult life, usually imagined in practical English or American terms as preparation for a job, romance and, eventually, a family.

---

13   George Bernard Shaw. *Pygmalion and Major Barbara*. Introduction, Michael Holroyd, New York, 1992., pp. 168-169.

If this is where your sight aims, then by 1970 or so, you face the following: an array of colleges or universities that will offer either a professional degree with a precise connection to a field or a liberal arts major which has a rather nebulous connection to procuring a job after graduation. If you don't aspire to a specific profession, you examine the ancillaries—status of institution, proximity to home, affordability, and, maybe, the kind of students that attend the college—and select an institution offering bachelor-of-arts or -science degrees. You can, at this point in time, probably ignore the general education requirements—what used to be the liberal arts core—because those requirements are pretty vague. Despite a small number of institutions maintaining structured liberal arts programs, if your imagination has been fired by parents or a church experience or perhaps a high school experience that has given you a glimpse of what college might be, you still have largely the same set of options.[14]

---

14   There were exceptions to this general situation among institutions that offered a strong liberal education: Chicago, Columbia, Eckerd College, Reed, Rhodes College, St. John's, St. Mary's College in Moraga, Shimer College, and, of course, the University of Dallas. With Columbia being the early leader of all but one of these institutions, each had reacted at some point in the 20th century to the dissolution of liberal education as an institutional-wide phenomenon. And each of these reactions resulted in a different core curriculum for each institution. But for the majority of students, the option to take a core curriculum was carefully disguised by the importation of the "menu" or shopping mall system of course selection into college life—an importation steadily, if slowly, adopted by college after college. The menu system, of course, does not get rid of the possibility of individuals taking a core, liberal arts curriculum, though when universally applied it eliminates the possibility that all students will take one that is shared by a large body of peers.

This system throws the burden on faculty members or professional advisors to supply the advice to students to take such a curriculum. Substantive advice, as opposed to credit-fulfillment advice, rarely issues forth, for faculty members who belong to departments tend to know only their own department's courses, and they, as do professional advisors, have a legitimate interest in seeing the student complete a major, but little interest in seeing the student complete a coherent liberal education.

This educational shape of the curriculum means, of course, that the students are relying on their own character, the tentative state of their desires and ambitions, and the limited experience they have in intellectual matters, science competitions of high school, work experience, voluntary activities or artistic endeavor to determine what they will take in college. Liza, in deciding to stay at Wimpole Street for her phonetics experiment, simply chose her local institution to get an education from, and, then, followed the advice of her advisor; she majored in what would get her what she wanted as she imagined it. Most students will do the same.

Though I believe we need to recognize the important elements of freedom, independence, and responsibility that fall upon the student within this arrangement, we can still say that much of the issue of educational character development had, thus, been transferred out of the general education curriculum to the student in the form of a very limited concept of choice; practically, the notion of providing institutional guidance among related courses from a variety of fields had been reduced to providing guidance for the major, each of which represented but a small subset of the entire institution's students.[15]

The Revival of Liberal Education as a Coherent Curriculum

When undergraduate faculty in the 1970's began to cope with students who simply had little or no educational experience in a coordinated liberal arts curriculum, some were driven to begin

---

15   We are likely to conclude that during the early 70's there was no liberal education because we don't see a whole curriculum. The truth of the matter is that a fractured liberal education could be achieved and that a whole one, for individual students, might be developed as well. I had a liberal education but I didn't know it was fractured—a fracturing from which I have never entirely recovered. Yet, it was at the University of Chicago, as a graduate student, that I began to get some idea of what a coordinated, coherent liberal arts education might be like. I suspect this kind of experience was repeated more often than we acknowledge.

to form better, more coherent, liberal educations for their students. These faculty did rely on their earlier liberal arts experience, but a new problem had entered the mix. Structures and incentives which had appeared in earlier liberal arts colleges no longer existed. By 1970, the idea of a faculty sharing a set of common *liberal arts* simply had vanished. Faculty were paid by departments and rewarded, that is—tenured and recognized, increasingly into the 21ˢᵗ century—for publishing in a huge variety of disciplinary organs wholly outside the institution and its control, none of which had any interest in building core liberal educations. So, as the 1980's faculty developed core curricula, the intellectual and practical knowledge of how to accomplish these programs and, in many cases, to fit them into the large institutional arrangements of disciplines and departments had to be re-invented.

Through the American Academy for Liberal Education, I conducted a national study on the development of general, liberal education in 66 institutions over the last 20 years, called "Assessing Trends in the Liberal Arts Core: A Vision for the 21ˢᵗ Century," (*Trends*) (later expanded to 81 institutions covering 24 years)[16] and I co-founded, in 1994, the Association for Core Texts and Courses, a professional liberal arts association to which Thomas More College of Liberal Arts belongs, I am proud to say. Both the *Trends* study and founding ACTC were projects of the mid-90's. What each independently indicated—*Trends* through its research, ACTC through the growth of its participating institutions—was that contrary to belief in both the education industry and wider public, liberal arts programs have been resurgent since the very late '70's—in the numbers of programs, in the size of the institutional curriculum that these programs occupy, in the coherence they display, and in the reliance upon great books or core texts that they entail. Between the research and the work of ACTC, I think we

---

16   The Final Report of "Assessing Trends in the Liberal Arts Core: A Vision for the 21ˢᵗ Century" by George Lucas and J. Scott Lee is available on Repondeobooks.com.

can draw some conclusions on how faculty and institutional supporters managed to rebuild liberal education.

Five factors became really crucial to any development of liberal education in an institution. These factors may help Thomas More College to see the truly remarkable achievement that constitutes the College. First, institutions relied on their specific traditions of education and of community, or faith, to help them to rebuild their liberal educations. Second, faculty crossed out of the departmental structures by establishing interdisciplinary programs—particularly across the humanistic disciplines and the social sciences of political science, history, and religion. Third, faculty committed to the liberal arts relied on the politics of collegial friendship and a sense of honor, often entailing deferral or sacrifice of career advancement, to entice other faculty to work in the programs. Fourth, institutions became aware of the market value of a sound liberal education program—reliant upon their specific traditions—in differentiating institutions for the wider public in a world of competitive educational offerings. Fifth, institutions and faculty rarely accomplished a complete baccalaureate degree based on a liberal arts core curriculum; they prudently and wisely settled for a coherent part of the general education curriculum or they offered coherent alternative tracks through general education. This was my alma maters' solution in 1980 and it was a tremendous improvement over what was offered by many other institutions and what was previously offered to the college's students.[17]

In this national context, the birth and longevity of the Thomas More College of Liberal Arts shines like a bright star. New successful colleges, except as expressions of state support, are rare. But the achievement of Thomas More does not simply rest in its growth and development. A successful college which is wholly devoted to the liberal arts is rarer still. Rarest is a college faculty whose rewards and recognition depend almost exclusively on their devotion to the teaching and learning of their students. And, finally,

---

17 St. Olaf College's "Great Conversation." "Asian" and "American" Conversations were, later, developed on this model.

unique in the nation is that crown jewel of the College curriculum, the four-year Humanities sequence. With these accomplishments in mind, we can further appreciate Thomas More's achievement in the context of liberal education as a national development.

To begin, I'd like to spend a little bit of time on how the religious traditions, particularly Catholic ones, helped institutions to reconstitute liberal education. Judeo-Christian religious traditions of any faith tend to strengthen a liberal arts curriculum by adding, at least, two to three courses to it, as with the two Theology courses here at the college. Religious traditions may further, deeply influence the mission, activities and life of the community that surrounds the curriculum. Catholic institutions are often said to be conservative because in their curricula there is a tendency to preserve older traditions, frequently identified with the liberal arts. I'm not sure the notion of "conservative" is very helpful, here. The political connotations of the term, often quite loaded with contemporary meanings, tend to collapse into a few current issues the preservation of a tradition of learning that extends back to pre-Christian times. The collapse also tends to ignore that even as an expression of Church doctrines, the tradition is interpreted by Jesuits, LaSallians, Franciscans, and lay Catholics in widely different ways. Seattle University, St. Mary's College of California, St. Bonaventure University, the University of Dallas and Thomas More College of Liberal Arts each have widely different, true liberal arts programs.

We can appreciate unique educations better if we approach them through how the colleges speak about themselves. Dr. Sampo's articulation of a distinctly Catholic interpretation of liberal education as an iconic movement toward "realiz[ing] the form we were meant to have" through the transformation of "heart and mind of each student" is a philosophic statement of the end toward which the education aims. But, inevitably, the College must employ means consonant with that end; the College's mission statement indicates the complex religious and cultural traditions which it uses as a resource to achieve the transformation it seeks, "As a school of liberal arts ... [the College] participates in one of the oldest enterprises in Western civilization: the initiation of youth into responsible membership in the human community." That is, it offers a *paideia*—a lived education whose transformation of heart and mind depends on a contemporary community—this College—open to a rich, civilizing tradition.

Interdisciplinary Humanities Courses and Their Function in a Core Curriculum

Given my very limited qualifications to comment on the College's Augustinian interpretation of the harmony of faith and reason, I would, therefore, turn my attention to that element of Catholic tradition that—the College notes on its website—upholds the value of secular forms and worldly pursuits, particularly as these are informed by a *paideia*, an educational way of life. Specifically, it is the worldly pursuits of disciplines and arts, and contributions to community that I am able to speak of.

Thomas More College of Liberal Arts offers (1) an interdisciplinary education through its Humanities course, (2) a rich exposure to arts, sciences, methods, and languages which the intellect may use to explore the mysteries of existence, and (3) a disciplinary development through its four majors. In my experience, a four-year Humanities sequence is rare in liberal arts colleges; no more than half-a-dozen may maintain such a sequence. The College is nationally unique and admirable in its involvement of *freshmen to seniors simultaneously reading the same texts in the same course sections in this sequence.* Given the Humanities' place in the curriculum, it is important to reflect on the relation between the disciplines and the interdisciplinary Humanities courses.

For two years, thanks in large part to Louise Cowan, ACTC was able to pilot a Liberal Arts Institute dedicated to curriculum development at the University of Dallas. Louise and I used to go back and forth over whether a liberal education should be founded on a disciplinary education. Not too long ago, in an exchange compounded of dinner conversations and emails, she wrote to me that

A discipline to [Don and me] was a mode of seeing, which built around itself a rich tradition of making, always open to the new. He always maintained that one's discipline governed one's way of viewing the world, no matter how many professions one entered.

For my part, I could hardly deny my own disciplinary training—at Chicago we worried deeply about forms of literature, principles and methods of interpretation, and the proper ways to construct histories of literature and bodies of criticism. Yet, though the Chicago critics were engaged in the enterprise of making their critical examination of poetry, drama, and literature "scientific" in a disciplinary sense, they relied very extensively on the vast history of liberal arts as a resource for their renewal of the arts of criticism and literature. That history is multi-disciplinary, or, perhaps more accurately, "multi-arted."

While scholarship will lend a deep understanding of history and its potential, prior to such scholarship a young mind must have a practiced appreciation of poetry, philosophy, religion, history, rhetoric, grammar, logic, the fine arts, and if that person can get it, he or she should also have a sense of geometry, mathematics, physics, and I would add, biology. These are, of course, the *topoi* of liberal education. And the practice of liberal education is to cultivate the ability of students to become familiar with this vast array of arts and sciences which shape human thought, action, and production *such that they may be related to one another by the activity of the person who has familiarity with them.*

Undergraduate students who have not yet experienced and may never experience graduate school, enter this rich tradition without a discipline. Inescapably, students find themselves in a sea of works and disciplinary demands that they must navigate for themselves if, like Liza, they are to have an education that is truly theirs. How much more challenging this education will be when, as at Thomas More, the students may start their navigation not at the beginning of a story of Western Civilization, but in its middle, or near its current terminus? Yet, at Thomas More, the Humanities sequence, at once, baptizes students in this sea of knowledge, while providing them a ship to navigate with. How is this reciprocal relation achieved?

The problem is not new. During that ancient war between Sparta and Athens, Pericles in his *Funeral Oration* extolled the wide diversity of experiences, arts, and activities which ordinary Athenians undertook, and he reminded Athenians young and old, that, despite this amazing diversity, it was in the common character of their habits of thoughtful deliberation --whether in the assembly, in the market, or in private decisions of soldiers facing the enemy across the battlefield—that they were enabled to take common action. It was through collective and personal deliberation that the Athenian way of life reached the soul of every citizen so that the wide experience and diversity of Athenians could be synthesized into common pursuits. This synthesis is the "versatility" which Pericles attributes to Athenians. Though I have not seen the Humanities course in action, everything I know about liberal education and the testimony of your alumni on your website teaches me that your Humanities course—which immediately involves new Thomas More students in thoughtful discussions with the more experienced and all three of the more senior classes of the community—will enable students to acquire this habit of democratic, versatile conversation.

The Necessity of Learning to Live Democratically and Corporately

Liberal education is the school of how we can learn to live democratically and corporately. A liberally educated person has the power, in voluntary associations, in the community, church, office, in artistic or scientific endeavors, to listen to the voices of others, to see the opportunities of bringing the wide range of experiences of others to bear on the solution of human problems, and to articulate reasons for possible courses of action, inquiry, or production. Liberally educated persons are the vital bridges within communities or between divisions of corporate bodies that can perform well, but do not know how to relate their various activities to a larger project or larger ideal. Without such voices—whether acquired through liberal arts education or through the practical life—we are lost.

Imagining with an Eye to Helping Others

The greater the coherent magnitude of the curriculum, the more the student is challenged by rich works of the mind, the better the chances that the activity of a student's mind will begin to resemble the artistic activity of liberal conversation which has almost universal application in solving the larger problem of democratic coherence in our communities and associations. Thomas More College of Liberal Arts clearly makes a rich provision for developing the art. In part, the acquisition of the art of conversation depends on the habit of studying a wide variety of disciplines; in part, possession of the art depends on the practice of perceiving questions and permanent problems that span disciplinary boundaries. There is simply no question that the art of conversation depends on the activity of engaging others in discussions, as well as debates, about their thoughts about the works of the human mind. And when one looks at the testimony of Thomas More alumni that speaks to the lived engagement of this education outside the classroom in the form of discussions carried on in the cafeteria, dorm, and in tending the college's communal resources, I can only say that I know of, perhaps, three or four places in the United States offering to students such a life.

But while habits and practices lay the foundation for developing the character of a liberally educated soul, they do not constitute the achievement of liberal education. This is the point at which the form of the core curriculum becomes important in cultivating an art. For these reasons, I admire the junior and senior projects and the comprehensive exam at Thomas More College of Liberal Arts because their purpose seems to be aimed at imaginative reflection in a student that will produce an artistic ability to converse. I can think of only a handful of institutions in the country which have anything like this opportunity, and these instances include some of the very best liberal arts colleges the country has to offer.

By enabling students to reflect *imaginatively* upon the whole enterprise of becoming liberally educated, student purposes are directed to acquiring the "art" in liberal arts. We have lost Aristotle's book on comedy, but what he says about the tragic synthesis may tell us why *art* is so important. Tragedy, as well as all art, takes what we know or recognize—be it history or an old myth—and turns it into something possible, something new. (9. 1451b27-33). For such invention, imagination is required.

As with tragedies performed, so with education learned. We cannot make our own history, that is, add to our civilization, without making something new, and the something new is for others, not just our own, particular development. That is, it is one thing to take a course of education and to perform well; it is quite another to ask oneself what is the fit between yourself and the world. In her battle with Henry Higgins, Liza has just such a moment:

Liza: If you can preach, I can teach. I'll go and be a teacher.

Higgins. Whatll you teach, in heavens name?

Liza: What you taught me. I'll teach phonetics... Now I know how to deal with you. What a fool I was not to think of it before! You can't take away the knowledge you gave me. You said I had a finer ear than you and I can be civil and kind to people, which is more than you can. Aha! That's done you, Henry Higgins, it has. (Act V)

This is the moment at which Liza assumes her full character—not when she decides to teach, for in fact she never becomes a teacher,—but when her education, talents, and natural dispositions are absurdly synthesized into an artistic capacity to reflect upon what she possesses and to imagine in her own life *and for others*—the future.

It was the invention, the making of Thomas More College, that gave such future opportunities to the students here and which is helping to shape liberal education, now, as we know it. The Humanities course at Thomas More is the unique, essential foundation for the imaginative reflection which turns habit into art during the capstone experiences, for the Humanities sequence brings into play the widest consideration of knowledge, actions, and productions that have made us what we are and might be.

For purposes of this talk, I wish to conclude by quoting from Thomas More's website a voice of an alumna who knows very well the value of possessing a liberal art of conversation both for herself and for those in the immediate secular world around her:

> Humanities is the basis for the community that is TMC ... it provides a level of equality that says everyone in this classroom is *capable* of doing what we are asking. ... Because of what I learned at TMC about *community, about teaching and learning from your peers,* and about *insight,* I am recognized as the best manager in my company. Companies hire me because I have an MBA, *but they move me to the top quickly and above others with more experience because of what I learned in Humanities.* [my emphasis]

This is a voice that Liza would recognize and would be pleased to hear, for this voice had a community to speak to that Liza never had in all her education.

Liberal education is a carrier of imaginative stories such as Odysseus' and Liza's and this anonymous alumna. And liberal education's institutions, such as Thomas More, are the halls where human beings gather to listen and learn from these stories, so that they might go out and give to others something new with a character artistically attuned to what can be done with all that we have been given. At Thomas More the story of liberal education is particularly, clear; the voices that sing it show great care for the community which they have built and serve; and the future for the College, its alumni, and its faculty seem as bright as the song is clear. Thank you for showing me the hospitality of your home so that I might learn from you how the song of liberal education is sung, here.

(Rev. Delivered 10/14/2004.)

CHAPTER 5

The Irreducible Case of Liza Doolittle

oday's conference call argues that the formation of character can be the business of undergraduate core text programs. Years ago, using Robert Maynard Hutchins', *Higher Education in America*, I argued at Shimer College that the core texts of college or university education needed to be incorporated into curricula so students might discuss rationales of liberal education. That said, the character being formed by Hutchins' proposal was the *professoriate's*—a character, experienced in teaching an extensive core text program, interdisciplinary in its research capacities, and philosophical in the questions asked that shaped that research.

Plato, Aristotle, Cicero and Hutchins provide a matrix of traditional liberal arts educational character concerns within higher education for the 20th and 21st Centuries. Among these concerns are the question of whether character is ethical, rhetorical, or poetic; the question of whether a liberal education should attend to cultural texts—Cicero—to performances—Aristotle—or to arts and sciences necessary to govern—Plato; and, last, but not least, should higher education be professional, and if it is, can it attend to character in a liberal fashion? Such questions are rarely raised overtly in our programs, and even if they are raised, the questions take the professors' or teachers' point of view on education—not the students'. One happy exception to that point of view, perhaps a great text to be added to such a matrix, is Bernard Shaw's *Pygmalion*, widely translated in Europe and familiar through the movie *My Fair Lady*. The play is a comic warning to students and to us about the education we jointly seek when our concerns are about character.

Liza Doolittle, seeking to raise herself out of cockney poverty in London, through her own initiative, comes under the thumb of the generous but imperious professor Henry Higgins who, in a ridiculous phonetics experiment, uses her education—'tuition free'—to prove his pet educational theory that all that stands in the way of anyone's rise are the social restraints that language imposes on a person's status, and, thereby, to win a bet with fellow linguist Pickering:

> [Under the Covent Garden portico during a shower] The Note Taker [Higgins]: You see this creature with her kerbstone English: the English that will keep her in the gutter to the end of her days. Well, sir, in three months I could pass that girl [Liza] off as a duchess at an ambassador's garden party. I could even get her a place as a lady's maid or shop assistant, which requires better English. (Act I.)[1]

After much trying phonetic labor, Liza—having won Higgins' bet by being taken for a duchess at a society garden party, just as Higgins grows disdainful of his whole social experiment—accuses Higgins of want of feeling, removes herself from his care, and, then, in a climactic battle between them over who knows Liza better, wins her independence, her freedom, by discovering, absurdly, what she knew all along: that from the first she has been an independent person.

Our purposes make us focus on the technical—Aristotelian—relationship of character to plot. After an outline of Higgins' and Liza's character traits and what the proposed experiment does to those traits, a focus on the relationship between plot and character is best done by centering on the comic disaster of an 'at home' at

---

1 All citations are from *Pygmalion and Major Barbara*. Introduction, Michael Holroyd. New York: Bantam Books, 1992. As is customary, Shaw's punctuation and spelling are retained in quotations.

Higgins' mother's house in Act III, the mutual discovery by Liza and Higgins of a loss of dignity in Act IV, and the reversal of their relations in the comic resolution of Act V, ultimately through Liza's absurd discovery of her independence.

Liza is inventive and a natural wit. Her clever industry in selling flowers on a curb in London she purposes to turn to good account—to become through language training in proper English a lady selling flowers in a shop. Though she 'extravagantly' decides to take a taxi with some of the pocket change that Higgins gives to her at Covent Garden, she thoughtfully chooses to go to Higgins' home on Wimpole Street, the address of which she overhears. In short, she has a good memory for hearing spoken language. Yet, Liza's experience of manners in her cockney world and almost total ignorance of polite society and its manners, of her financial resources vis-à-vis Higgins, and of how to conduct a simple request for services nearly sink any fulfillment of her desire for self-improvement:

> The Flower Girl [Liza] I know what lessons cost...and I'm ready to pay.
>
> Higgins: How much?
>
> The Flower Girl: Now you're talking! I thought youd come off it when you saw a chance of getting back a bit of what you chucked at me last night. (*Confidentially*) Youd had a drop in, hadnt you? (Act II)

Further, her purposes can be diverted toward defenses of her character, especially her pride, through her emotional sensitivity to insults, as when Higgins refers to her as a 'guttersnipe.' Yet, not surprisingly, once accepted into Higgins' household, she is forced to bathe and to dress in new clothes, all of which she is more than happy to have done.

Higgins's expert knowledge and social position constitute a world Liza cannot know, provide a range for his frankness and un-mindfulness of others to roam, and, thus, indicate that he prizes his own judgment over the judgment of others, saving someone like Pickering. He is apt to insult, sometimes not quite realizing it, because his enthusiasm for his profession leads him on. However, when Liza offers out of her half-crown income per week to pay a shilling to him for lessons, we see, then, a professor, who through proportional reasoning about the fees millionaires pay out of their incomes, generously discovers that he has, in principle, found a student who desires his instruction in his subject more than any student he has ever had. His enthusiasm for the lessons is fired, carrying him past his profession's boundaries in his decision—made before Liza—to make a faux duchess of this "deliciously low, horribly dirty...draggle-tailed guttersnipe" who the judgment of society, which he disdains, will accept (Act II).

Higgins and Liza become united in a folly that comically attacks everything about them. Higgins is now committed to a social performance he disdains precisely because it seems to him so empty. Further, Liza has laid herself open to constant striving to improve in areas she knows little about—language and social grace. In other words, this performative education substitutes acquisition of prescriptive language and social manners for their ethical character, subordinating and suppressing some of their better and worse habits. Consequently, we will see that teacher and student are engaged in an attack on human dignity through taking such an educationally 'constructed character' seriously, as more valuable than a dignity based on the virtues which worthily define their character.

Technically, of the four "attributes" that any character must have to be of any value in a play, the most important is that the character be useful to the plot. Here, the basis of Liza's character—her pride and desire to improve herself—has not only been subverted by the experiment, it has also been rendered useless to discovering that she is attacking herself so long as the experiment directs her intentions. Much the same may be said of Higgins' generosity which underlies his dignity. Further—for purposes of the experiment—the appropriateness or propriety of all that is essential to Liza has been subordinated to non-essentials. For example, her pride is no longer vested in character but in new clothes, and her industry and emotional sensitivity in becoming an artificial duchess. This is, then, an inversion of character. True, these inversions are useful, appropriate, probable, and consistent with the farcical disaster in Act III, when this educational inversion openly attacks their dignity. But none of this would work, as presently constructed at this point in the play, for a discovery of loss of dignity for both characters and a regaining of it in Acts IV and V. In short, the plot must re-invert their characters for the play's comedy to become humane.

In Act III, when Higgins arrives at his mother's at-home to give Liza her first test outside Wimpole Street, Higgins tells his mother that "I've got her pronunciation all right; but you have to consider not only how a girl pronounces, but what she pronounces..." It is clear from the rote practice sentences that Liza utters in the Act—such as, "the shallow depression in the west of the islands is likely to move slowly in an easterly direction"— Higgins' concerns are not about reciting a memorized dicteé learned in his house. Neither polite language nor proper topics for an at-home are on his mind either, for Liza, we learn, has been restricted by Higgins in her topics to the weather and people's health, while bad language never makes an impression on him. No, Liza is always at his breakfast table, using her Cockney habits of grammar to ask for butter or anything else. And that Higgins notices. Moreover, Higgins thinks of his mother as a good female model of society and its conversation. So, Higgins takes Liza to use his mother to help transfer Liza's memorization of language to her *thinking*; can she use her training to get beyond memorization in polite society to speak proper grammar?

After the arrival of the Eynesford Hills, who had met Liza under the Covent Garden portico in the guise of a flower girl, Liza enters gracefully, beautifully dressed. When Mrs. Higgins mentions the weather, Liza's industriousness blossoms as she offers her practice sentence on this permitted topic. Freddy Hill, her age, becomes delighted by her speech without recognition of her or she him, and Liza mistakes his laughing delight for chastisement.

Immediately, her thought swings toward pride in her defense, "I bet I got it right," but Mrs. Eynesford Hill swings the conversation back to permitted topics by remarking that she hopes the weather will not turn cold during influenza season. Compelled by circumstances to *think* of something to say because she has no practice sentences on the special topic of influenza, Liza's wit rises to the point where she sees that, if she can speak of an experience, she can do so without the practice sentences. Liza delves into her memory and ventures her "dark" suggestion that her aunt did not die of influenza, as was said by neighbors; the absurdities of the education explode:

But it's my belief they done the old woman in.

With perfect enunciation, at the exact point where her grammar begins to fail, she begins the preposterous proof of her aunt's murder through the woman's tolerance of gin, generously provided by all her relatives, and a missing hat that should have come to Liza at her aunt's death. The education, designed to elevate all the non-essentials of her character—her bodily grace, her diction, and even her grammar—has ignored everything essential about her. Not only have Higgins and Pickering patently failed to prepare her for the conversation of society, but they have failed to anticipate how Liza's pride, cleverness, and background would shape a situation outside of Wimpole Street. As Freddy offers to walk her home, in full bloom Liza's pride in her accomplishment swells to bursting with an obscene exit:

Walk, not bloody likely. I'm going in a taxi.

And, then, Higgins "eagerly" asks him mother:

Well? Is Liza presentable?

It becomes patent that not only have Higgins and Pickering failed to prepare Liza for the conversation of society, a primary goal of the education, but they have failed to anticipate how Liza's cleverness, pride and background would shape a situation outside of Wimpole Street. This absurd education forces Liza's essential traits to demolish completely her dignity which now rests on taxis, clothes, tone, and pronunciation. Through his blind enthusiasm for the language training in the education, Higgins' dignity takes it on the chin, too. Not only has the education produced a creature which contradicts its whole purpose, but it has so completely absorbed its participants that all are blind to the fact that that it is making a mockery of the traits of character most important to them.

Let's pause for a moment to think about dramatic and, particularly, Shavian comic artistry. From the standpoint of cultivating student capacities, of their use of resources available for a future that they produce, the inversion and re-inversion of character are examples of why we want to examine artistic form and technique, not just 'ideas,' in texts. We want students to think about such techniques even in their present. We could ask, "do you think your education is shaping and manipulating you for ends that academics think are worthwhile? Do you think education is developing a 'character' for you through this shaping?" Other questions could follow, but the sharpness of the inquiry depends on seeing the technique.

To return to the play: when we watch a play's plot develop, what we are seeing is a little like watching a person perform a job. Does the character have the requisite traits to perform what the plot (or play) asks her to do? Liza's character has been inverted by her education, precisely so that she can pass her seemingly final test (off stage) at the garden party. She passes. But is this the measure, or more pointedly, the end of her education as, frankly, most education would have it for undergraduates? No, rather, the test is an accelerant for the further destruction of her and her teacher's dignity through the education's constant upping of the ante for Liza until, as Pickering puts it to Higgins after Liza's successful triumph,

> the garden party, the dinner party, and the opera! Rather too much of a good thing. But you've won your bet, Higgins. Eliza did the trick, and something to spare, eh?
>
> Higgins: Thank god it's over! (Act IV)

Gone is the inspired folly or proving his profession's worth and in its place is the realization that it takes more than phonetics to make a lady. The manners, the polite topics, and the routine of teaching these things have subjected Higgins to a social involvement he cannot stand. Liza, on the other hand, discovers her apparent worth to Higgins not through her achievement as a lady, nor through the small services she provides for him at his home, but through her value, her utility, to his experiment:

> Liza [breathless] ... I've won your bet for you, haven't I? That's enough for you. I don't matter I suppose.... [pulling herself together in desperation] What am I fit for? What have you left me fit for? Where am I to go? What am I to do? Whats to become of me?

This question begins the mutual discovery of their loss of dignity and, ultimately, a reversal for Liza and Higgins of their relations to each other completed at the end of Act V. Thus, to Higgins' suggestion that his "mother could find some chap or other who [would marry you,]" Liza replies, "We were above that in Tottenham Court Road...I sold flowers. I didn't sell myself." Liza, also, returns the favor: "Please, will you tell me what belongs to me?...This ring [is] the one you bought me in Brighton. I don't want it now." To which Higgins rejoins, "... damn my own folly in having lavished hard-earned knowledge and intimacy on a heartless guttersnipe." (Act IV)

After leaving Wimpole Street in the night, Liza retreats to Mrs. Higgins' where Higgins and Pickering find her the next day. The subsequent conversation between Higgins and Liza is very carefully structured, driven by the interaction of the consequences of the education and their respective character. First, upon reflection over the night, Liza has discovered that the manners she cultivated can be of use to her in addressing Higgins with composure, aplomb, and precise needling. She has also discovered Higgins' private preference for his vocation over Liza's as a lady. And she uses both to attack him by trivializing his efforts:

[My education in phonetics] "was just like learning to dance in the fashionable way." (Act V)

At this point, Shaw has brought the education of Liza to an end in regard to the maximum use she can make of the non-essentials of her character. In proclaiming her own profession's worth through her manner of conversation, in pursuing satisfaction for an injury, she has discovered she is not worth something because she has those traits, but that the traits are worth something because she has them. Put dramatically, the plot has reversed the priority, ethically and technically, of Liza's character traits—essential and non. But it has yet to unify those traits for each person. Let us see why it must.

The pursuit of satisfaction for an injury leads Liza to strive to define her character in the polite treatment she receives as exemplified by herself and others. But Higgins justly rejoins that he treats everyone the same: "I treat a duchess as if she were a flower girl." Liza's subsequent reply, "I don't care how you treat me, but I won't be passed over" brings her manner to the service of her feelings, yet she makes a mistake in assuming that certain manners of a human being are congruent with the feelings of the heart. And, in this mistake, she turns to the question of purpose: "What did you do it for if you didn't care for me?" Now, it is important to recognize that Liza is not asking for romance, but, as she puts it,

> I want a little kindness... I did [the experiment] because we were pleasant together and I come—came—to care for you; not to want you to make love to me, and not forgetting the difference between us, but more friendly like.

Most teachers, who have worked with students over time, know that this feeling is not uncommon. Perhaps, most teachers might elide the request with some gentle words of 'deflective assurance'; perhaps, a few would deflect abruptly and rudely; some would wait years before accepting the friendship. But, given their conversation, Liza is challenging Higgins' worth—"what did you do it for if you didn't care for me?" This might be her purpose, but it is not

Higgins'. One of Higgins' chief character traits, his enthusiasm for his work, carries him to an attack on Liza's purpose:

> You find me cold, unfeeling, selfish, don't you? Very well, be off with you to the sort of people you like... If you can't appreciate what you've got, you'd better get what you can appreciate... Do you not understand that I have made you consort for a king?[2]

In each person, we have a process of unification of character for the sake of the other's understanding, but with a difference. At over forty, Higgins *never felt such a need until Liza successfully attacked him,* but she, near twenty, *must define herself if she is to be anything other than he created.* In telling Liza that she could be a real duchess, Higgins' makes the mistake that he has made all along—trying to shape Liza's character. She thinks differently:

> You think I like you to say that...But I won't be coaxed round as if I were a baby or a puppy. If I can't have kindness, I'll have independence... I'll go and be a teacher.
>
> Higgins. What'll you teach in heaven's name?
>
> Liza. What you taught me. I'll teach phonetics... I'll offer myself as an assistant to [your rival] that hairy-faced Hungarian.
>
> Higgins. [rising in fury] What! That imposter!... that toadying ignoramus! Teach him my methods, my discoveries! You

---

2   Higgins uses in this speech and elsewhere such terms as 'go back to the gutter' and 'impudent slut' to describe Liza either as she suffers or as she triumphs. He can easily, possibly justifiably, be called a sexist, and his size and the patriarchal power of Wimpole Street can as easily be raised in a classroom, though Mrs. Higgins' domicile, Liza's rise and triumph, and, of course, her physical posture in this last scene, especially as Higgins "lays hands on her" need to be taken into account. To have such discussions is apposite, but they are not the fulcrum of the play, for the play turns on the humanity that develops between Liza and Higgins as she becomes an independent person.

take one step in his direction and I'll wring your neck. [He lays hands on her]. Do you hear?

And with that, all of Liza's re-inverted traits are unified to serve her purpose:

Liza. [defiantly non-resistant] … Aha! Now I know how to deal with you. What a fool I was not think of it before! You can't take away the knowledge you gave me…Oh, when I think of myself crawling under your feet and being trampled on and called names, when all the time I had only to lift my little finger to be as good as you, I could just kick myself. (Act V)

The final reversal: Not only do we have Liza triumphant through the most unexpected resource, Higgins' profession, but the whole sequence of her sufferings is made ridiculous through the suffering of her triumph. Liza discovers comically that all along she mistakenly looked elsewhere for her worth, her dignity. She only had to look to herself to be the independent woman she always was. And, so she is.

So, what character did the education produce? As long as Liza moves towards being an artificial duchess, as long as we can assess her progress as we saw in Act III, we have to say that being a lady is what this education produces. But it produces such a character at a cost, in this case reducing Liza to her training—linguistic facility, bodily posture, new clothes, even professional development—while temporarily convincing her educator that all these accoutrements are worth the effort, which, frankly, reduces him, too. When, upon reflection, together they question what they were doing, the education allows Liza to use her acquired traits in ways to suit her character and allow her to be freely herself. Yet, while Liza acquires a complete education, it was not by design, but the action of the education shaped by the substantive character traits of each, just before the experiment begins and after it ends.

Universities and colleges are some of the most powerful instruments humans have developed and a liberal education can be part of that power. If liberal education embraces character development beyond the acquisition of judgment, it must recognize that for each student, *it is their personal education*, as Act III and Act V absurdly show. Higher education risks a reduction of character to some enumeration of cognitive developments, or it may reduce the diversity of character to a few, uniform, traits. Worse, foreseeably, it may develop 'assessment' that will 'compel' programs and, ultimately, students, to have a 'virtuous' character as a college or university sees it. A fourth alternative presents itself: universities and colleges may offer resources—imbued with articulation, discussion, and application of techniques—for character development, but they will have to recognize that such traits as pride, industry, wit, emotional sensitivity, and personal purpose—as well as many other character traits—*should* and *will* shape the education offered. Put differently, it is not for the power of liberal education to make even 'ethically right' people, but, rather, for it to offer people the choices and opportunities to make themselves.

Beyond that, since we control so much of our own educational message, we ought to admit frankly what this control can entail, including development of 'character'—whether conceived ethically or artistically. Some self-conscious examination of why we would have core text education or what that education might lead students into is for the students the right curricular thing to do. After all, we all know they are thinking about why they are taking these courses. If they read something like *Pygmalion*, they may get beyond thinking their education is something being done to them. They might see that liberal arts education can help them, humanely, to become who they are.

(Rev. Delivered 10/18/2019 at the Universidad de Navarra during the III European and Liberal Arts Conference on "Caring for Souls: Can Core Texts Educate Character?")

CHAPTER 6

Globalizing the Core through Core Texts

The Association for Core Texts and Courses (ACTC) exists to help institutions build core text programs in undergraduate education. ACTC adopted two modes of providing that help. The first mode was to provide a series of summer seminars, which faculty teams from institutions attended to read core texts in the sciences and humanities, participate in pedagogical and curriculum development, and seek to reinvigorate the use of liberal arts, ancient and modern.[1] The other mode was by institutional invitation extended to one or more ACTC members to describe the educational purpose, curricular organization, pedagogical principles, and principles of textual selection for 'start-ups' in institutions that did not yet have core text programs. Beginning near the turn of the century, a number of these invitations came from Central Asian institutions.[2] The institutions inviting ACTC visits were located in the Caribbean Basin and in China. Prior to these particular invitations, ACTC had worked with Central Asian institutions. Later on, European institutions, working in cooperation with ACTC, organized core text conferences in European venues.

---

1   See Chapter 7, "Bridging the Gap Between the Humanities and Sciences" syllabi, and the "Rejuvenating and Reinventing the Liberal Arts" summer session syllabus in the appendix.

2   For our Central Asian efforts, see "Final Report to the Mellon Foundation on the Aga Khan Humanities Project" available on RESPONDEOBOOKS.COM.

In these locales the educational conversation which has been ongoing in North America since about 1920 is unknown or only, sometimes, just being discovered. Because of this, working with such faculty allowed an examination of principles of education and primary texts illustrating those principles. This chapter is developed from papers delivered in Colombia and China which reflect arguments made on behalf of core text curricula in both parts of the world. However, the two areas represented different core text curricular problems. In the former, aside from *Don Quixote*, faculty were unfamiliar with any texts of the Western tradition before mid-19th Century, that is, before Marx, because, generally, curricula have been conceived of as 'revolutionary' in these countries. In China the contemporary absence of any core text curricula and the sense of a 2500 year history of Chinese arts and letters suggested to more than one institution the idea of matching Chinese texts with Western texts—a curricular development that is much harder in the West because of entrenched patterns of largely Western texts.

The purpose in all visits was to honor an institution's specific cultural tradition, to relate the core texts of arts and sciences to liberal arts education, and most importantly to work reflexively and inductively from possible core texts to a position of how to read with students given texts from one's own or another tradition. Most 'texts' we considered are books. Each of these problems was approached from a reflexive point of view, derived largely from Aristotle's *Poetics*, of what a curriculum of texts or books implies about principles of construction and reading, adapted to specific traditions. Of course no construction takes place without a faculty conversation, and in almost all of the passages, herein, the question of what a faculty and, later, students might discuss frames this chapter.

Aristotle

There is a suggestion in the *Poetics* and elsewhere in the Aristotelian corpus how a pluralistic conversation about core texts might be governed. The suggestion is intellectual, not political. The *Poetics'* last three chapters are discussed as problems (*problematon*) and solutions regarding poetry. Aristotle also wrote in his *Topics* about "dialectical problems" (*problema...dialetikon*) which are inquiries into either choice and avoidance or truth and knowledge."[3] Neither of these alternatives is the object of poetry; rather, the successful completion of the work qua tragedy, comedy, or some other form is.[4] The problems of the *Poetics*, conversely, do not appear as the problems of the *Topics*. Yet, quite clearly, what is arranged by the *Topics* and *Poetics* is the back and forth of criticism, reply, and conversation. This strongly suggests that Aristotle thinks that there is an artistic, intellectual, conversational space which <u>adapts</u> itself to the inquiry of the texts it examines and is not the same as the consideration of a work by any specific discipline.

That space is what Aristotle knows as *paideia*, or general education. In our own terms, it might be described as a culture of education. *Paideia* is an educational conversation which is crafted to the vast variety of textual artifacts which cultures produce. To be critical in this sense is to be capable of examining the works of most branches of knowledge, less with a view to truth, for that is a discipline's concern, as with a view to the construction or exposition of the text.[5] The last chapters of the *Poetics* are where the

---

3   Poetics 25, 1460b6 and Topics, I, x, 104b1-7

4   The implication of the *Poetics* chapters 25 and 26 is not that objections of various disciplines are forbidden, for they are, in fact, enumerated, nor that the completion of a text seals it off from the rest of the world, for while what is being discussed is making and possibility, it is still true that something may have happened historically or should come to pass in relation to the text. Rather, the implication is that we can know the difference between what are the effects of completing a work of art—a *poetike techne*—and what are the effects of disciplines, morals, natural possibilities or probabilities, technical virtuosity, and linguistic usages of various fields.

5   In his *Parts of Animals*, Aristotle simultaneously conducts two types of investigation: what would be the proper way to conduct an inquiry, that is, produce a scientific treatise on living animals, and what are the possible educational stances which students may legitimately take toward such treatises. Book I Chapter 5 begins the investigation of living natural phenomena proper. In the first four chapters, Aristotle lays

most radical implications of Aristotle's doctrine of inquiry into works may help to form a broad-reaching, interdisciplinary core text education in colleges and universities. All works, ancient or modern, in so far as they are works separate from their authors, are subject to principles of investigation as artificial objects and subject to their own principles of completion. In examining such texts, we are looking at the past, present and future that humans have opened for themselves.

A Turning Point in History

We are at a turning point in history, where societies, connected across the globe by easy communications and relatively inexpensive travel, are deciding on nearly every continent what from their cultural past they will bring with them as a resource for the future. This decision resonates, I believe, with José Ortega y Gasset's conception of the University: as well as a center of scientific research and of teaching the professions, it was to be the institution most responsible for the transmission of culture.[6] Ortega y Gasset conceived culture as a "system of ideas, concerning the world and humanity, which the man of that time possessed... a repertory of convictions which [can] become the effective guide of [a person's] existence." Will universities and colleges fulfill such a role into the

---

out considerations of how to inquire not only over possible natural phenomena, but over the methods of inquiry which natural and productive sciences often employ. These considerations are distinguished as "independent of the question whether the statements made [in a scientific treatise] be true or false." They are, instead, directed toward a judgment "as to the goodness or badness of the method used by a professor in his exposition." Aristotle argues that the judgment formed of exposition is that of "an educated man" and that "to be educated is in fact to be able to do this; and the man of universal education [paideia] ... is thus critical in all or nearly all branches of knowledge." (639a1-15, esp. 8). See Chapter 10 of this book for more on the use of the observations in this passage in structuring a liberal arts education for freedom and joy in learning.

6   Ortega y Gasset, *The Mission of the University*, 1992, Transaction Publishers, p. 33.

future? This is the educational issue we are called upon to decide in universities. This meeting in Cartagena is part of those decisions.

Recently, the New York Times ran several articles that congregated around the issues of culture, canon, curriculum, and texts. "Many young professors" one article noted "aren't interested in teaching outside their narrow specialties, nor are they generally prepared to do so."[7] Of course, the converse is that they construct courses narrowly tailored to their disciplinary interests. Mark Lilla, at Columbia University, notes in this article that to read only our most recent works—the works only of the current state of our discipline, or only the recent productions of our country or culture—is to make each reader the least "alienated" of all individuals, and, by implication, the least open-minded. Is there an educational alternative to this situation?

In the early and mid-20th century a group of teachers, scholars, and administrators centering on Columbia University, the University of Chicago, Notre Dame, the University of Virginia, and St. John's College offered a variety of educational plans which explored and expanded liberal arts education based in reading great books or core texts. In 1943 Mark Van Doren, of Columbia University, in his book, *Liberal Education,* implied that a faculty strengthened itself through such exploration,

> ...the job of educators during the days ahead is a job of discussion. No curriculum will emerge unless this discussion is constant and fundamental. But the one thing necessary for that is a common desire among teachers, corresponding to a common desire among men [i.e., young students], for the clearest obtainable notion as to what the human mind can be and do. The best circumstances would be those in which several men [faculty] who were already engaged in educating one another, as friends do, met regularly in search of a rational curriculum... [8]

---

7   Rachel Donado, "Revisiting the Canon Wars." *New York Times Book Review,* 09/16/2007

8   Mark Van Doren. *Liberal Education.* New York: Henry Holt & Co.,

Since it is obvious that not only the present but the past expands the scope of the mind's possibilities, Van Doren added that "no function of the discussion is more important than that to know itself, education needs to know its history."

Since then, faculty at many U.S. and Canadian institutions have undertaken the kind of discussions Van Doren called for. These discussions have mostly focused on providing general education courses, which include many seminal works from across the curriculum and which are staffed by colleagues from many different departments. Often, these are interdisciplinary courses that draw their texts from the Western and world intellectual heritage. So, on the one hand, Van Doren's vision of cooperating faculty engaged in educational discussions has come true at some institutions. On the other hand, I am less convinced that his vision of engaging in a discussion of the history of education has been realized because part of that history is the story of the production of books, a story we often lose track of. This is the story about writing books, how books tell us how to read them, and about building educations around them. This story is written in core texts. I am convinced that as liberal artists or humanists we cannot lose for ourselves, students and the public a sense of the importance of these, for our sense of what a civilization is, perhaps the very constitution of civilization, is dependent on such artistic products.[9]

I propose to examine four texts that might be read in an interdisciplinary core course and that present important features of the story of books and education: I've chosen the Bible, Plato's *Phaedrus*, Confucius' *Analects*, and Cervantes' *Don Quixote*. The story of books is vitally linked to four ideas which have changed cultures, made us who we might be, and are inevitably linked to

---

1943, p. 111.

9 Especially since I am convinced that liberal arts students can read scientific texts, ancient to modern, with appropriate education, what I am saying here goes for those scientists and defenders of science who argue that the weakness of humanistic education lies in reading books. See, e.g., in Chapter 2 the discussion of Pinker and in Chapter 7 the discussion of the use of the liberal arts and the rise of science.

founding core text programs: canon, art, disciplinary-and-interdisciplinary education, and the innovation.

The Bible

Consider for a moment the Bible from the perspective of a student. It's one book, isn't it? Or, is it? Those who know of the complex scholarship that began to accrue around the Bible from the 18th Century onward, will easily remember the multiple-author hypothesis for the Torah or Pentateuch. Our students who read this text will probably have little such background, but they can easily see evidence in the text of the differences in language, matter, order, and overall emphasis of the two creation stories in Genesis 1 and Genesis 2 & 3. I cannot speak for Spanish translations of the Bible, but in English the Deity is referred to as "God" in Genesis 1 and as "Lord" in Genesis 2 & 3. This linguistic sign indicates the Priestly and Yahwist traditions of Biblical composition. The origins and order of creation differ, and the important universals of these chapters differ. Such analytic observations may take us to what the _sequence_ of the Biblical text does. Since, the sequences of texts can be marked textually by the linguistic and ideational signs of original difference, it is fair to posit for students the idea of an editor that brought the two texts together to unify them, and to ask the students why the editor thought they could be merged, given their differences.

One sequence to select from within the Torah/Old Testament are the materials which provide much of the history of Israel. Pushed far enough, considering the sequential construction of this history implies the Bible can be seen by students as a book of books, a canon. Canon is very much a part of the story of the Pentateuch and the Bible. The writing carries not only the Ten Commandments and various laws for the Israelites. Traditions such as the Passover or the common experience of the wilderness are crucial but insufficient to assure the continuous future of this Jewish nation without the legacy of the written word. Just before Israel loses Moses, according to the text, he "finished writing down in a book the words of this law to the very end," admonishing the Jews to "'take this book of the law and put it beside the ark of the covenant of the Lord your God … as a witness against you. For I know how rebellious and stubborn you are'." (Deut 31, 24-27).[10] Acting as a check on their national character and kingly rule, the Torah stands ready, as does a prophet, to correct a people's future actions.[11]

The Torah, or Pentateuch, that we have is arguably the work of the priest Ezra, or a redactor like him.[12] Ezra upon returning from Babylonia to Israel, apparently backed by the authority of King Artaxerxes, read from the Torah before "both men and women and all who could hear with understanding."[13] If Ezra was reading the Torah, the significance of the narration of this incident is that the audience—as a whole—had never before heard this synthesis. The Torah seems to be a case in point of a literate group—priests with political ambitions—assembling a text precisely because they understood the power of narrative and law in written words to change the future of a people. We can ask students why such a moment might be important.

We don't want to be naïve. Ezra and the Levites were in a political fight with earlier returnees to Jerusalem. Ezra came with gold and, no doubt, the troops of Artaxerxes, for whom it was an advantage to settle a dispute about governance in a province of the empire. But we don't want to be jejune either. Ezra was a scribe, a scholar. He had studied the texts of Jewish traditions. He did not bring one

---

10   All quotations from the Bible come from The New Oxford Annotated Bible: New Revised Standard Version with the Apocrypha. 4th edition. Editor, Michael D. Coogan. Oxford University Press, 2010.

11   Further passages in Ezra, Nehemiah, the Gospels, including the beginning of John, and Paul's Second Letter to Timothy all clearly point to the growth of the Bible.

12   New Oxford Annotated Bible, *The Pentateuch*, xxxv, and Richard Elliot Friedman, *Who Wrote the Bible?* New New York Harper and Row Publishers, 1989, pp. 223-225

13   Nehemiah, 8.2.

text expressing only one of those traditions. He brought, instead, a synthetic version which contained recognizable stories out of each tradition. And he read to an audience composed of members of each of those traditions.[14] What, then, was the power of narrative and law in written words to change the future of a people?

That's what the Torah as canon does: it not only presents different traditions, it promotes synthetic thought among readers about the alien as well as the familiar. In thinking about others as well as themselves, Old and New Testament authors added texts. Through expanding readership, they expanded the extent and scope of their communities, their religious worship, their understanding of God and humans and the sweep of cultures and history they would consider. The idea of the Bible, a book of books, a canon, is, a great idea and one which students should come to appreciate through study and discussion precisely because the growth of books, reading, and thought lies at the heart of growth of community into the future. In developing core text curricula, we offer our students a canon. This is not a lesson about books that either we or our students should ignore.

Plato

There is a difference between discussion that focuses upon one work, however extraordinarily capacious, and discussion that focuses upon many works which remain distinct. One person who faced this issue was the philosopher Plato. Within the ancient Greek tradition, unlike the Judeo-Christian tradition, we have a glimpse not of a formed canon, but of how to form a canon. The Greek discussion is philosophical and projects what a state and its educational institutions would look like from either a curricular or instructional point of view. The Greek educational discussion emphasizes not what was decided upon as canonical, but the principles of decision.

The Greeks, of course, had their texts of Homer and Hesiod,

---

14   Friedman, 225 ff.

who Plato tells us, were "the poet[s] that educated Greece" offering teachings "that one should arrange one's whole life in accordance with."[15] Their stories formed the underpinning of a cultural, artistic tradition that shaped Greek private education from childhood through adolescence. Plato took exception to this education and its texts. He and philosophy were not part of the canon, and, frankly, Plato wants in. He offers two divergent textual paths to examine and reformulate education. One is through the political treatises, for example, *The Republic*. The other path is through what I will call the artistic dialogues. I have in mind the *Ion*, *Symposium*, *Protagoras*, *Cratylus*, *Gorgias*, *Phaedrus*, and, perhaps, *Timaeus*. In the former, politics and philosophy compete with poetry for pre-eminence in a curriculum dialectically formed by laws. Plato politically deconstructs and transforms the cultural education of his day, easily anticipating 19th-21st Century revolutionary thought, and, then, he constructs a new education, in the process making room for philosophy and philosophic texts. In the artistic dialogues, overt *curricular* discussions recede. Nevertheless, there are educational gains. The contemporary cultural life of Athens, particularly as it is shaped by teachers and students of competing intellectual arts, rises to the fore. Additionally, a profound question which shapes all academic life is more interestingly explored: what is it to have an art or discipline?

For students in the first two years of college, I think the magnitude of the *Republic* is very tough going. To make their way easier, we often select isolated snippets, such as the Cave and the Divided Line. This alternative, that arouses *our* passions, cuts off the images of the Cave and Divided Line from the discussion of imitation or how the true or false in the poetry of Plato's day might affect character development in education. These isolated images give students a vague glimpse of ideals in education, but they do not speak to the passions that concern students.

The Phaedrus in its concern with sex, love, including gay love,

---

15   *Republic of Plato*. X 606e, Translator, Allan Bloom. Basic Books, NY: 1968.

gods and a kind of heaven, speech, rhetoric, poetry, the soul, and philosophy at least begins with something that students can grasp. The *Phaedrus* moves through three speeches centering on love, and offers a dialogic exploration of criticizing and formulating the art of speaking. Invoking both the poetic traditions of Greece as well as Athens' contemporary disciplinary competition among teachers seeking students, the dialogue argues for the philosophic life through a hierarchy of preferred forms of speech: the living speech within the soul and the living exchange of speeches between souls that give rise to the spread of wisdom and understanding are to be preferred over written speeches—laws, addresses, and poetry, even philosophic dialogues—which give honor to and receive acknowledgement from the public sphere.[16] The *Phaedrus* mediates the transition between student concerns and their particular choice(s) of intellectual life through exploring what an art is.

The dialogue begins with Phaedrus' recitation of a speech by Lysias, a rising democratic political star, in Athens. Written as an exercise in wit since it argues that an adolescent should give his favors to an elder non-lover, instead of a lover, the speech is, essentially, a list of topics applied to the benefit of a sexual liaison with someone who has no emotional attachment to the adolescent. Phaedrus' enthusiasm leads him to describe Lysias as "the best of our writers," a judgment from which Socrates must demur. Subsequently, Socrates composes two speeches, the first of which uses Lysias' theme.

Since both Lysias' and Socrates' first speeches amount to offenses against love, Socrates mounts a third speech, this time in favor of the adolescent choosing the lover. Love is re-defined as a madness of soul that is a divine gift. The soul is described as a chariot "driver ... in charge of a pair of horses, ... one [of which] is beautiful and good and from stock of the same sort, while the other is the opposite." The soul's function is to nourish itself, train its parts to respond to command, and to take care of

---

16   *Plato: The Complete Works*, ed. John M. Cooper. "Phaedrus," trs. Alexander Nehemas and Paul Woodruff, 278e.

the inanimate bodies it may come to inhabit. The soul feeds on the grass in the meadows of heaven, a metaphor for the perception by intelligence of ideas that govern the universe—including human actions. When it fails to train itself well enough, the soul falls from heaven and alights in a body on earth, where, if it did have some care for the truth of ideas in its prior existence, it continues to seek the same beauty it found in heaven. On earth, it finds such beauty in an adolescent, for through the adolescent a lover glimpses the beauty and truth of the universe. It is that beauty and truth which he still seeks, while the boy becomes recognized as an image of a god. Caught between yearning for the sight of beauty and the painful absence of that sight whenever the adolescent is not present, the lover begins to exhibit the madness of love. The question of behavior revolves around the direction the lover can give to himself in his madness; in the philosophical lover all the energy of love is directed toward giving to the adolescent the education which leads to love of beauty and truth. But the lover must contend with the horses of his soul, particularly the dark horse, and so, it is possible that the lover of truth and the adolescent may yield to carnal desire, particularly if what is loved is honorable ambition, instead of truth. In this case, there is consummation, though accompanied by moderation, and the life lived is philosophic in the sense that true friendship is[17].

Now, if the first two speeches do not capture our student readers, this last should be enough to make them sit up and take notice. And the question of the dialogue, indeed, the question of much learning, is why should we be fascinated? To point to the content, as I have just done, is to give ourselves assurance that we are fixing upon what can provide an answer, but it is to offer no <u>way to answer</u>, nothing approaching a road to reading. Put differently, to recite the content is to love the speeches without knowing why. It is here that the question of art—in general—enters the dialogue, specified throughout the *Phaedrus* as rhetoric, but exemplified by medicine, poetry, music, and dialectic. Art and artistry give shape

---

17   Ibid., 256ff.

to the examination of the speeches within the dialogue. Thus, the second half of the dialogue is an imitation of an artful conversational answer seeking a road to reading.

The first sign of art is whether a speaker can discriminate appearances of truth through shades of similarity and difference.[18] No one—for example, pleaders or assembly members—could be successful or avoid deception or tell if their opponent was succeeding, if they were not able to tell when another speaker was discriminating likenesses and differences truly. But the problem with founding art on truthful discrimination is that it assumes the very thing which is, at best, an end product of developing artistry and art—i.e., truth.

So, Socrates repositions the search for art, particularly a rhetorical art, by examining whether it is possible to discriminate the import of words which arise from the entire field of discourse. The inquiry starts with words which are clearly understood by an audience—words like "'iron' and 'silver'"—and words which are ambiguous or open to considerable latitude of understanding—words like "justice," "good," "love," "art," "knowledge." Thus, an art is, by this analysis, actually a way of attentively recognizing a permanent fact of life: i.e., there is a huge realm of human concern which occupies a wide dispersion of thought and ambiguity of reference.

The search for art (or artlessness) moves from words to the entire arrangement of speeches, with Lysias' scattershot, topical arrangement of arguments indicating a kind of artless construction. Socrates' two speeches present an alternative approach of offering a definition and a trail of argument leading away from the definition which follows "the natural joints" of the subject. Socrates makes an important observation about the combination of these two features: "Whether its definition was or was not correct, at least it allowed the speech to proceed clearly and consistently with itself."[19] A further mark of art, then, is not its tie

---

18   257e-258e.

19   265e-266d.

to truth, but its ability to structure its effects for observers as a delineated framework for consideration.[20]

The dialogue, thus far, has examined three candidate speeches for signs of artfulness. Socrates next calls into question much written theorizing, i.e., textbooks about rhetoric as an art.[21] We are thus taking up Athenian disciplinary competition for students. Put in today's terms, the competition takes the form of a concern over thoughtless instrumentalist education—producing its repeatable effects upon our audiences, businesses and consumers, culture and politics—with little regard to anything other than the effective use of the techniques themselves.

The discussion should present a challenge to both liberal arts

---

20   Post-modern 20th Century thought has tended to see this intellectual move as an erasure of accident and a subservience to purpose and *telos*, at the expense of historicity, particularly as the critical demands on works move toward a sense of the fullness of the work, and particularly as the examination of critical and original works centers upon the post-Enlightenment. Derrida's early work is unusually clear on this point and relevant to this dialogue, particularly:

> "To be a structuralist is first to concentrate on the organization of meaning, on the autonomy of form and idiosyncratic balance, the completion of each moment, each form: and it is to refuse to relegate everything that is not comprehensible as an ideal type to the status of aberrational accident. [For example,] The pathological itself is not the simple absence of structure. It is organized. It cannot be understood as the deficiency, defect or decomposition of a beautiful, ideal totality. It is not the simple undoing of *telos*." 'Force and Signification' in *Writing and Difference*, University of Chicago Press, 1978, p. 26.

Much of this is true, but just as clearly, Plato and Socrates are engaged with a spectrum of works which may have structure and form in admixture, and, thus, admit of much chance and accident; further, the "anxiety about language—which can only be an anxiety of language, within itself…" which is the very origin of the modern concern with structuralist erasure is at the heart and conclusion of this Platonic dialogue, p. 3. "Difference" in approach there might be, but similar concerns seem more informative, here, than currency of thought.

21   *Phaedrus*, 266c-d.

students and teachers, for here we touch upon a very common justification, one which I think is very weak, for core text, liberal arts courses. The justification is that they teach skills—which are said to be useful in the marketplace or for citizens, but never seem to be directed toward anything specific. Of course, we want liberal arts citizen-students to emerge from any study with techniques of construction and thought. But what Socrates is complaining about is the use of technique—in any field—as a guarantor of effects—the eventual harms, benefits, or nature of which remain unexamined by either the texts or teachers within an education. The objection to the rhetorical treatises and their author/teachers turns on the failure of them to examine the ordering of rhetorical techniques to production of persuasive speeches, or their failure to examine persuasion as such.[22] In sum, Socrates expands the question of structure in art to include the purposes of any teacher or learner of an art. What purpose is to direct technique? What direction marks an art?

What Plato offers as an alternative to instrumentality may seem weak to our colleagues outside humanities and liberal arts departments. Socrates, somewhat ironically, remarks, "all the great arts require endless talk and ethereal speculation about nature: This is what seems to give them their lofty point of view and universal applicability. That's just what Pericles mastered, aside from having natural ability" and, we might add, extensive practice.[23] This speculation is given direction and specificity as Socrates joins a subject to teaching rhetoric: "it is clear that someone who teaches another to make speeches as an art will demonstrate precisely the essential nature of that to which speeches are to be applied. And that, surely, is the soul."[24]

With this, 2000 years of developed disciplines rise up and say:

"good grief, we not only know, with precision, at the expense

---

22   269c.

23   270a.

24   270e.

of centuries and careers of effort in acquiring techniques and systematic method, what things like gravity, life, politics, culture, the psyche, and brain are, but we have precise definitions, tested arguments and procedures, replicable experiments and survey results, and vast arrays of peer-reviewed evidence and argument about what these terms mean. We've done what Socrates wanted far better than he ever could. What we don't need is ethereal speculation; we need, instead, to solve the problems of our disciplines, to advance the frontiers of knowledge and get on with educating the students."

This is true and should be conceded. But there is a problem in education which does not seem resolvable in this way: what discipline will the student choose and why? The *Phaedrus* addresses this issue by arguing that art, not science, is needed to answer this problem. Put into student terms, for Phaedrus is a student of speech, a great art such as dialectic or rhetoric has as its ultimate subject the nature of the human psyche or soul because the aim of *acquiring* an art is education, not in the sense of disciplinary discovery, but to explore, systematically, what can be known, which arts and sciences are worth knowing, and, thus, what knowing through various disciplines might do to someone. In short, education is a permanent problem.

In view of some historical scholarship, it is arguable whether Plato or the Greeks were forming a curriculum through their discussion and debates about education. But it is not difficult to say that the *Phaedrus* is consonant with a liberal arts education today. A student may, of course, be thinking in his or her fashion about the education to come. Not only from books but from all manner of technical recording devices, as Socrates says, they "will be enabled to hear many things without being properly taught, and they will imagine that they have come to know much," perhaps even what their education should be.[25] But when, as in this dialogue, a book, a teacher, and an art are employed to discuss loving, speaking and learning with a student, for Plato and Socrates the

---

25   275b.

chance encounter with the artifacts of culture becomes a living exploration known as philosophy.

If, as representatives of educational institutions and disciplines, we don't want to tell the students what to take, we do, at least, owe them the opportunity to see what is at stake, how difficult yet artful the choice is, and why they should not make a thoughtless decision. For that, the *Phaedrus* is perhaps one of the best books on education that can be read and the reason why it deserves to be included in the canon of works in core text, great books courses.

Confucius

The *Analects* is a similarly great book; it has a deep concern with learning, teachers, and student–disciples. There is much in the way of dialogue. But Plato constructs his text as a narrative sequence of speeches and thoughtful criticism of them. The way that the *Analects* explores a thoughtful life is not Plato's way. Thus, if as students we are really interested in learning what might it mean to be educated, what is worth knowing, and how teacher and student might be related, the *Analects*, particularly Book I provides an alternative to Plato's way—one that ought to be considered by students in core text courses.

The *Analects* does have something in common with both Plato's dialogues and with the *topoi* of rhetorical handbooks.[26] At first sight, the chapters of each Book of the *Analects* may appear to a Westerner's eyes as fragmented dialogues. Legge's alternative translations of the title as "Discussed Sayings" or "Digested Conversations," however, approach a better sense of the dialogues' function. The apparent fragmentation is really a distillation, a device to interrupt the flow of dialogic conversation, so to speak, by focusing on distinct episodes between students and teacher which call for thought. Thus, each chapter becomes literally a "place" to

---

26   These would include, as well, Aristotle's *Rhetoric* or Cicero's *De Inventione*, treatises which had the benefit of being written after Plato had rendered his judgment about earlier rhetorical treatises.

go to think. That is what *topoi*, or commonplaces, in the better ancient Greek and Roman rhetorical treatises were: they were short sentences, arguments, and, occasionally, examples which one pondered in order to understand a situation or the nature of something.[27] No matter how separated they were in a handbook, you were encouraged by these collections of commonplaces or *topoi* to put them together to form your thought, to understand something.

What I want to understand is Confucius' sense of learning, particularly in the relationship between teacher and disciple-student. I don't pretend to offer any scholarship about Confucius or any advancement of his thought. I recognize how reliance on English translations of Chinese characters may erase multivalent meanings. Mostly, I will be like a young student who doesn't know the tradition of commentary. Yet, in speaking so, I hope to illustrate how a student, including an educated teacher new to Confucius, encountering this work for the first time in undergraduate education, might come to see why it, too, is a core text—a text worthy of both ancient and his or her own contemporary study. I believe that this approach that honors Confucian thought converges with the American classroom approach in using core texts in that it allows for the student's naiveté to plumb the depths of the most serious human questions.

The very first sentence of the *Analects* speaks to studying or learning. In Legge's translation we find, "The Master said, 'Is it not pleasant to learn with a constant perseverance and application?'" Ames and Rosemont translate, "Having studied, to then repeatedly apply what you have learned—is this not a source of pleasure?"[28] With two translations, we have two possible interpretations. For

---

27 The textual basis of a homily or sermon tends often to function similarly.

28 Confucius. *Confucian Analects, The Great Learning, and the Doctrine of the Mean.* Translated with Critical and Exegetical Notes, Prolegomena, Copious Indexes, and Dictionary of All Characters [by] James Legge. Dover Publication, 1971., p. 137. Roger T. Ames and Henry Rosemont, Jr. *The Analects of Confucius: A Philosophical Translation.* Ballantine Books, 1998, p. 71.

non-Chinese speaking students, providing two translations might be a good device to a get a conversation going among the students. That conversation should open up three great themes: first, the Master, perhaps this book, is deeply concerned with study, and questions are central to his Mastery; second, there is a relation between studying and application which necessarily involves pleasure, probably unattainable without these two poles of human endeavor; and, third, maybe most importantly, the question as a form of dialogue between a master and a student is designed to make one think in relational terms about him or herself and the world. Though chapter 1 involves studying or action, it is about the *relation* between the two in a person.

The second sentence seems to draw a parallel between the pleasures involved in study and application and the journey of friends from distant quarters to pay a visit. The clear question we are to address is "why is pleasure in studying and application like seeing old friends whom we have not seen for quite some time?" This parallelism is the kind of leap of thought that the topical arrangement of the *Analects* requires of students of Confucius, and it represents a miniature education in growing student thought. I mean that the text requires students to see a connection between studying and the world which they normally would not see, and it presents the example of a mind actively searching the world for unsuspected parallels. If a teacher asks students what might be the similar pleasurable relation between friendship and studying, the students might reply that their friends' sense of their journey enhances their appreciation of the visit itself. Finally, the students in class might recognize that the journey itself is nothing but pro- logue. The real reason for the journey is so that as friends they can share themselves and their conversation. So, the students might begin to think of the pleasure in studying and application as some- thing like a journey, which is really a prologue to sharing the fruits of study, of learning, with friends, who bring from "afar" possibly unexpected insights. Learning, in this sense, becomes not merely a private pleasure, but a social activity.

The third sentence extends our students' thought even further:

"Is he not a man of complete virtue (*junzi*) who feels no discomposure though men may take no note of him?" Here again—at least for most Western students—a leap of thought is required. Confucius has asked a question about the *junzi* which presents studying, learning, and application in a light *opposite* to the second sentence. An exemplary or virtuous person embodies excellence, yet that excellence often goes unnoticed. We might ask students, how might a person who is serious about learning feel as a result of his or her study and application of learning, particularly when "others" cannot and do not recognize the rewards of studying, learning and application? For students who are by nature social, we could, then, ask, what about studying, learning, and application might actually lead to a character like the *junzi's*?

Thus, in the first three sentences the *Analects* continues to probe what studying and learning involves by asking our thought to make leaps between the world and self. By the very application of our thought to try to make some ties among the first, second, and third sentences, we may, indeed, be experiencing that pleasure of study of which the first sentence speaks. And, finally, we have already begun to think relationally, to tie together passages of this text in application to ourselves as students.

A topical arrangement of distilled dialogues invites further leaps. Instead of proceeding to Master Yu's sayings in the second chapter of Book 1, suppose that we ask our students, "is there an example in Book 1 of sharing the fruits of study with friends and is there an example of the comportment of a scholar whose learning may not at first be recognized?" Perhaps one of the students would leap to Book 1, Chapter 15: in which Zigong, one of Confucius' favorite disciple-students, and Confucius engage in a dialogue comparing thoughts and character, ending in Confucius' appreciation of Zigong's thought and conversation.

Legge notes that Zigong's question, "'what do you pronounce concerning the poor man who yet does not flatter, and the rich man who is not proud?'" is about Zigong's own experience. Ames, on the other hand, translates as if Zigong were asking not about his own character, but about the adequacy of statements: "What do you think of *saying*: 'Poor but not inferior; rich but not superior'?" [my emphasis]

Ames translates Confucius' reply as "'Not bad, but not as good as 'Poor but enjoying the way (*dao*); rich but loving ritual propriety (*li*)'." This reply as a statement, something said in response, is an improvement in statement. Zigong's statements, whether about himself or about how to say something, lack a way for one who was poor or rich to know that one's character was properly oriented. This is what the references to the *dao* and *li* provide.

Instead of silence or an expression of disappointment in the correction, Zigong—the thoughtful student—interprets Confucius' statement with a reply from the *Book of Songs*, "Like bone carved and polished / Like jade cut and ground. Is this not what you had in mind?" These are products of art, of assiduous study, of something made valuable by the application of repeated, careful actions. What is enjoyed, what is pleasurable is a repeated process of learning that shapes the character of the raw materials. As Zigong is speaking about humans, the metaphor or parallelism invites a curious thought for our students: *dao* and *li* are like the work of artistry, not on some foreign materials, but upon oneself. It is Zigong's actual use of the *Songs'* artistic statements to understand the way in which *dao* and *li* operate that Confucius commends, for Zigong's reply is like a further stroke of artistry upon the conversation. Zigong and Confucius have initiated a wide-ranging conversation about studying, learning, character, the wider world, and artistry in mutual appreciation of each other's contribution to the conversation—a thought that returns us with greater appreciation to the very first chapter in this first book of the *Analects*.

If, at this point, we begin to reflect with our students on Plato's *Phaedrus* and Confucius' *Analects*, we can see how their mutual use in a general education, core text course would complement each other because they would expand student thought. Both are concerned with study and learning. Both are concerned with how statements and conversation may be used to broaden and deepen student thought. Plato's way, however, is not that of the *dao* or *li*, but artistry. Plato wished his students to investigate the soul. Plato's concern in the *Phaedrus* is how competing disciplines or arts will structure the education of students and their relation to teachers. Plato writes one narrative dialogue which calls into question the worth of having a conversation with texts that cannot speak back, and the dialogue persuades towards a preference for the living, artistic conversation, the specific disciplinary education between student and teacher which is known as philosophy.

Confucius's students assembled the remembered, distilled conversations between Confucius and his disciples as a way not simply to record history, but to stand as a lasting source of continued thought and conversation for the future. The *Analects'* first Book concentrates on the relationships of studying and application, teacher and student, statement and life, and relational leaps of thought.[29] Confucius congratulates his student on knowing how to think and speak about shaping the soul by using the analogy of the arts. But the arts are an analog to the way *dao* and *li* work in the world; they are not the substance by which one comes to knowledge. Partaking of *dao* and *li* is the true path to study. Plato and Confucius represent two perfectly respectable forms of approaching education. Plato's world in the *Phaedrus* is much like our disciplinary world of departmental education—in which we urge our students to take a course of study with a teacher who has a specific discipline to offer—e.g., either rhetoric or philosophy. Confucius' world in the *Analects* Book I is much more like the interdisciplinary world of core texts courses, particularly in general education, where analogies of the various arts and the broader applications of study to the wider world are considered. Yet, both of these texts belong in core text courses, for they open the minds

---

29   Legge notes that the Lun Yu, the *Analects*, came to be absorbed under the term *Ching*, a "term …of textile origin, [that] signifies the warp threads of a web, and their adjustment," p. 1. A web is a good metaphor for the <u>functional</u> structural construction of the *Analects*. The association of the term "web" with this book and the electronic "world wide web" strongly suggest that 21ˢᵗ Century students may, in fact, be more prepared to read the *Analects* than we may be inclined to give them credit for.

of students to what the world of study and education may involve. And both of the texts in combination indicate how an imaginative, not historical, conversation between East and West might proceed in a 'world' core text curriculum.

Cervantes

Great books programs in United States universities and colleges are often Western focused, with a decided bent toward Northern European science and art. While today's curricula are increasingly international, inheritors of these curricular programs owe a debt to Mortimer Adler's and Robert Maynard Hutchins' *Great Books of the Western World*, a product of late 40's and early 50's curriculum work at the University of Chicago. *Don Quixote* appears in the Adler collection and is read at many U.S. institutions which have these great books programs. In a historical progression that is employed by many of these courses, *Don Quixote* will appear about 60% of the way through a 2800-year span of works. A little closer examination will note that *Don Quixote* is the last work of Mediterranean and Spanish origins in the Adler collection, and that the works after it all derive from Northern Europe or the United States. Certainly, historical movements of the Reformation as well as North American educational needs and cultural preferences have played their part in this collection, but *Don Quixote* was on the cusp, the borderline of inclusion. Why was it included at all? I don't mean to answer this question historically. Instead, I want to answer the question pedagogically, from the point of view of a faculty member who is thinking about why this book should be added to a syllabus for a great books course. What are the advantages of teaching *Don Quixote*?

It turns out that there seem to be formidable disadvantages. First, if taught in the U.S., the work will have to be translated, losing many of its beauties and subtleties. Second, it is long. Third, there's a vast literature of secondary sources about the book itself; perhaps students and teachers should read this to prepare. Fourth, there is the knowledge of all the historical conditions that contextualize the work that seem requisite for intelligent reading. Fifth, there's the current research agendas of intellectual inquiry; does *Don Quixote* fit into programs exposing the strategy of textuality that erases the marks of oppression, or does *Don Quixote* adequately signal the more important questions of colonization, race, class, gender? Sixth, finally, if cultures not authors write works, almost all these approaches could be required before one could approach the work intelligently. Of course, all these approaches exalt the authority of professors in the classroom, while displacing the participation by students in the main text—*Don Quixote*—towards a struggle with 'the literature' of myriad criticism.

All of these difficulties are, of course, specialist objections to core text programs. Is there a way to meet these objections? The way to think about these, I believe, is to look at the book itself. Even with a cursory inspection, it seems to me that reading Homer's *Iliad* and *Odyssey*, Plato's *Republic*, Aristotle's *Poetics*, The Bible, a bit of Ptolemy, Horace's *Ars Poetica*, Longinus's *On the Sublime*, Virgil's *Aeneid*, Ovid's *Metamorphoses,* excerpts from Marie de France's *Lais*, perhaps selections from Aquinas, Dante's *Divine Comedy*, the *Morte D'Arthur*, selections from Lope de Vega, and a romance by Shakespeare would all help to prepare for and contribute to a reading of *Don Quixote*. I mention these works because I think Cervantes indicates directly or indirectly a familiarity with them or their kind, and most of these works have appeared in liberal arts, great books-based programs at one time or another.

A book's evident contact with works from other fields, eras, and languages seems to me to approach a first criterion for including it in a core text syllabus; in other words, it is in conversation not only with its own time but with many, many works and ideas that come before it or follow after it. Such works are Cervantes' most appropriate context. But other criteria are necessary. A book also needs to promise artistry of considerable magnitude (that is both size and excellence); that's a matter of inspecting the work. While works dating from the Enlightenment might seem to be all we would need, works of the ancients, Middle Ages and Renaissance deserve serious consideration for they provide sources of thought, often unavailable or badly represented in strictly modern discourse. I have in mind here something akin to the notion that a rhetorician is known by the use of the available means of persuasion. Similarly, an educated person is known by his or her use of available resources for thought—ones often ignored by modern minds. These three criteria seem to me to imply a fourth: a work in this collection should be innovative, whether as most excellent in kind or simply distinguishably original. It seems to me that *Don Quixote* satisfies all four of these criteria.

Such criteria also begin to outline what we might expect students in such a course of study to achieve. With these core texts, we ask students to become prepared to encounter and develop a sense of excellence in artistry, attention to and memory of the extended connections of works, a growing sense of the interconnected relations of most fields of knowledge and ability to see them—often in unfamiliar clothing—in a vast variety of contexts. We seek from them an ability to weigh and suspend immediate judgment about arguments and actions found in works, an openness to the breadth of human accomplishment, and an emotional sensitivity that comprehends what can be at stake in human endeavor. In short, we ask student to confront the dignity and worth of humans, even in such comic works as Cervantes's novel.

These same principles of selection and hopes for our students' achievements might be approached through examining the innovation of *Don Quixote* in a pedagogical manner, even if the work is not in the repertoire of one's expertise. One critic remarks that "when Cervantes was creating his masterpiece there really was no such thing as a novel as we now know it."[30] Aside from Rabelais' *Gargantua and Pantagruel* the Adler Great Books collection tends to confirm this statement, for all its other novels, six in number, follow Cervantes. If so, then students are being confronted in a

---

30   Edward H. Friedman, "Introduction," in Miguel de Cervantes Saavedra, *Don Quixote*, tr. Walter Skokie: NY, Signet, 2001, p. 22. All quotations from *Don Quxiote* are taken from this translation.

course of Western intellectual traditions with a new art form, an invention. What difference might this make? Certainly, sprawling works like the *Iliad* and compounded poems like Chaucer's *Canterbury Tales* plus critical works like Aristotle's *Poetics* will prepare students who have read these works to read a lengthy complex novel. But I would insist that *Don Quixote* marks a difference here. Aristotle is right when he remarks that an epic can contain two or three stories and that an incident might be used for a wonderful, Homeric, digression. Further, Chaucer's unfinished tales certainly deliver a collection of short stories that might have, had they been completed, filled out a pattern of the lives of each of the pilgrims. But even with these works in hand, it is hard to think of a narrative work before *Don Quixote* that relied on a consecutive plot interrupted by so many tales told by characters, some of whom impact the protagonist and some of whom do not. Not even the Pearl Poet or Shakespeare matches this extraordinary magnitude of tales in one single work.

For our students this book's magnitude has considerable implication for the development of their thought. To grasp *Don Quixote*, they must take seriously our same critic's observation that "Cervantes does not simply write a novel to entertain the reader with an intriguing plot, but he uses the occasion to make the reader think seriously about the act of writing and the act of reading."[31] Put differently, I think, a core text course, a proper orientation of the curriculum should almost inevitably raise these activity-of-making questions for students, since these are curricula about books. In Chapter 47 the curate and the canon are in debate over how to regard books of chivalry. The canon remarks:

> I have never seen a book of chivalry with a whole body for a plot, with all its members complete, so that the middle corresponds to the beginning and the end to the beginning and middle. Instead, they are composed of so many limbs that they seem rather to have been intended to form a chimera or a monster than a well-proportioned figure…They are devoid

---

31　Ibid.

of all art and intelligence and deserve to be expelled from a Christian republic as a useless race.

Admitting, however, his own attempt to write a chivalric romance, the canon progresses to an alternative which might very well allow such works into a Christian republic:

> [the canon] said that in spite of all that he had said against them, he discovered one good thing in them, namely the opportunity that they offered a good intellect to display itself. For they presented a wide and spacious field through which the pen might run without any obstacles... "The author might show his knowledge of astrology, or his proficiency in cosmography and music, or his experience in affairs of state... He may display...all those attributes to create the model hero, sometimes placing them in one single man at other times sharing them out among many. And if all this is done to in a pleasant style with an ingenious plot... the author ... will achieve the end of these works which as I said is to instruct as well as entertain."[32]

If students have read the *Phaedrus, the Poetics,* and *Ars Poetica,* they should be in a position to recognize that the canon has presented an important critical debate for the birth of the novel. Clearly, the argument that the chief effects of a work depend on plot coherence presents a tremendous challenge to anyone who is trying to write a novel, and it would seem that Cervantes' found a solution in Roman rhetorical traditions which saw structure as less a matter of specific effects than as a qualitative display of the intelligent character of the author. The passage above suggests that Cervantes' basic principles of construction for Part I of this work seem to be that he will write a consecutive plot, but he will *distribute the primary attributes of his hero among many protagonists* such that multiple stories will be required to fill out the work. Since multiple stories would yield a display of intelligence but

---

32   Cervantes, p. 478-479.

overwhelm the coherence of a plot, an "ingenuous plot" will have to be constructed to overcome the difficulty.

As a teacher deciding with other faculty whether to include this work in a core text program, I would be inclined to pursue the following questions as ways to inquire into the ingenuousness of Cervantes' work. Is Don Quixote's madness caused, as seems the case in the first few pages, by reading the chivalric romances, a cause which seems to affect no one else in the novel, or in that first few pages is there some yearning on the part of Don Quixote that more nearly touches his peculiar form of madness? I would be inclined to ask, why are love and valor so important to Don Quixote's knightly adventures and to the various love stories that fill the novel's pages? Through these lines of inquiry, I would probe for a comprehensible connection within the novel such that if the romances were removed, we would not only lessen the novel by reducing it as a collection but lessen the story of Don Quixote as well.

Such questions lead me to conclude that the novel invites us to explore whether this work is merely a clever collection of love stories embedded into an absurd adventure of a middle-aged man in a mid-life crisis that he refuses to accept, or whether the novel is using the knightly adventures and embedded love stories to explore how precious and, even, governing is the regard of human beings for each other. Whatever the case, my job both in deciding *with* my fellow faculty members to include the book in a course and in teaching the work to students does not involve an obligation to persuade my colleagues or coerce my students into accepting my interpretation of this work. Rather, I need an interpretation in order to develop questions that effectively relate this work to others in the course and the parts of this work to itself as a whole. What should, then, ensue out of such questions—whether in the classroom or in faculty offices—is a discussion which explores the greatness, the magnitude of this work within the *intellectual* development of the West (and, perhaps, the world).

What is important, here, is that while such questions are an essential part of faculty decisions about inclusion of works, they are questions which students themselves could address in class discussions. In other words, the decisions for constructing such programs should have everything to do with how the students, not a given discipline or set of disciplines, could approach these works in light of other works and modes of education exemplified in the books themselves. Put differently, *liberal education is about itself,* and its scope ranging through the cultural core texts of various traditions or, even, the world, gives it appropriate license to be so constructed.

Therefore, our job is to facilitate the exploration by students of the scope of the work and its relation to other works through *their* give-and-take, *their* debates, *their* discourse. Core text or great books courses are rarely, if ever, intended as a representation of what is acceptable in a discipline, nor are they representations of the collected special interests of a professor. Instead, ideally at least, they are representations of the collective educated judgment by a faculty that these works should be explored by students so that a program in liberal arts may, through the students' own discussions, cultivate persons who look to the future through an acquired command of the past. Cultivating the ability of students and their intellectual artistry through questions which can provoke widely varying discussions is absolutely central to students developing such command. Ultimately students should become the ones who are asking the questions as they seek to build their own interpretations and their own sense of the links between works from across the range of Western or other traditions of thought.[33] Such command means that when students graduate from such programs, they *know* what to look for in a book or work of art to inquire about their future because they possess the art to do so. Perhaps, what is at stake is something as serious as what Cervantes achieved, for

---

33   One way to do this might be to assign repeatedly in different courses an essay to justify removing one work in the syllabus and replacing it with another—perhaps drawn from a bibliography supplied by the professor. Such an assignment might not only begin to build a sense of construction by students, but also orient them toward asking what is the nature of their education.

Cervantes did not simply write a comic novel which made him famous; he was a primary player in expanding our minds' capacity for thought and in changing the map of literature—forever. It seems as if Don Quixote's sallies were indeed a serious comedy.

Changing the Map of Education

For our part, we may not be able so uniquely to change the map of education, but we should not underestimate our ability to do so. We are cartographers of the mind. When the faculty of the University of Chicago began to design the Great Books collection, the world was a more fragmented place, teetering on the brink of World War II. The designers of that collection admitted that there were conversations among books and authors in countries and civilizations that this collection did not touch. Some greatness, it seems, was unrecognized.

Now, the world is changed and higher education has been a serious participant in that change. American institutions have developed a more pluralistic outlook of what belongs in liberal arts programs. They have included works from other major world civilizations which intersect with Western thought, and they have re-examined the Western heritage to expand the works which a cultivated citizen should read. Today, Gabriel Marquez's *One Hundred Years of Solitude* or *The Chronicle of a Death Foretold* are often included in these programs as modern continuations of the Western liberal arts tradition of great books or core texts. Faculty discussions have brought in women authors, and also the experience of African-Americans. For our own part, we meet today in a North-South dialogue on Colombian soil on the continent of South America. I hope this dialogue will extend the scope and, perhaps, reach of liberal arts programs both here and in the United States, particularly with regard to Hispanic literature, history, and philosophy. I hope it will help to expand the cultural conversation of the liberal arts and the nations of the earth.

(Selected and revised from speeches delivered in Colombia in 2006 and 2008; in Taiwan, 2009; compiled and revised 1/7/2020. In translation, portions of the Confucius section appeared in *University Education Science* No.1, 2014 and were reprinted in *Higher Education* (Remnin University) No.6, 2014. Translator Yaqun Zhang.)

CHAPTER 7

Enriching Liberal Education's Defense

Liberal Arts, Invention, and Technē

Part I: Seeking a defense of liberal education

For a number of years, it has struck me that people who write about a "liberal *arts* education" rarely write directly about the arts. They write about political, religious, and moral dispositions; they write about the rise of the sciences; they write about cultures; and recently, they write about the conditions of education. Sometimes, they write about books and core texts within the tradition of the liberal arts, but these books and their associated arts are written about as exemplars of politics, morals, science, and culture—rarely as exemplars of arts.

A recent spate of writings defending the humanities and humanism, the college and the purpose of education—by Martha Nussbaum, Tony Kronman, Andrew Delbanco, and Patrick Deneen—all mention liberal arts education. They defend the fine or liberal arts, but none of these authors ground their defenses of liberal arts education in art per se.[1] All of these writers sense an

---

1 Andrew Delbanco hardily approves of Anthony Kronman's great books curriculum for the ideas it raises, and he cites the *artes liberales* ideal of education that Bruce Kimball has extensively documented as a tradition of aristocratic European liberal learning that opens the mind. But it is America's "attempt to democratize" this tradition through its collegiate educations that really interests him (*College: What It Was, Is, and Should Be* [Princeton: Princeton University Press, 2012], 33.) "Working to keep the ideal of democratic education alive," Delbanco, in an extensive analysis

ebbing of liberal education correlated with the economic, scientific,

---

of the past and present social conditions of colleges as institutions, ultimately locates the "universal value of a liberal education" in the belief,
derived from the nineteenth-century religious college, that "no outward
mark—wealth or poverty, high or low social position, credentials or lack
thereof—tells anything about the inward condition of the soul" (171). He
transmutes this belief, today, into a liberal education whose "saving power"
(171) allows students to "ignite in one another a sense of the possibilities of democratic community" through "the intellectual and imaginative
enlargement [college] makes possible" (172). He concludes, "we owe it
to posterity to preserve and protect this institution. Democracy depends
on it." (177). Martha Nussbaum begins her "manifesto" in defense of the
humanities and arts with a crisis in which "the humanities and the arts
are being cut away in both primary/secondary and college/university
education, in virtually every nation in the world." This entails "discarding
of skills that are needed to keep democracies alive." In the survival of the
humanities and arts within educational institutions "the future of the
world's democracies" is said to "hang in the balance" (*Not for Profit: Why
Democracy Needs the Humanities.* [Princeton: Princeton University Press,
2010], 1-2).

Notwithstanding a very serious concern with "ideals of freedom,"
Anthony Kronman is less focused on the links between democracy and
liberal education than on the links between the humanities and our culture (*Education's End: Why Our Colleges and Universities Have Given Up on
the Meaning of Life.* New Haven: Yale University Press, 2007). He stresses
particularly the humanities' abandonment, within colleges and universities, of the search for meaning in our individual lives, and he warns
against our scientific culture's way of aggrandizing our technical powers
without setting them within the limitations of human finitude. The combination, he believes, yields a kind of spiritual desiccation.

Oddly similar to Kronman notwithstanding their published differences,
Patrick Deneen argues that before the rise of the New Sciences, whose
authors often belittled ancient books, greatness rested in a "predominant
understanding" of cultivated endurance and an acceptance of the limits of human power, knowledge, and ambition. The modern great books
program contains many scientific, political and economic works which
support the idea of transformation. So Deneen asks, might there be an
alternative way to think about the core texts of the ancient to medieval
Western tradition, ultimately as a way of restraining our scientifically
released *pleonexia* for mastering and transforming our world? He suggests

and technological conditions under which we live. Nearly all find that the present responses of our institutions to these conditions impede rather than aid the robust maintenance or development of something like a liberal education. Most of their arguments rely on research, though their positions on whether research—scientific, bibliographic or otherwise—within a university favors or harms undergraduate liberal education tends to range Nussbaum on one side and Delbanco, Kronman, and Deneen on the other. In contrast, each author attempts to revive traditions of the liberal arts by linking them to current conditions of democracy, spiritual needs of cultures, or ethical understandings of faith. All believe that the souls of our students and our citizens are at stake, though of course they disagree about the constitution of the soul and the education designed to nurture it.

A common concern among these authors is whether our cultural assumption that we can transform almost anything, particularly through the technology of science, is good for our souls and good for liberal education. For Nussbaum, technology appears as the attractive image of students in a lab—instead of pictures of students "thinking"—that administrators use to lure students to universities.[2] Delbanco notes the advantage that the sciences have over the humanities in public evaluations: technological landmarks of progress, accompanied by an occasional historical or philosophic "breakthrough."[3] For Kronman and Deneen, technology is the differential gear which imparts varying force to science, culture, and education. Further, Kronman and Deneen come very close to each other in noting the meretricious effects upon our character and our sense of limits that technological achievement unleashes in the form of *pleonexia*. The humanities currently fail to oppose it (Kronman), or worse, education encourages it through a

---

great books might be justified by recovering this earlier understanding's humility ("Against Great Books," in *First Things* [January 2013], 35.)

2   Nussbaum, *Not for Profit*, p. 133.

3   Delbanco, *College*, p. 95. Apparently, literature does not rise to breakthroughs.

philosophy of transformation, of creating original knowledge and innovations through research (Deneen).[4]

---

4   At one point, Kronman and Deneen come very close to saying—and meaning—the same thing. Kronman's case for the humanities in large part rests on controlling technology through a recognition of human limits: "We have a desire for control that can never be satisfied by any degree of control we actually achieve. We always want more. This is the human condition, which is characterized by our subjection to fateful limits that we can neither tolerate nor do without. The most important thing about technology is not *what* it does but what it *aspires* to do... Technology encourages us to believe that the abolition of fate should be our goal... Technology discourages the thought that our finitude is a condition of the meaningfulness of our lives ... It makes the effort to recall our limits and to reflect upon them seem less valuable and important" (Kronman, *Education's End,* 230-233). For Kronman, the research ideal is, of course, partly justified in the sciences by the "fruit"—both in discovery and in technology—that it produces: "The research ideal is today the organizing principle of work in every academic discipline... In the natural sciences, the research ideal has proved remarkably fruitful. The new discoveries that pour from our college and university laboratories every year and the clear sense of progressive movement toward an objective understanding of the structure and mechanisms of the natural world testify to the productive fit between the natural sciences and the modern research ideal." Whereas in the humanities "understanding," but *not a productive technology* character- izes research results: "In the humanities the benefits of research are less uniform or certain" (ibid.,130-133). Nevertheless "research in the human- ities has produced results of lasting value. It has added importantly to our understanding of the historical, literary, artistic, and philosophical subjects with which the humanities deal." The demands for specialization and for teaching to that specialization ought to be less insistently felt in the humanities: "What must be resisted is the imperial sprawl of the research ideal, its expansive tendency to fill every corner of each discipline in which it takes hold and to color the expectations and judgments of teachers in these disciplines regarding what they do. Admittedly this is asking a lot... But ...it is merely asking for a somewhat greater degree of humility on the part of those in the humanities who first allegiance is to this ideal" (ibid., 248-249).

For Deneen, the (current) point of a philosophy of education is not to admire the world, or suffer its limits, but to change it, to transform it. To Deneen, since the Enlightenment, greatness seems to rest in

Finally, while all these authors seem to be convinced that the products of arts are essential to any revival, and while they are skilled fashioners of argument in areas where no single discipline can claim precedence, the discussion of fine or liberal arts and their products is not in terms of art, but in the terms of the political, cultural, or religious end sought. For example, Nussbaum devotes large portions of her book exploring arts and a whole chapter to "Cultivating the Imagination: Literature and the Arts." In the latter, we learn that "in order to be stably linked to democratic values, [both the artistic cultivation of capacities for play and empathy in

---

transformation. So he asks, might there be an alternative way to think about and assign terms to the core texts of the Western tradition, ultimately as a way of restraining our excesses in transforming our world? He begins by accepting a stasis in the political, moral, religious, and poetic inheritance of books that extends from the ancients through the first stirrings of modernity: "Great books such as *Paradise Lost* sought to inculcate a sense of limits, ... we could look at a dominant understanding of a long succession of great books from antiquity to the Middle Ages ... to conform human behavior and aspirations to the natural or created order" ("Against Great Books," 35). By way of Baconian, Cartesian, and Hobbesian repudiation of books, Deneen elaborates the argument that he feels undermines the "'human limits" understanding by trying to discriminate two kinds of liberty. The first, associated with great books, is a "liberty ... of hard-won self-control through the discipline of virtue," which often animates defenses of great books as materials in preparing for citizenship. The second is a liberty with "the stress ... upon the research, creative activity, scholarly inquiry and the development of new knowledge" (ibid., 37). The former constrains our desires, the latter endlessly satisfies them through "the human project of mastery." The latter pursuits were justified by the arguments of Bacon, Descartes, and Hobbes, reinforced by Dewey, which depended on the idea "that a larger number of natural forces and objects [could be or] have been transformed into instrumentalities of action" in the West than in cultures which did not exploit the natural resources available through scientific technology (ibid., 36). Deneen concludes that we do need to teach these two competing notions of liberty through the great books, but defenders should exchange the notion of "greatness" for a notion of "humility" derived from the earlier works of the intellectual tradition represented in the West (ibid., 38). Humility might, then, restrain our excesses in regard to transformation.

159

a general way, and the treatment of particular cultural blind spots] require a normative view of how human beings ought to relate to one another ... and, both therefore require selectivity regarding the artworks used."[5] A catalog follows of the failures of artworks, of "defective forms of 'literature',," to cultivate the sympathy that Nussbaum desires. Undoubtedly, Kronman's understanding of the search for meaning and his discussion of civilizational "conversation" depends on art; Delbanco's distinction between research and reading instances canonical works from ancient to modern times; and Deneen's argument is concerned with a residuum of teachings that earlier great books leave us. Yet, in these social-moral defenses, an entire line of argument concerning the arts is, for the most part, relegated to an instrumental, supporting, or ancillary role in a discussion that might be titled: "Social Conditions, Educational Institutions, and Individual Capacities: Whither Liberal Education?"

I wish to suggest now that the ecology of liberal education defense could be enriched by also focusing on the *arts* of liberal arts education, invention, and *technē*. Please note that my preceding remarks are not meant to imply the absence of artistic works in liberal arts programs, nor that some parts of those programs are not structured by the arts. For example, Yale's Directed Studies program has courses explicitly divided into three groups: Literature, Philosophy, and Historical and Political Thought. Clearly literature is art. Columbia's Core's program has the Literature/Humanities and the Contemporary Civilization sequences, not to mention the Music offerings. Again, no one doubts that this program involves art. What I am interested in are the rationales and justifications for programs using core texts that can be grounded in the liberal arts.

Why is it important to develop a line of argument about arts to the point where we might see them in the guise of an end, not just a means, to liberal arts education? Do you remember, about forty or fifty years ago, if you aspired to a bachelor's degree, you chose either a bachelor-of-science or a bachelor-of-arts? No one

---

5   Nussbaum, *Not for Profit*, p. 108.

today questions whether a student possesses a science if she or he earns a B.S. What art or arts, however, do our students possess if they have earned a B.A.? So, if we claim to offer a liberal *arts* education in undergraduate bachelor programs, it might not be amiss to ask what arts are our students learning and what arts are teaching. And asking such questions can enrich our view of liberal arts education using core texts—whether of the Western tradition or not.

Part II: The problem of accommodating liberal arts education

When educators of any stripe are seeking renewal, they often resort to an examination of the past, so I thought the best place to begin a search for a renewal of liberal-arts education might be in a book by Bruce Kimball first published in 1986: *Orators and Philosophers: A History of the Idea of Liberal Education.*[6] The book's judicious consideration of a vast number of core texts, curricular materials, and the scholarly production surrounding liberal education make this work a seminal contribution to its history. Kimball has paid much more explicit attention than any current author we have examined to the educational curricular ideal of the *artes liberales*, the citizenship-oriented use of liberal arts and the tradition of associated texts. This ideal he contrasts to the research ideal—or, as he styles it, the *liberal-free* ideal in education, developed by him with the same care. With the important exception of an unstable "*artes liberales*' accommodation" in a very few universities and colleges between these two ideals—Chicago, Columbia, St. John's College being the primary examples—his extended history gives little comfort to the conviction that liberal-arts education, particularly in relation to democracy, has much of a chance of revival in most of today's universities or colleges, precisely because of the

---

6 Bruce Kimball, *Orators and Philosophers: A History of the Idea of Liberal Education* (New York: Teachers College, 1986; rev. ed., New York: College Entrance Examination Board, 1995).

success of the ideal of research throughout academe, and its allied notion of freedom.[7]

Kimball's history, which extends from ancient Greece to late twentieth-century America, reflects a two-fold tradition reaching into modern education. A rhetorical liberal arts tradition complains about disarray and divisions of undergraduate education, while an epistemic, research quarrel among the fields of science, social science, and the humanities over "definitions of knowledge and culture" influences undergraduate education. These two educational traditions—the *artes liberales* ideal for citizenship and the *liberal-free* ideal for specialization—compete in public, graduate, and under-graduate contexts. To bring this competition down to earth at the undergraduate level: Kimball finds "it is supremely difficult for an undergraduate major ... to coexist with a thorough [curricular] commitment to citizenship, virtues, the republic, and the appropriation of the textual tradition of a community."[8] The reason is that these two polarities, or ideals, are systematic: they entail different ends, characteristic qualities, and, ultimately, curricular expressions. The "*artes liberales* accommodation" is unstable partly because it cannot readily convince academics that classics are necessary to a critical intellect, and partly because its insistence upon exploring ancient texts "conflicts with the liberal-free mind" in its desire to range where it will.[9]

---

7 The importance of these institutions to the "*artes liberales* accommodation" is inferred from, not stated in, Kimball's text. What matters for inference is whether institutions or those who constructed curricula advocate "classic" texts be used in liberal education. What also matters is whether Kimball or 'the literature' cites these advocates frequently, in the debates and discussions about liberal arts education. Cf. p. 3 (Chicago and Columbia), pp. 220 (Chicago and St. John's), pp. 186, 279 (Hutchins and Gideonse), pp. 236-237 (Frankel and Kristeller at Columbia), pp. 275-276 (McKeon and Booth; particularly important here is Kimball's interpretation of their 'voluminous' position on the 'history of liberal education' as a singular *philosophic* tradition, subsuming rhetoric.)

8 Ibid. p. 286.

9 Ibid. pp. 223. The instability of programs, aside from the three

To varying degrees, then, Kimball anticipates the ambivalence that Kronman and Delbanco feel about reading great texts at the undergraduate level with modern research in mind. Kimball also anticipates Kronman and Deneen's concern with the way in which the rise of science has shaped our educational institutions toward a research ideal and away from a reflective, character-building liberal-arts education. In a strange twist of fate, Kimball also recognizes the role of the liberal-free ideal in harnessing science and research to the democratic and market-based national project of the United States. And in this he anticipates Nussbaum's and Delbanco's attempts to have our educational institutions, committed as they are to the research ideal, serve the national or international life of democracies—a role formerly reserved for the *artes liberales* ideal.

In sum, historically and philosophically, with research and disciplines firmly entrenched by the rise of science in the modern university, all of these authors find themselves in a very difficult position. They sense a pervasive cultural and ethical emptiness related to the very institution of education to which their lives

---

institutions mentioned above, is inferred from the following passage concerning the *artes liberales* accommodation and attacks against it in academe:

> The reliance on sanctified classics fundamentally conflicts with the liberal-free mind, and the artes liberales accommodation, in attempting to bridge the two ideals, incorporates within itself the source of its own negation. (223)

This goes beyond a dialectical or intellectual contradiction to an institutional struggle usually leading to the disappearance of a liberal arts curriculum, which would include those based on an artes liberales accommodation:

> All the [current higher education] reports complain about how departments and specialized majors have devoured liberal education. But none of them have tried to conceive of an undergraduate education without departments or majors. (287)

Kimball suggests that setting up opposed faculties (i.e. different colleges) within one institution "dedicated to one or another conception" of liberal education might be feasible. (289)

are committed. They resist this emptiness by offering an alternative end to liberal education—call it citizenship, democracy, humanity, or faith—something other than research. All of these supporters of liberal education are faced with an institutional history that is well documented and that holds out little hope (but let us not say no hope) of successfully wooing to the ends of liberal education the disciplines and departments that mark universities and colleges.

As I indicated above, in these analyses the arts, including the liberal arts, are relegated to a secondary role. The defense of liberal arts education might change considerably were the end of liberal arts education seen differently. The seeming instability of the "*liberales artes*" accommodation is significant for understanding an entirely different end for the liberal arts than is usually supposed, as well as an historical continuity for these arts that is not fully appreciated. Such an appreciation offers important steps away from the corner out of which liberal education defends itself. The liberal arts sources outside academe and the persistent attempt by higher education faculty to devise curricula composed of 'classic' or core text works strongly suggest that *invention and innovation have become the end of liberal arts development and its education.*

Part III: Inventing new arts, sciences, and education outside the academy

Before and after the innovative congregating of lecturers into medieval universities, education in liberal arts was often done outside an institutional context.[10] This "outside" development

---

10   Kimball tends to find considerable influence within universities by academics supporting the liberal arts during the rise of Renaissance humanism. He relies on the facts of co-curricular teaching, institutes, and reform plans, as well as traveling scholars who promoted humanism to include liberal arts instruction in universities. Universities, since their inception, have been centers around which intellectuals have congregated or traveled to, but this is different than being a faculty member of a university constructing and delivering instruction as a matter of a formal degree. Ibid., pp. 82-84 ff.

matters because in one way or another almost all of our authors acknowledge institutional atrophy at various points in the history of liberal education. And if, today, liberal arts education is institutionally "strangled" rather than atrophied, that is all the more reason to examine sources outside academe, or sources within academe that are not currently predominant in models of education for inspiration in renewing liberal arts education. In particular, the transition from Aquinas to Bacon has as its *backdrop* the rise of universities—but the actual *stage* was filled with liberal artists outside of academia who were actively developing new educations, arts, and sciences. The work of these liberal artists provides us with generative—perhaps even transformative—models, grounded in the classics, that can contribute appreciably to institutional revival of the liberal arts.[11]

---

11   As the medieval universities rose, the *septem artes* diminished in importance, largely owing to Aquinas's dictum that "the seven liberal arts do not sufficiently divide theoretical philosophy," as well as the emergence of new studies in graduate programs. This led to a distinct separation of the seven arts from philosophy within the curriculum of new medieval universities (Ibid., pp. 66 and 71). That said, the philosophic medieval rediscovery of the ancients seems not to have been an exercise in "freedom from a-priori strictures and standards" nor "a critical skepticism" linked to "scientific method." (pp. 120-121).

On the other hand, the humanists' interest in oratorical skills allowed the liberal arts to flourish successfully *outside* the universities during the twelfth and thirteenth centuries. Beginning with Petrarch's interest in Cicero and Quintilian, the *artes liberales* ideal leads to a revival and spread of enthusiasm for literature among the literate general public, but a widespread revival of studying literary classics in the curricula of universities did not take hold until the middle of the fifteenth century (p. 80).

A similar historical development occurred in the emergence of modern science, notwithstanding Newton's appointment at Cambridge, the pursuit of philosophy in the name of the New Science of Bacon, Descartes, Hobbes, and Spinoza led to a blockade of natural philosophy from the curricula of universities. The philosophically based liberal-free ideal emerges *outside* of the universities, relying for its support on widespread Enlightenment attachment to freedom and rationality. The ideal

Leonardo Bruni's fourteenth-century letter to Lady Battista Malatesta of Montefeltro on "the Study of Literature," has importance for the ideal, the curriculum, and the goal of education. Bruni is addressing a woman who must "leave the rough-and-tumble of the forum entirely to men." What, then, is she studying for? This turns out to be "human excellence," which transcends the historical circumstances of political life: "There is, indeed, no lack of examples of women renowned for literary study and eloquence that I could mention to exhort you to excellence." Here Bruni cites Cornelia, Sappho and Aspasia.[12]

The point of Bruni's urging is to form a liberal education outside the university and the common expectations of men.[13] In consequence, Bruni does not recommend a technical study of rhetoric, but rather a grammatical and broad "knowledge of sacred letters", philosophy, and poetry. What Bruni is doing is *explicitly* substituting for the Ciceronian, highly developed, technical elaboration of rhetorical distinctions and artifices (no "practice of the commonplaces" nor study of "knotty *quaestiones* to be untied") the broader literatures of history, philosophy, and poetry, which are exercised in writing.[14] While his treatise's intellectual roots lie in grammatical

---

does not shape curricula until it combines with the re-organization of German universities under the research program in the late eighteenth and early nineteenth centuries.

Since the rhetorical ideal and its foundational art, rhetoric, was excluded from universities in the twelfth and thirteenth centuries, while the philosophical, liberal-free ideal and its new sciences were excluded from the sixteenth to nearly the end of the eighteenth centuries, the faculties shaping university curricula for long periods in the West have excluded one or another version—or, at least, significant portion—of what could be termed "liberal education."

12   Leonardo Bruni. "The Student of Literature To Lady Battista Malatesta of Montefeltro," in *Humanist Educational Treatises*, trans. Craig W. Kallendorf. Cambridge, MA: Harvard University Press, 2008, pp. 47-63; p. 47 for Aspasia.

13   Ibid., pp. 47-48.

14   Ibid., pp. 53-55.

considerations of such authors as Augustine and Isadore, Bruni is accomplishing a re-ordering of liberal education that is innovative. It is neither directed toward philosophy in the medieval sense, nor directed toward salvation in the Christian sense, nor directed toward statecraft and citizenship in the Roman sense. Instead, the character one achieves is that of a fine artist.

This kind of re-ordering of the liberal arts extended past literature to the generation of the New Sciences. To see this, we must first look at invention's role in the classical liberal arts. Invention is the principal organizing part of Ciceronian, and indeed Roman, rhetoric. Invention is the discovery or devising of things ('res,' subject matter), arguments or signs, to render a case probable or true.[15] Commonplaces or topics are central to invention and one of principal technical features which dialectic shares with rhetoric is the use of commonplaces or topics.[16]

Machiavelli's *Prince,* in its operational concerns, its focus on the problem of new states, and its topical organization of how to analyze a state or ruler's situation falls well within the traditions of expedience and invention characteristic of the rhetorical tradition. Galileo's *Starry Messenger* is the application of dialectical commonplaces derived from observation of nature. The moon is examined first as whole, which is light, and then as a whole which is dark; its parts are, then, divided into light and dark, and its boundaries into continuous and discrete.[17] The entire treatise continues in similar fashion as it produces its four major discoveries. Finally, Bacon, readily acknowledging in the *New Organon* that current philosophy and arts are "use[ful] for supplying matters for disputations

15   Cicero, Marcus Tullius. *De Inventione,* Cicero in Twenty-eight Volumes. II. Trans. H. M. Hubbell. Loeb Classical Library. Cambridge, MA., Harvard University Press, 1960, 2000, I, vi, 9, p. 19.

16   *Cicero, Topica,* II. Ibid., I, ii, 6-8, p. 387; *De Partitione Oratoria* Ibid., Trans. H Rackham, 1942, 1968, II, 9, p. 313.

17   Galileo Galilei. "The Starry Messenger," in *Discoveries and Opinions of Galileo,* trans. and ed. by Stillman Drake. New York: Doubleday, 1957, pp. 21-58, esp. 31.

or ornaments for discourse," distinguishes between "methods [of] cultivation" of those matters and "*invention* of knowledge" which he is engaged in developing. The sciences should be "methods for invention or directions for new works."[18] Yet, much of his analysis is directed less toward the experimental manipulation of phenomena, than the re-ordering of the mind, or "intellectual operations" by frameworks properly adapted to nature.[19] The analysis of the blocks to scientific progress, occupying the first book of the *New Organon*, is presented as a series of "aphorisms," a dialectical term indicating definitions or important distinctions. These aphorisms either move toward properly orienting the mind or showing that current systems of disputation, philosophy, and experience distract the mind. Indeed, Bacon sounds something like Bruni, for he says that, "my purpose [is not to 'found a new sect of philosophy' but] to try whether I cannot ... extend more widely the limits, of the power and greatness of man."[20]

By converting the principal part of rhetoric, invention, into an *end*, the aphorisms take on the character, not of persuasion or eloquence, but discovery. The "Interpretation of Nature" in Book II, which is either to increase man's powers over natures or to discover the form of a nature, is carried on in aphorisms. And, in illustrating discovery which is subsumed under the invention of knowledge, Bacon outlines a procedure of collecting physical instances, instead of opinions, forming tables of instances (of the presence or absence of the nature in question), and, then, applying "induction"—that is, separation, inclusions, and exclusions of the sought for nature from other natures—based on the table of instances.[21]

Bacon criticized the arts and philosophies of his day as useless in the production of knowledge. Galileo tired of "long and windy debates." Machiavelli pitted imaginary constructions of polities

---

18   Francis Bacon, "New Organon," in *Selected Philosophical Works*, Indianapolis: Hackett, 1999, 63-206; p.88; aphorism 8, p. 90.

19   Ibid., aphorism 18, p. 92.

20   Ibid., aphorism 118, p. 138.

21   Ibid., aphorism 21, p. 178.

and ideal descriptions of human behavior against the usefulness of his treatise based in "realities." Bruni not only found scholastic subjects to be useless, but also clearly tried to provide a liberal education for a woman while wondering whether the standard rhetorical arts educated men at all. I want to stress here that in the hands of these authors the liberal arts were essential in challenging and criticizing the learning that came before. Yet, however much all these authors argued their separation from the past or their differences with current versions of education, none of their protests can obscure *the continuity of art that tied the past to the present.* So the transition from Aquinas to Bacon was actually a roadway paved by innovation as individuals attempted to *extend* the liberal arts into many different areas—including, apparently, areas university curricula simply wouldn't touch.[22]

We are speaking of the simultaneous development of the New Sciences, the Humanities as separate disciplines, and the liberal arts. Kimball acknowledges that in that the development of the *artes liberales* educational ideal incorporated a critical skepticism, yet, in the end, this skepticism "misse[d] the point of the scientific method: any conclusions inferred become new hypotheses and are always subject to challenges and criticism."[23] Certainly, no one doubts that the hypothesis and challenges are foundational to scientific method. While the hypothesis may well be essential to the *science* of a liberal-free ideal, is it the hypothesis or the continuous growth of knowledge that is essential to the *liberal-free ideal as a whole?* Depending on how one answers, the *liberal-free ideal* and the *artes liberales ideal* of education tend to separate or merge.

Kimball was not the first to conclude that the German research university changed American institutions toward something like the liberal-free ideal. And research—not hypotheses or laboratories per se— is what changed higher education from within:

---

22   The liberal arts did not cease to be inventive and innovative in the transition to the Enlightenment. See the syllabus of "Rejuvenating and Reinventing the Liberal Arts" in Appendix 3 of this volume.

23   Ibid., pp. 121, 172; see also pp. 225-226.

Visiting American graduate students and professors returned from German universities enamored of the specialized scholarship, the commitment to speculative research, and, above all, the atmosphere of freedom they had seen in their host institutions. Particularly this latter aspect—*Lehrfreiheit* (freedom to teach what one wishes) and *Lernfreiheit* (freedom to study what one wishes)—impressed the Americans. [The atmosphere of freedom] was seen "to follow from the searching function, the presumption that knowledge was not fixed or final," a presumption underlying all aspects of the idealized German university that the Americans took to be "dedicated to a search to widen the bounds of knowledge rather than merely to preserve the store of knowledge undiminished."[24]

The question of whether hypotheses or the growth of knowledge is essential to the liberal-free ideal is not without significance. The former, representing science, tends to draw a firm distinction between the humanities and the sciences; the latter, representing the humanities, tends to admit that instances of significant mutual influence shape education and knowledge. The former tends to restrict criticism to specialists. The latter tends to make criticism and critical thought dependent on broad views of knowledge.

If in their artistic inventions Bruni, Machiavelli, Galileo, and Bacon were using the liberal arts, then, they were "proving opposites" by simultaneously attacking the past and building the future. But they were not simply constructing arguments opposed to works of the past. They were constructing extensions of the arts they knew, the liberal arts. They thought that they were breaking with a past of instruction and knowledge in the liberal arts; yet, *because arts proceed by invention, not hypothesis*, these artists refashioned liberal arts ends, principal parts, techniques, and devices, and made them suitable for new discoveries of knowledge, new feats of action, new methods of production, new formations of character, and new explorations for expanding the bounds of human inquiry. In other

---

24   Ibid., p. 161, quoting Carl Diehl, *Americans and German Scholarship: 1770-1870* (New Haven: Yale University Press, 1978).

words, *invention is the characteristic response of the liberal arts to the project of continuing the quest for knowledge.* In our context, *invention* provided the bridge between old and new knowledge, while it simultaneously constructed both the distinction between past and future, as well as the distinction between the sciences and the humanities. Thus, in the transition between Aquinas and Bacon, liberal arts invention provided as much continuity as discontinuity. The foundation for an accommodation between the liberal-free ideal and the *artes liberales* ideal appears, therefore, to be *inherent* in the development of the New Philosophy or New Science, and, more deeply, inherent in the liberal arts and modern higher education themselves.

Part IV: Liberal arts and the foundations of disciplines

The liberal arts projects of Bruni, Machiavelli, Galileo, and Bacon suggest that the places to look for liberal education not only include institutional curricula, but in the education of *individuals*. All of these authors were learning via the liberal arts; only one of them was doing it in a university, and he found few who embraced his extension of dialectical methods. No curriculum for women existed until Bruni devised one for Lady Battista. No widespread articulation of scientific method existed until Bacon. At the time of publication, it seems Machiavelli's handbook simply didn't impress rulers. Yet, these examples of individuals practicing and acquiring liberal education outside of an academic institution show that an "*artes liberales* accommodation" might have deeper educational roots than we think.[25]

All of our authors demonstrate an acute awareness of the work of predecessors, and each of them is attempting to build new

---

25 Kimball does acknowledge that a plausible argument for roots of the *artes liberales* accommodation exists, p. 221. This chapter takes a different route than Kimball's historical outline of the plausibility, acknowledging earlier liberal arts achievements and, then, moving to the 19th and early 20th Centuries.

knowledge. Thus, it seems the liberal arts brought us research in its nascent form, before it reached the universities. Is there, then, an illustration of humanities research requiring liberal education by an individual after research reaches the universities? Such an example is depicted by Henry Adams in his book, *The Education of Henry Adams*.[26] Adams was a man groomed by lineage and by a stale antebellum, Harvard liberal arts education to become, later, one of America's foremost specialized historians of the nineteenth century at his alma mater, during the very time that Harvard made the transition from a college to a research university.[27] Yet, the *Education's* first person narrative shows that in the opening of his specialized historical study to any source of knowledge or human achievement, an opening which begins in the 1890's well after his undergraduate education and his life as a professor had ended, Adams exhibits some of the finer uses of liberal arts, core text study. His service in Great Britain during the American Civil War, followed by comic revelations, some thirty years after the fact, by principals of the British government about their real motives in considering entering the war on behalf of the South in 1862, con-vinced Adams that private experience, or even, a research career devoted to historical analysis of American Presidencies, was too small a scale for adequate judgment of the motives of men—or, what was the same, "a chart of history."[28] This conviction was aug-mented, in part, by his friendship with John Hay, the Secretary of State, who quickened Adams's interest in the international scale of human relations—the true locus, Adams ultimately decides, that determines the motives of human beings. Only as Adams moved from the local to the remote, only as he took an interest in symbols, only as he began to study seriously not only politics, but science, art, religious thought, and their core monuments—at

---

26   Henry Adams, *The Education of Henry Adams* in *Adams: Democracy, Esther, Mont Saint Michel and Chartres, The Education of Henry Adams.* New York: The Library of America, 1983, pp.715-1181.

27   Ibid., p. 777 and 993-997.

28   Ibid., p. 1105.

Chartres, in the theology of Aquinas, in the dynamo, in the discoveries of Curie, in the art of LaFarge—and added these to his store of diplomatic and governmental knowledge—only then did he discover the Education of Henry Adams.[29]

The education Adams garnered towards the end of his life was a preparation for inventing a new theory, a new art, a new science of history. But let us make a quick induction using all of the authors we have discussed. The proper use of education, and particularly the liberal arts, is to render students capable of making available to themselves the world's cultural resources in order to construct a future. Adams's employment of cultural history as the means for his re-education suggests, as do the works of our other authors, that no one should presuppose education begins with firm, well-grounded disciplinary assumptions and then proceeds to the mastery of the discipline's tools. Actually, it seems to be quite the opposite: if we are to offer students real education, then we are obliged to abandon the presumption of given disciplines and invent a curriculum in which students may explore and conceive the foundations of disciplines for themselves.[30]

Part V: Invention, books, and *technē*

We have touched upon inventing arts of knowledge. Now, we turn to inventing objects of knowledge. Invention is just as important

---

29   Ibid., pp. 1066ff and 1109ff.

30   I mean to suggest that by continuously returning to the principal parts of liberal *arts*—poetic and rhetorical invention, as well as dialectical discovery—the liberal arts and their associated core texts played a significant artistic role in developing the new philosophy or new science. In the same way, they may continue to develop human innovation today. This argument can be extended across civilizations backward in time, and forward toward the present-day sciences, particularly in their use of the humanities and liberal arts to explain themselves. Examples are: Darwin's *Origin of Species;* portions of Einstein's *The Meaning of Relativity;* Skinner's *Beyond Freedom and Dignity;* Feynman's *QED;* Margulis and Sagan's, *Acquiring Genomes,* Pinker's *Enlightenment Now,* Wilson's *Consilience.*

in the latter as in the former. Invention is the justification for core texts which is, perhaps, essential if our moral, cultural, political, religious, scientific and artistic perceptions of the past's resources are to be made available to us in a way that is promising and fruitful. Often, we read core texts from many disciplines to explore *ideas* as a way to enlarge student experience. This is laudable, but in exploring great ideas, it seems to me that we don't want to lose the thread of our own story—I mean the story of making books. The production of books is part of the larger story of made things, the story of art, *technē*. *Technē* has been a chief source of change in civilization almost since its inception, and if you want to learn how and why culture, religion, literature, philosophy, morals, and science change, you must read books of great depth and invention across genres, disciplines, cultures, and eras.[31] When we do present the story of making books—and, more broadly, the story of inventing and developing arts—and when we build an education around them, it is not only our students who gain a powerful resource for building the future. We, the educators, do so as well.

In constructing such curricula, there is an obvious need for liberal arts education to select core texts. This brings us back to several arguments mentioned earlier: namely, that ancient, medieval, and early modern moral teachings can be reduced to restraint; or that a proper selection of texts can promote the correct democratic values and skills; or that the limitlessness of technology is destroying our culture and character. Each of these serious arguments may be true, but they simply don't come close to expressing the fullness that a liberal arts education can offer. The liberal arts have never been only moral, ethical, political, and cultural. They are fundamentally *inventive* and *transformative*. We remember that Aeschylus disapproved so much of the blood-bath at the end of the *Odyssey* that he devised a tragic trilogy, the *Oresteia*, to celebrate the creation of the jury trial,

---

31　By a book I mean any written work that comes down to us, and which, of course, may be found in many different media—scrolls, velum, hypertext, and someday, I suspect, inexpensive holographic-imaging devices replacing tablets.

in which justice, and not merely revenge, could be felt by all. We contemplate in wonder as Sophocles' Antigone, constantly debating Creon, suffers unjustly, tragically, for merging the gendered male role of retrieving and honoring the dead with the gendered female role of love of family. We recall the attempt in Plato's *Republic* to replace Homer with philosophy, and rhetoric with dialectic as the basis of education—and, perhaps, of society. We remember Aristotle writing—in a society that seemed unaware of human rights in general, and of the right of expression in particular—a treatise on art which defended its own governing principles. We recall that the *Aeneid* not only artfully incorporates the two Homeric epics, but in having Aeneas gaze upon the artfully wrought wall of Carthage, upon Vulcan's shield, and upon the wrought belt of Turnus, Virgil incorporates art as essential to the education of his hero— an education into a vast enterprise *beyond his ken*—in a way that neither Homer nor most of the Biblical writers employ. We recall the importance of books—scriptures—to ancient Jews and Christians, not only in the canon that became the Bible, but in the remarkable synthesis of writers and texts that Ezra seems to have read to the people of Jerusalem as he united them after their second exile. We remember from the opening "archaeology" of Thucydides' *History of the Peloponnesian War* the kind of works one reads matters. And we recall the sharp contrast between the Athenian virtues of Pericles's "Funeral Oration" and the Judeo-Christian virtues of Christ's "Sermon on the Mount"—the importance of the soul in each, together with the enormous differences of those souls and their purposes. And we remember Augustine's struggle with the uses of the liberal arts and the wealth of pagan works his society possessed as he came to be not only one of the greatest expositors of the Bible, but also one of the chief agents who synthesized Athens and Jerusalem into a single educated culture. *The technē of books, of arts, and of genres and forms invented all this and much more. Without them, acknowledged or not, we would be nothing.*

Arts are instantiations of *technē*, that intellectual virtue concerned with making something out of the world of the variable, bringing something into existence that otherwise might not be. And the essence of a liberal arts education is the development of artistry in relation to making—*technē* in relation to *poiēsis*. This consideration seems to have implications for liberal arts in research universities and colleges. If, as we have seen, it is plausible that liberal arts, invention, classical or core texts, and a productive, but not stifling, link to research have persistent, stronger, intellectual ties to education than might be suspected, then we should see these ties in histories of institutions as well as the inventions of individuals.

Part VI: Inventing liberal arts curricula

In an important sense, professors who teach in any university setting are almost defined by this relation—of bringing into existence a product, a course or curriculum, that otherwise might not be in virtue of their capacities for making. Yet, there are hinderances—institutional and disciplinary—to building innovative curricula. "*Assessing Trends in the Liberal Arts Core*" (*Trends*) was a three-year study of 66 institutions' patterns of general education development over twenty years (1978-1998; originally conducted through the American Academy for Liberal Education; The Association for Core Texts and Courses (ACTC) extended the study with 15 more institutions to 2002.)[32] *Trends* addressed the question of faculty cooperation across the sciences, social sciences and humanities as a structural framework in which causes of change in general and liberal education could be discovered. Data collection analysis, derived from catalogs and generalized into course and curricular patterns, was followed up by reports tailored to 36 institutions' general education histories. On-campus interviews with hundreds of administrators, faculty, and students at the 36 institutions confirmed or disconfirmed facts and plausible speculations of causes for change on each campus found in the patterns and reports.

---

32   The "Final Report of Assessing Trends in the Liberal Arts Core: A Vision for the 21ˢᵗ Century" by George R. Lucas and J. Scott Lee submitted to the Fund for Improvement of Post-Secondary Education is available on the Respondeo Books website, respondeobooks.org.

The array of purposes and constructions by faculty of different fields tended to indicate where invention and innovation played a role in course development in general and liberal education.

Physical scientists were concerned with the practice of science per se; they did not find historical or philosophical purposes for their general education courses to be primary, though they would admit them as secondary. However, the practice of science, preferably laboratory based, certainly was not and could not have been the most up-to-date laboratory techniques or the most recent theoretical advances. So, repeatedly, we heard in our interviews that scientists teaching general education wanted to teach "how scientists think" and the "problem-solving method."

Invention and innovation arose as matters of 'rigor.' Could rigorous courses for general education be constructed that were not leading to the major or into science-based fields such as medicine? The answer appeared to be, yes. Mike Ruiz, chair of the department of physics at the University of North Carolina at Asheville at the time outlined the case:

> The community of physicists realized about a half century ago that to reach general students you cannot expect them to know calculus (needed for the intro physics sequence for majors), or for that matter trigonometry (needed for the pre-med physics). You have to create new courses—courses not for the major—without math. Thus, at professional meetings (the American Association of Physics Teachers and the American Physical Society) for over four decades now, physicists have thought and thought—giving paper after paper—sharing with each other the results of innovative courses for general students[33]

The disciplinary model of general education was, unquestionably, dominant in science general education courses. When we spoke with scientists of "interdisciplinary" courses in general education in the sciences, outside of environmental science, we would

---

33   Michael Ruiz, Correspondence, 5/19/00.

be speaking of either history of science courses, topical courses, or "mixture" courses, the latter being a science course that attempts to treat physics, chemistry and biology as a whole. Occasionally, "mixture" courses which tend to incorporate a bit of history as a way to bring non-scientists to the world of science were successful. Boston University's two-semester, Core Curriculum Natural Science sequence was a rare example of a stable course.[34]

Humanities were governed in general education, in so far as we are speaking about disciplinarity, by skills concerns, which fell to English, speech, foreign language and, sometimes, philosophy departments. This was the 'rigor' concern of the humanities. Of course, "introductions to" the various disciplines were a dominant mode of course delivery, but this began to change in the early '80's. The tendency of the arts to be "philosophic" in the sense that they are concerned with what might be possible, invented, or connected by analogy led to interdisciplinary courses, while the difficulty of reading texts across so many disciplines satisfied a yearning for skills development, as did the usual papers that were required of students. Moreover, in view of the actual courses that were developed, the humanistic impulse towards broad views of knowledge was also satisfied by such courses. That said, there can be little question that the humanities and social science faculty who developed these courses were driven in textual selection by a sense of (artistic and scientific) 'human achievements,' or 'seminal works.'[35] In many respects, then, such core texts courses, developed in the 80's and 90's by political philosophy, history, religion, English, and language departments were unquestionably inventive in their

---

34   When physical scientists control the general education committee, they are deeply skeptical of interdisciplinary courses in other fields on two related grounds: they expect courses to be in a hierarchy which leads to a progression of study and they expect courses to be taught by authorities. Interdisciplinary courses have problems in both regards.

35   E.g., Lloyd Chapin, "The Core Curriculum at Eckerd College," in Michael Nelson, *Alive at the Core*, San Francisco, Jossey-Bass, 2000, p. 98-99.

curricular formation, and the core texts that were employed in them were innovative in Western and other major civilizations.[36]

The findings of *Trends* raised some persistent and uncomfortable questions about higher education. Scientists and humanists knew very little about each other's fields or the courses being offered. This amounted to advisors to students in one field simply being ignorant of the courses offered in or the requirements of general education outside their discipline. And, more broadly, the characteristic rigor of the sciences or humanistic innovations of interdisciplinary courses in general education, which tended to be influenced by liberal arts concerns, did nothing to ameliorate mutual disregard, if not disdain, by faculty of the sciences and humanities. Finally, if either a bachelor-of-science or a bachelor-of-arts degree were of any significance beyond the major, there were few ways in which faculty of a given institution might actually understand the degree as awarded by their institution.

Taking a cue from C. P. Snow's famous *Two Cultures* argument and the findings of the *Trends,* ACTC brought together nationally respected experts in the sciences and the humanities with faculty from ten institutions to develop humanistically-based, liberal education core curricula and courses in three, two-week summer seminar sessions, from June 2003 through June 2005,

---

36   Social scientists might participate in interdisciplinary courses in general education, but this depended on several factors: (i) did the departments use general education course to recruit students? (ii) did the social science faculty think of their disciplines as 'new' sciences, whose disciplinary boundaries had to be protected? (iii) did the social sciences of an institution think that theory was converging between the social sciences and humanities so that interdisciplinary work was more appropriate for seniors than for (social science) general education students? (iv) Otherwise, were the considerable differences in principles of the various social sciences compatible enough to attempt a cooperative general/liberal education program?

The social sciences faculty apt to think that general education students could benefit from interdisciplinary, cooperative courses came mostly from the political science (i.e., political philosophy), history, and religion departments.

The title of the project was "Bridging the Gap Between the Humanities and Sciences: An Exemplary Education Model of Core Text, Humanistic Education" (BTG) supported by the National Endowment for the Humanities (NEH).[37] The participating institutions crossed the standard Carnegie classifications, secular and religious affiliations, and private and public incorporation. Participating institutions sent teams of two humanists and one scientist, one of whom was also an administrator in a general education program, to the seminars. These faculty returned to their campuses, both to develop course models and to conduct faculty dissemination and training projects. The overall objective was to establish on campuses the groundwork for conversations between science and humanities faculty for purposes of understanding each others' fields and, more particularly, for changing the content and, possibly, structure of general education courses and curricula.[38]

> The three years of readings engaged in by scientists, humanists, and administrators included difficult but accessible readings from classical to modern times in geometry, physics, biology, scientific technology, social science examinations of science, philosophy, epics, poetry, dramas and other forms of works.

Did the faculty intellectually engage across 'the gap' and were the liberal arts in service of that engagement? The project had a project evaluator for each of the summer sessions for three years.[39] Extracts from one of her evaluations convey an answer to that question:

---

37   The syllabi for the project can be found in the appendix to this volume. The Final Report to the NEH is available at RESPONDEOBOOKS.COM.

38   The following passages are drawn from the "Bridging the Gap" project final report.

39   Patricia Cook, then of St. John's College.

Year I
Discussions of Readings

….This session was the intellectual climax of the [first year] seminar. We discussed how Isaac Newton wove the various strands of natural philosophy of Copernicus, Galileo, and Descartes into a comprehensive solution to the issues of celestial mechanics. Perhaps the greatest moment was when one participant "demonstrated" Newton's Proposition I , Theorem I (roughly that a line joining one heavenly body to another sweeps out equal areas in equal times) at the blackboard. This is an extremely elegant proof with a beautiful construction. Everyone worked through the steps together, discussing their mode of understanding and/or assent to each move in the argument. This, it was said, is what it is to make a persuasive case and what it is to really understand an argument.

The demonstrative mode is perhaps neglected in contemporary pedagogy. Many of us had never tried to demonstrate a theorem for an engaged audience. We had neglected earlier opportunities in this seminar (e.g., to demonstrate propositions of Euclid).... Now it seemed to us that demonstration involved unparalleled rigor on the part of both the demonstrator and the (interactive) audience. Though time-consuming and difficult, many participants believed that this demonstrative mode belongs in our college classrooms to create a benchmark for what it is to clearly understand…

An extract from survey responses by the participants confirms the evaluator's judgement:

With an eye to understanding the histories of physics and astronomy, and the development of the 'scientific method,' I found Euclid, Galileo, and Descartes to be most intellectually interesting. What interested me most about Euclid was the way that he proceeds in the *Elements*—his effort to demonstrate particular 'enunciations' from very few postulates. I was impressed to see Ptolemy in the *Almagest* and Newton in the *Principia* pursuing substantially the same method…

Innovative, cooperative curricular construction crossing fields to this extent cannot be done in one year; this project took three years of teams from ten institutions returning to each summer seminar, and, then, to campus to learn how to work across the gap between the sciences and humanities. So, it is an arduous process. Still the data from the project indicated that it is possible, not only to construct new courses which house humanities and science core texts, but also to reshape entire general education curricula. In several institutions by the third year—either by faculty vote or through the spread of core texts by faculty through curricula in core programs—core text, humanities-and-science curricula or core text curricula in the humanities became the structural model of delivery for general education.[40] The following passages extracted from the final report of the project to NEH indicates what was accomplished in curricular construction:

> Curriculum and course development followed several varying patterns and applications. In one case, a whole curriculum was revised by introducing new, commonly required, core text courses. Though no science texts were introduced, bridging syllabi and faculty were central to establishing this new curriculum. In most cases, curricula were revised by "infusing" core texts into already established courses. In other cases, common courses were completely or partially revised in light of the project. In some cases courses, which were not commonly taken but which were available in general education curricula, were revised. Finally, *who taught* courses began to change at some institutions; scientists and humanists cooperated to teach courses; or courses were paired across a curriculum, requiring the coordination of humanities and science faculty.

---

40   Further, at ACTC annual conferences over three years, core text science/humanities papers increased from eight (8) in 2004 to twenty-seven (27) in 2006, and core text humanities-science panels increased from four (4) to (11).

Year III: number of courses launched:

		New	Textual Infusion	Total Courses
Core/Gen Ed	Whole Curricula Revised	1	7	
	Honors		3	
	Regular Common Req'd Core	2	4	
	Regular Distribution		1	
	Alternate Track through Core		1	
Electives/Upper Level			1	
Majors				
Course Totals		3	17	20
Total Courses All Three Years		15	35	50

Curriculum and Course Building. *Based on the course-building minimums of two-pilots per institution, the number of courses generated by this project vastly exceeded minimal expectations (by as much as 2.5–3.5 times) and "permanent" courses became the norm.* Based on the budget allocation by NEH of the original grant for seven participating institutions [subsequently expanded to 10], the figure of 6 institutions producing new or infused courses fell short of goals by one institution, but of the remaining four institutions, the content of some instructors' required humanities courses were moved toward core texts and science materials, and two more instructors did produce new BTG-inspired courses.

The range of success at once supports the idea that it is very difficult for texts of the liberal arts tradition to become integrated into institutional curricula, but, also, that faculty with sufficient support will respond both by trying and succeeding at some institutions.

It is true that many of the science and humanities *Bridging* and *Trends* interdisciplinary programs no longer exist, but many still do, as indicated above. Subsequently, others have been developed through ACTC's "Tradition and Innovation" summer seminars.[41] Stability is partially dependent on the clash of ideals of higher and liberal education, but it is also a matter of institutional support, deriving from careful hiring and rewards, administrator and faculty courage, purpose, care, and enculturation of new faculty. Of course, if liberal arts disciplinary or interdisciplinary courses based on "classics" were eliminated from the face of the earth, there would be no question of persistence. But, in fact, invention of these programs is a persistent feature of higher education, whatever their vicissitudes in particular institutions. And, this fact of persistence strongly implies that an important segment of faculty pursue significant invention which introduces a broad understanding within institutions of what a bachelor degree is *as a matter of liberal arts*.

The pursuit of invention and innovation have generated a plethora of *artes liberales* accommodations in institutions around the world. To point to just a few: Boya College of Sun Yat-sen University, the Chinese University of Hong Kong, the Erasmus Institute, the Liberal Arts College of Concordia University in Montreal, Shimer College (now a division of North Central College), Saint Mary's College of California, Thomas Aquinas College, the University of Dallas, and the University of Notre Dame's Program of Liberal Studies are all in some way closely or distantly intellectually, educationally, and personally related to Columbia University, St. John's College, or the University of Chicago. Many of these institutions have had self-reflective faculty who have published materials on some aspect of liberal arts education. One of them, The University of Dallas, developed a great books program in literature unrelated to Chicago/Columbia/St.

---

41   Seminars were held in 2014 and 2016 at Columbia University (Kathy Eden) and Yale University (Norma Thompson), and Columbia and the University of Chicago (Richard Strier) with Roosevelt Montás, Columbia, and Scott Lee, ACTC directing the project with the support of the Teagle and Bradley Foundations, and the ACTC Liberal Arts Institute. A description of the 2016 project can be found at HTTPS:// WWW.CORETEXTS.ORG/INSTITUTE/TRADITION-AND-INNOVATION.

John's, and then welcomed Straussians to teach in the University's core. All of them have different configurations of curricula, different internal organizations, different purposes for a baccalaureate, and different relations between general education and research.[42] The accommodationist ideal has, in fact, persistently stimulated rejuvenations in institutions and innovative programs

---

42 Prior to arriving at Chicago, Richard McKeon and Mortimer Adler were involved together at Columbia with the professors who developed the Contemporary Civilization core sequence and, later, the Literature-Humanities core sequence. Ultimately, each of the Columbia sequences replaced the departmental offerings of general education courses that, in the early twentieth century, had been a part of the requirements for graduation. To this day, Columbia offers a bachelor's degree without a major. Scott Buchanan passed through Chicago on his way to St. John's College which developed, partly, out of this complex of institutions and personalities. St. John's curriculum entirely eschewed the departmental-disciplinary basis of the Chicago program, while it retained the liberal arts, explicitly identifying its program with the great books and authors of the Western world. In 1953, Notre Dame, in large part through the work of Otto Byrd, whose teachers included Adler, McKeon, and Etienne Gilson (Otto Byrd, *My Life as A Great Bookie*, [San Francisco: Ignatius Press, 1991], 46 ff. and 66 ff.,) organized a three-year major called the Program of Liberal Studies on the basis of disciplinary courses that stretch across all the divisions of knowledge found at Chicago, but the Program retained the idea of interdisciplinary reading seminars that characterized St. John's program. A 1941 article by Adler, delivered to the American Catholic Philosophical Association's Western Division, on "The Order of Learning" (in *The Moraga Quarterly* [Au- tumn 1941]: 3-25) sparked at first a short-lived attempt (1943-44) and then the enduring establishment of classics-based liberal arts education programs at Saint Mary's College of California; this ultimately resulted in a St. John's-like program for a major, alongside a four-semester great books program taken by those who majored in a discipline. (See *What Is It To Educate Liberally? Essays by Faculty and Friends of St. Mary's College* [St. Mary's College: Office of the President, 1996], 1-28). Though modified, both programs are still running. Shimer College adopted one version of the Chicago-Hutchins, or "new college," curriculum, but it had no departments and, for the baccalaureate, only four general concentrations, including one in science; it has carefully staged integrative courses and requirements in every year of its curriculum.

that are enormously different. Rhodes College's "Search" courses

---

Straussians graduated from Chicago and went, in particular, to the University of Dallas. There, in conjunction with literary specialists who formed a core sequence of genre studies unrelated to political science that was conceived by Louise and Donald Cowan (who were in turn influenced by southern critics at Vanderbilt), the university faculty formed a disciplinary core leading to majors that had no interdisciplinary courses but was founded on great books. The University of Dallas founded the only graduate program explicitly using the Western Great Books, which offers three PhDs in political science, philosophy, and literature. Its graduates not only have staffed institutions across America, but also have helped to re-organize the New England Political Association so that there is a "core text/political philosophy" section of the Association's annual meeting that contributes more than a third of the papers at the meeting.

Meanwhile, at Columbia, William Theodore deBary rejected Adler's and Hutchin's contention that great books education had to consist only of books from the Western tradition. For over fifty years, and continuing until his death, deBary has translated or collaborated in the translation of Chinese texts, and had argued for the inclusion of these texts in some courses of the Columbia core. Although his work took place during the period when China has risen to threaten the U.S. while at the same time destroying its own cultural traditions in the Great Leap Forward and the Cultural Revolution, deBary's work has no tinge of cultural superiority about it, for it is not rooted in Greek education or Enlightenment political philosophy as is Strauss's. St. John's, motivated by its own experience in teaching great works, has also developed at its Santa Fe campus a masters degree in Eastern Classics, reading and discussing Indian and Chinese texts.

In 1978, Frederick Kranz, a graduate of Columbia, along with Harvey Shulman and Geoff Fidler, establish a three-year liberal arts baccalaureate college founded on the Western great books tradition at Concordia University in Montreal. In the Far East, the Chinese University of Hong Kong, under the direction of Cheung Chan Fai and Mei Yee Leung, recently developed a two-course sequence in the humanities and sciences based on great texts of the West and East, which owes part of its development both to Chicago and to Columbia.

Since 2014 institutions in Europe instituted core text programs, particularly Universidad de Navarra and Winchester University, which have no outright lineage as many of the institutions above but which, also, testifies to the persistence of these efforts in core text, liberal arts education.

(formerly "Man" courses) and Yale University's Directed Studies Program illustrate innovations not depending on personal contact with the complex of "Great Books" institutions above, yet still emerging from an awareness of problems and solutions in general education.[43]

Part VII: Inventing a future for liberal arts education

We can change our defense of liberal education programs through paying more attention to the interplay of *technē* and invention. We not only have stories to tell, but a case to make. The Association for Core Texts and Courses is both a result and a proximate cause of the accommodations and innovation[44] that we have illustrated

---

43   Michael Nelson, ed., *Celebrating the Humanities: A Half-Century of the Search Course at Rhodes College* (Nashville: Vanderbilt University Press, 1996), 3-31, begins with a post-World War I narrative of Charles Diehl's attempts to bring liberal education to Southwestern (now Rhodes) College between the 1920s and 1950s. This program was based in Christian traditions, but with an awareness of the educational innovations at Columbia, Chicago, and Vanderbilt. Justin Zaremby's *Directed Studies and the Evolution of American General Education* (New Haven: The Whitney Humanities Center of Yale University, 2006), 32ff., says that Maynard Mack, educated entirely at Yale, helped to devise and found the program with Dean William Clyde DeVane. Mack was seeking to solve the problems of "choice" that had arisen in general education, which were the cause of the differences between Hutchins and Dewey.

44   A precursor to this paper was delivered as a speech entitled "Accommodating the Core Texts Tradition of Liberal Arts in Today's Universities: History, ACTC, and Marroquín—An International Phenomenon," to the faculty of Marroquín University in Guatemala, in September of 2012. At this point in the text, the speech noted that

> the Association for Core Texts and Courses was co-founded by Stephen Zelnick and myself in 1995 in order to bring together programs that used common readings, taught in common courses, by shared faculty. The idea was originally Zelnick's, who was Director of Temple University's Intellectual Heritage Program—a two course sequence of texts from the sciences, social sciences, and humanities

in liberal arts education. There have been two chief vehicles for ACTC's growth, both related to liberal arts. The Annual Conference is the first vehicle, the Liberal Arts Institute, the second, illustrated earlier. As a pluralist, my goal as director of ACTC was to maintain cross-disciplinary, 'liberal-arted' discussions notwithstanding higher education's habits of narrow disciplinarity. Part of what is at stake in having such discussions is readily apparent: faculty members get exposed to ways of thought about their disciplines that they will rarely encounter at disciplinary conferences.[45] Another

---

stretching from ancient to modern times required of every Temple undergraduate. He had discovered that the wide variety of professional associations at the time did not really address educational issues of these kinds of programs. As the organization grew, it encouraged faculty and institutions to develop and use their own core text programs in their own fashion for their own institutional missions.

After the first organizing conference, under my direction, ACTC conferences took on the following structure: originally, paper proposals were organized into panels over two days with each session exclusively devoted to one of four categories: Interdisciplinary Questions, Science, Social Science, or the Arts & Humanities, accordingly characterized by texts, problems, or disciplines discussed—but not by faculty presenters. That is, if you were a humanist and wished to address Newton's *Principia*, that was fine. After about seven years, the membership voiced a desire to have panels of the four categories appear in each session. Generally, this movement by the membership was an effort to allow conferees to attend panels of the fields, perhaps the disciplines, which they were most comfortable with.

45   A note sent to me after the 2015 conference captures this crucial aspect:

"I really enjoyed the ACTC conference. I attended an American Chemical Society conference just two weeks prior to ACTC, so I was in a unique position to compare and contrast. What I really enjoyed about ACTC was the group discussion that followed each round of papers. Discipline-specific conferences, like ACS anyway, don't generally provide such opportunities. Yes, there is maybe 5 minutes for questions tacked on to each 20+ minute presentation, but it is hardly discussion. I also very much enjoyed the fact that the attendees I interacted with, while specialists in their own right, were also "generalists"

part of what is at stake is more subtle, though it can be found in almost all the works I have discussed. Many core texts serve a dual role in intellectual history: on the one hand, they help to found or articulate a discipline; on the other hand, their ideas, deep-seated attitudes, or basic techniques migrate across disciplines. In both cases, they are innovative. This is true in regard both to Eastern and Western texts. So, for both of these reasons, the determination to keep discussing great texts at ACTC conferences plays an essential role in maintaining the liberal arts orientation of the organization.

ACTC does not have a list of canonical texts. There is an insistence that every paper address a core text of each conferee's choosing for at least three quarters of a page in a five-page paper. The treatment of the text is up to the conferee. But what is most important is whether a given text within a proposal, or a set of texts within a collection of proposals, will spark an exchange of ideas about programs, the texts, teaching, or other matters of liberal arts concern. This is a matter of perception, not a matter of doctrine, established argument, or disciplinary governance. Most panels actually cohere quite well using texts as the starting point for potential inquiry and extended discussion—whether the panels are disciplinary or interdisciplinary in focus.

These considerations speak to the *technē*, the art, of ACTC members. ACTC is filled with accomplished scholars and teachers, but it exists to promote conversations about texts among faculty

---

capable of contributing thoughtfully to discussions outside of their primary areas. My session that centered on biology attracted a handful of philosophers, for instance. I contributed to some discussions that centered on Christianity. It was great!

Personally, I am much more of a "generalist" than a chemist! I design and teach interdisciplinary courses about as often as chemistry courses, I direct our first year seminar program, I am an outspoken advocate for the liberal arts (ask anyone on campus!), and my scholarship is much more interdisciplinary in nature. Bottom line: I got much more out of ACTC than I did ACS, I think because ACTC does the types of things I like to do, and attracts people like me who enjoy learning for the sake of learning."

members across institutions, programs, and disciplines. Here we enter a fertile field deeply furrowed by a distinction Bruce Kimball discusses at the beginning of *Orators and Philosophers:* the distinction between *ratio* and *oratio*. Used in the context of liberal education, these are distinctions in *technē*. Disciplinary conferences exist to offer extended versions of the *ratio* of a discipline—long papers and complex panel sessions marked by highly specialized arguments, which, frequently, offer little actual time for serious questioning and discussion. ACTC's conferences exist for a quite different reason. The first sentence of Aristotle's *Rhetoric* is, "Rhetoric is the counterpart of dialectic." The Greek word translated here as "counterpart" is *antistrophē*—as in the return dance of the chorus that leads to their exit from the stage. This, of course, makes dialectic into the *strophe*, and this has important implications for the relation of these two verbal arts.

First, one needs to know which direction one is headed in. This is not always easy to figure out, given the nature of language and the closeness of the two arts. Because the intention of the conferences is to produce serious discussion around the seminar table, the brevity of the papers leaves the direction of the conversation open. Second, even if a presenter's argument is either mainly rhetorical or mainly dialectical, the ensuing conversation will likely lead, at least, to reflections on what the argument would look like from the viewpoint of the other art. Since there are no list of canonical works and no standard set of disciplinary preconceptions that contain conversations within pre-set boundaries, ACTC presenters are asked to consider a rationale for why their text should be considered a world classic or a text of major cultural significance. If this *defense* were being made to a disciplinary audience, it might well be entirely dialectical or highly specialized, since the audience already agrees on the basic outlines of what belongs within the discipline's boundaries.[46] But because the audience at ACTC's conferences are

---

46   First time attendees often present (shortened) papers which are shaped by disciplinary distinctions, current arguments, and technical terminology. In short, they are not papers that reach out to other disciplines

interdisciplinary, such defenses must be at least partly rhetorical, insofar as they are aimed at persuading listeners from many disciplines to consider a text for inclusion in a liberal arts program. Even here, however, such a defense would become dialectical if it focuses on what the liberal arts, a particular program, a discipline, a text, or an idea contributes to our understanding of liberal (arts) education.

Today, understanding is not enough, but the opportunities for changing the defense of liberal arts education are in our hands. At the close of *Orators and Philosophers*, Kimball makes a well-pointed observation. In the academy

> there is rarely a recognition that the means to accomplish the resuscitation of the community of learning lie in elevating and emphasizing the study of expression, rhetoric, and the textual tradition of the community. Yet the means are self-evident. A community is, after all, a group of people who talk to each other and do it well. This view of community was dear to Socrates, no less than to Cicero.[47]

We may go further in the current situation of humanistic liberal arts education where defenses are wanted. *The community of liberal arts learners will need to re-vision its future as one that is devoted to and embraces techné and invention. After all, inherent in these programs is the widest record of invention available through education.* This is what ACTC promotes: the opportunity for faculty members, through the liberal arts and its traditions across all disciplines, to cooperate in discussing, planning, and implementing liberal arts curricula. Beyond the invention of courses

---

or an interdisciplinary audience. These papers sometimes have trouble fitting into the discourse of panels, though they may provide the opportunity, particularly for graduate students, to learn how to present at a conference. However, the first time experience, particularly of younger scholars, suggests a liberal arts alternative to the specializing of their advanced degree.

47   Kimball, p. 240.

devoted themselves to the inventions of texts, liberal arts advocates, including faculty and administrators, will need to be very much interested in *oratio communicated to the public* that concerns the artful origins and possibilities of invention for the future. As with humanistic liberal arts education, so with ACTC. The future success of its mission may well depend on those who not only share aims promoting the invention, enrichment, and development of more core text, liberal arts programs in universities but also express this inventive orientation to a wider public. If it does, the students of the future will have the opportunity to become innovators no matter what their life calls them to.

(Rev. Originally published as, "Enriching Liberal Education's Defense in Universities and Colleges: Liberal Arts, Innovation, and *Technē*." St. John's Review, Fall, 2014, pp. 14-47.)

SECTION III

Curricula as Objects of Art

CHAPTER 8

What Has Been Wrought
and the Effects on Faculty

I am honored and delighted to be invited to participate in this conference: "Core Curricula in the 21st Century" at Columbia University and to be part of this distinguished panel. I wish especially to thank Roosevelt Montás with whom I have had a number of productive conversations, and of course Columbia University's Columbia College with which my organization, the Association for Core Texts and Courses (ACTC), has had an enduring relationship for many years.

The conference hosts, Columbia lecturers in Literature/ Humanities (Lit/Hum) and Contemporary Civilization (CC), have a special claim to attention: supposing their interest in, perhaps love of liberal arts core text courses, what is the future of such courses in the 21st Century? Through a U.S. DOE Fund for Improvement of Post-Secondary Education research project, *Assessing Trends in the Liberal Arts Core* (*Trends*), and through the growth and variety of ACTC-affiliated programs, I think that we can fruitfully approach this question. *Trends* focused on the evolutions of general liberal education, including the type of core curricula represented by this conference. The study put core curriculum education in relation to institutional identities, baccalaureate degrees, program development, faculty support and enculturation, and core curricular review. Together with the ancillary confirmation derived from ACTC's growth and projects, we can now indicate to this audience the wide extent to which core curricula tied to core texts have shaped the landscape of undergraduate liberal arts education and the careers of faculty in the last quarter of a century. I think some of the lessons learned from these sources are about the future as well as about the immediate past. The lessons interweave four themes: faculty cooperation, institutional authority, faculty scholarship, and rewards for faculty in their careers.

First to origins of the *Trends* project: A start-up accrediting agency during the Clinton administration, the American Academy for Liberal Education (AALE), was empowered to accredit bachelor-of-arts and -sciences degrees based largely on general education programs. For years AALE's President Jeff Wallin, heard presidents of colleges and universities tell him that specialized accrediting agencies were demanding changes in general liberal education which increasingly fractured a common core and along with it the possibility that an entire faculty might somehow share its collective knowledge. In 1996 Wallin approached George Lucas, a philosopher, to write a grant proposal to learn if this pressure and fracturing was in fact the case. In short, the idea was to search for liberal arts education by looking into the pool of general education.[1]

---

1 The study's proposal incorporated a review based on the literature of general, liberal education. This review included the rise of specialization and professional degree programs. In addition, the proposal was contextualized by the cultural controversies and studies of the time which debated the fracturing of the core curriculum. On the one hand were such figures and organizations as Lynn Chaney and the National Association of Scholars (NAS). The former produced a report, *50 Hours*, of exemplary institutions that still had core curricula totaling nearly 40% of the curriculum. The latter had published a controversial college catalog study, the *Dissolution of General Education*, in 1992. It traced a century-long decline at 50 of the elite colleges and universities in the percentage of course-taking in a bachelor-of-arts degree devoted to general education. Within this sharp decline, it also noted the dissolution of structure within the these programs. The NAS study chose four years, spaced roughly 20-25 years apart, from which to select its catalogs: 1992, 1965, 1939, and 1919.

On the other side were figures like Lawrence Levine who, in *The Opening of the American Mind: Canons, Culture and History.* Boston: Beacon Press, 1996, claimed that required core curricula had never played much of a role in American higher education and certainly should not in a diversifying country, and figures like Clifford Adelman who, working at the U.S. Department of Education, produced *The College Course Map and Transcript Files: Changes in Course-Taking and Achievement, 1972-1993.* U.S. Department of Education, 1995, a census of courses taken by students in institutions across the country, which purported to show that students were taking an empirical core of courses, 31 out of 35 of them being introductory, through more or less wide-open curricular menus.

Until the rise of the German university model in America, most if not all of the courses of a liberal education, however widely divergent from institution to institution, were taken by all of the students within an institution. Philo Hutcheson argues that "the prescribed curriculum faded away, [but] it did not die. Aspects of its nature—including in some instances the conception of unitary knowledge argued by Newman and Hutchins—persist...in the form of general education," in "Structures and Practices" in Gerald Gaff, *Handbook of the Undergraduate Curriculum*, San Francisco, Jossey-Bass, 109. Earlier, then, a liberal baccalaureate education had little to do with the diversities of specialization we see today.

Now, the baccalaureate degree is an umbrella, often, which has as its virtue the tendency to specializing, becoming more and more imitative of graduate schools. It is nearly universally acknowledged in educational industry publications that, after the introduction of the German university model to this country's educational establishment, professional and disciplinary majors programs expanded enormously in surges after both World Wars, partly in response to government and industry demands for a trained and booming workforce, and partly in response to opportunities for survival or expansion on the part of institutions of higher education.

This pattern of expansion strongly suggested an accelerating replacement of traditional liberal arts curricula with general distribution programs, amenable to double-dipping major or professional courses, followed by specialization in a subject or profession. See: Frederick Rudolph, *Curriculum: A History of the American Undergraduate Course of Study Since 1636,* The Carnegie Foundation for the Advancement of Teaching. San Francisco, Jossey-Bass, 1977. Professional accrediting agencies had developed along side these new programs, and, with the exception of the major business-school accrediting agency, the Association to Advance Collegiate Schools of Business (AACSB), it appeared that after World

AALE won the FIPSE grant to study and disseminate the results of the evolution of general education in a widely diverse set of 66 colleges and universities over 20 years, from 1978-1998. I was appointed as the principal investigator and devised the database and performed the research into that evolution. [2,3]

The *Trends* hypotheses were:

- Between 1978-1998 we would find decreasing size and increasing fracturing of general education, including core programs
- The cause would be demands by specialized accreditors placed upon faculty to carve up curriculum

To test the hypotheses, we not only proposed to do a catalogue study, but to visit 21 of our 66 institutions and to interview hundreds of faculty, administrators, and, even, students who had been

---

War II professional accrediting programs encouraged expansion into four years of education and that they tended to diminish general education. It followed that if we wanted to locate anything like a coordinated liberal arts education similar to the multidisciplinary curricula of traditional programs, we would do best to examine general education.

2   Even with $ 350,000 of grant support, costs of input and staff prohibited a truly randomized study. Instead, the study had a "surface validity." The proportions of Carnegie classes, as they stood at the time, and affiliations of institutions matched the national proportions of class and affiliation with respect to institutions offering four-year bachelor-of-arts and science degrees, except that we had to take in a disproportionate number of research universities to generate any data at all.

3   Later, we were encouraged when our findings for 1978 also tended to match findings found in earlier empirical studies that led up to 1978. The figures are largely consistent with figures on the "percentage of [bachelor's] programs consisting in general education" which Arthur Levine published in 1978. At that time he found the plurality of Research Universities and Comprehensive, Masters' Universities, and Liberal Arts Colleges used 31 to 40%, while the plurality of Doctoral Universities, the Carnegie class with the fewest data points in our study, used 41-50% of their program's credits for undergraduate education. Levine, *Handbook on the Undergraduate Curriculum. Carnegie Council Series*, Table 2, p. 16.

or were then involved in general education. This way we could confirm or disconfirm our database findings, and we could discover and coordinate faculty and administrator views on the *causes* of change in general education.

Ultimately, our *Trends* study disproved our own hypothesis. The study found that *within* the bachelor-of-arts and bachelor-of-science degrees of colleges of liberal arts and sciences, increasing percentages of the overall curriculum were devoted to general education. There was also greater articulation, that is, increasing course and track structure, in the growth of general education, including core programs. And our study uncovered a far wider variety of causes of change in general education curricula than the unmeasurable, anecdotal influence of specialized accrediting agencies.[4]

When we examined the expansion and articulation of general education structures, we were encouraged to ask the fundamental question of whether liberal arts education intentions were evident. *Trends* found:

---

4   In the face of the facts of the industry literature and the controversies of the times that preceded this study, how and why could this be so? If your unit of analysis is an institution, on the assumption that universities historically expanded from their origins as colleges, then with the proliferation of professional degrees and schools in universities and former baccalaureate colleges, the liberal arts curriculum which all students once took will seem to have permanently disintegrated. If, however, your unit of analysis becomes a bachelor-of-arts or -sciences degree in a college of arts or sciences within a university, or a stand-alone college, or a general liberal arts curriculum taken by all students attending an institution, then the demise of coherent general education curricula can be seen to have been reversed by 1998.

Table 1. Requirements in some subjects were increasing, others decreasing:

1978:	1998:	
30.2% require Lab	59.1% req Lab	+ 28.9 pts
30.2% require separate Math	59.1% req sep Math	+ 28.9 pts
04.8% require Diversity or other Culture Studies	33.3% req Diversity or other Culture	+ 28.5 pts
22.2% require WC/GB/IH	50.0% req WC/GB/IH	+ 27.8 pts
28.6% require Fine Art	51.5% req Fine Art	+ 22.9 pts
54.0% require Natural Science	75.5% req Natural Science	+ 21.8 pts
03.2% require WAC/WI	24.2% req WAC/WI	+ 21.0 pts
34.9% require Foreign Lang	51.5% req Foreign Lang	+ 16.1 pts
1986: 34.8% require Lit	25.7% req Lit	- 12.7 pts

This is a table of increases in schools requiring categories or sub-categories of courses taken for graduation with a bachelor-of-arts or -sciences degree. The four categories which have been increasingly required for students were separate lab science courses, math courses, diversity courses, and WC/GB/IH or Western and World Civilization, Great Books, or Intellectual Heritage courses. The latter courses are grouped together because of the nearly universal concern with traditions of civilization shared by all these courses.[5]

I consider this particular comparison of categories or sub-categories of subjects taken in general education to be the most significant statistical table I showed to faculties at colleges and

5   The statistics in the lab and math requirements, being identical, look "funny" but they did come out this way and are probably closely related in any event, for schools which tended to require lab also tended to separate the math requirement from the natural sciences requirement.

universities in the campus visit, dissemination phase of this project. Hidden in it are many tales of liberal arts revival, interdisciplinary courses, migrations of subjects moving around the curriculum, subtle stories of disciplinary competition and increasing faculty cooperation. In order to focus on liberal arts intentions, I would like to dwell for a bit upon WC/GB/IH and Diversity.

There are many interpretations of how to approach Western or World Civilization, and there are many interpretations of what liberal arts education can be, but no one doubts that programs which involve great books, primary sources, or core texts—that is, world classics or texts of major cultural significance—are driven by traditions and motives of liberal education which are traceable to what is commonly known as Western Civilization. Despite a considerable literature decrying the loss of the classics, we found by 1998 that of the Western/World Civilization programs, courses in great books or intellectual heritage were represented in as much as 36% of our Trends institutions and required in 29%—an 18 point increase between 1978 and 1998.

All of you will remember the culture wars. Faculties were often divided over whether to add Diversity or some version of Western Civilization. But the opposition of the rhetorical debate often failed to reflect the solutions faculty found. Often faculty paralleled both categories in one institution: Columbia and Colorado College come to mind. Others found a solution much like Eckerd College's title for its core text sequence: Western Heritage in a Global Context. In any event, a surprising outcome of the Trends study was that the competition of the culture wars seems to have contributed to greater size and articulation of general education curricula and greater "liberal-artedness" within the curriculum.

We now consider the causes for change. Viewed from a national perspective, the culture wars were certainly not the primary motive or cause of change in general education curricula or even in the relative positions of Diversity and Western Civilization within curricula. Put very generally, the primary cause was faculty desire to improve undergraduate general education at each institution to which they belonged. Our interviews on campus identified eight causes of change, but the ones relevant to the creation of core curricula, particularly with core text programs, mostly depended on forms of faculty cooperation rather than oppositions. Four such causes were:

- academic leadership in times of institutional crisis or institutional redefinition,
- institutional traditions of affiliation and academic offerings,
- disciplinary differences in concepts and aims of knowledge, and aims of general education
- rewards to faculty for participation in general education development.[6]

Faculty cooperation is the truly amazing story of *Trends*. Faculty from every discipline worked together to develop new general education curricula. Administrators working with faculty and student tutors then focused student recruitment, orientation, housing, alignment of courses into learning communities, co-operative faculty learning teams, and the development of supplemental instruction (especially for at-risk students) in the general education curriculum. I said earlier that we were looking in the pool of general education to find liberal education. Though often not liberal-arted in the curriculum, the cooperation I just outlined was nevertheless motivated by concerns for the students that were very much like the traditions of the liberal arts, particularly in core curricula where common courses and readings are found.

Faculty cooperation in creating core text courses is really the beacon which lets us see the liberal arts affecting the whole of general education and core curricula. Our interviews with faculty and administrators on 21 campuses indicated that in the case of those institutions supporting core text programs, these were

---

6 The four others were:
Departmental need for students.
Generational change in faculty.
Organizational structure and general education review processes.
Government/system regulations.

primary examples of a new <u>degree</u> of faculty cooperation, particularly across the humanities departments but extending into the social science divisions housing political science, history, religious studies and occasionally drawing as well on faculty members in the sciences. The degree of cooperation was new to institutions because of the cross-disciplinary focus on developing and teaching common courses with common core texts taught by such a wide group of faculty. Such efforts became models of cooperation across less text-centered parts of a core program. Conversely, core curriculum reform which had at its center core-text faculty cooperation, often extending over three to five years of new program construction, resulted in career-defining experiences for participants. We repeatedly found tenured faculty telling us that the scope of cross-disciplinary inquiry, when combined with curricular formation and pedagogical invention, was more attractive and intellectually stimulating than pursuit of further specialized inquiry. Interviewees often referred to founders—both administrative and faculty—who shaped intellectual principles of the programs. Perhaps not surprisingly, there often was a graduate of Columbia, Chicago, or St. John's involved.[7]

The net result of this faculty cooperation was <u>not</u> a lot of look-alike baccalaureate educations. One extremely important reason for these variations was that core text programs were designed to express institutional traditions—interpretations of liberal arts core text education. Put in market terms, institutional identity was at stake. Three institutions represented on this panel (Columbia University, St. John's College, and the University of Chicago), which share a common educational heritage by no means have the same core programs. No less is true on the national scene. True, the common, if variously fore-grounded, feature of these programs is a statement of the importance to the education of undergraduates of

---

7 Readers should remember that I was addressing a Columbia University audience. I have detailed in Chapter 7, "Enriching the Defense of Universities and Colleges," that many institutions 'started up' core text programs, often independent of these three institutions.

their becoming familiar with challenging, thoughtful, diverse great works of Western and other, world civilizations. But the variable particular relations to this wellspring of works and civilizations turns on institutional traditions, the use of disciplines and arts, the specific works employed within each institution, and the size and scope of both program and institution. With the cooperation of 21 institutions, after the work on *Trends* I conducted a study of the purposes of those institution's core text programs, curricula and pedagogy, and administrations.[8] I'll summarize briefly the variations in purposes. All of these variations are accompanied by programmatically distinctive scope of application to a student body, curricula and pedagogies, and employment practices.

The various purposes of programs included: developing wide-ranging perspectives on the disciplines, divisions, and majors of a university; developing a person who can reason and communicate about traditional problems of disciplined learning to an audience outside the academy; developing life-long habits of learning through the examination and conversation about whole products—from sentences to books to musical compositions; developing the power to act as a citizen; developing the power to

---

8   The study examined the core curriculum and core text programs of 21 institutions, 10 in *Trends*, others from ACTC, ranging from research institutions to community colleges. A questionnaire was devised to which the deans, directors, or principal faculty responded, mostly with narrative responses which were, then, edited into program descriptions. Unfortunately never published, the study, however, indicated the wide variety of such programs. Five examples might suffice: St. Johns College which still has a required curriculum for four years; the Program of Liberal Studies at Notre Dame University, which offers a major based in great books that last three years and is usually taken in conjunction with another major; Boston University's Core Curriculum, which is offered as an alternative track through general education and takes two years, the then-existent Intellectual Heritage program of Temple University that offered a one-year, two course sequence all students took to graduate, and, finally, the Lynchburg College Symposium Readings which are 'infused' in courses, designated as LCSR courses (i.e., core text infused courses) in the catalog.

investigate higher revealed truths through the uses of various languages derived from disciplinary genres; and developing personal integration that becomes a student's authentic voice, certified by the ability to critique cultural heritages.[9]

I sum up this scanning of program purposes simply by noting that we must take seriously the effort that institutions go through to distinguish their programs one from another. The distinctions are real and consequential.

It seems to follow necessarily from the nature of both general and liberal arts education that institutions themselves, not a single discipline nor external lists of works, are the determining *authoritative* factor in how great books/core text curricula are constructed. This principle extends to core curricula in general. The relation between core programs and the authority of institutions has profound implications about curricular invention, hiring, promotion, and faculty careers. Depending on the importance of a core curriculum to an institution, *a core curriculum can function as a post-graduate institute*, partnering established faculty with new faculty in intellectual inquiry into the liberal arts. This can affect scholarship. I am particularly concerned with that fruitful

---

9   A superficial view of core curricula or core text programs within core curricula might contend that the aims, outcomes and even books of these programs are much the same, but we would not do well to lump them together. Indeed, an interesting study relying on ACTC as one of two sources for its conclusions restricts itself, for the sake of studying "tensions" in programs, to structurally similar programs of usually of one- or two-course length. This is probably perfectly fine for studying tensions, but it restricts the full diversity of such programs. Mike Axtell, "A Survey of Multi-section, Trans-disciplinary Courses with a Common Syllabus" Wabash College: "An examination of the basic structure of the sequences shows a high degree of similarity. 16 of the 20 schools had one or two semesters of common courses with 10 schools following the two semester model....The very nature of these courses, common and transdisciplinary, invites one to inquire into their purpose within the curriculum....Perhaps unsurprisingly, the nature of the responses rested upon the description of the course being transdisciplinary and common." HTTP://PERSWEB.WABASH.EDU/FACSTAFF/AXTELLM/CARNEGIEPROJECT.HTM

scholarship that unites discussion of core texts with programmatic development and philosophical principles of education. Chicago illustrates such scholarship with effective articles and books on liberal arts programs: Richard McKeon and Martha Nussbaum come to mind. More broadly, there seems to me to be a not wide-ly-known bibliography combining intellectual questions and programmatic liberal arts development. I have in mind here five instances: a documentary history of the liberal arts that ACTC encouraged and helped Bruce Kimball to publish, *The Liberal Arts Tradition* and his well-known *Orators and Philosophers*; Timothy Cross's recently published book entitled *An Oasis of Order: The Core Curriculum at Columbia College*; a collection of essays and bibliography on the liberal arts that has not received wide circulation which Saint Mary's College of California faculty pro-duced[10], *What Is It to Educate Liberally*; the scholarship of Eva Brann beginning with her *Paradoxes of Education in a Republic*; and the almost innumerable white papers in the archives of liberal arts programs across the continent which express an individual's or faculty's scholarly wisdom in founding and constructing core text programs.[11] We at ACTC intend in the next couple years to make titles, bibliographies and papers centrally available on our website. Their significance rests in the unique combination of the-ory, practice, and production that such scholarship holds for not only the careers and efforts of faculty across the continent, but the very character of institutions with core curriculum and core text programs.[12]

---

10   Through the editorship of Kenneth Cardwell and Steve Cortwright, who have compiled the bibliography in two editions separated by 20 years time.

11   Since this paper was delivered, the Donald and Louise Cowan Archive at the University of Dallas has been established in part to "make available their published and unpublished essays, lectures and notes on literature and liberal education, as well as their annotated library, to the general public." HTTPS://UDALLAS.EDU/CENTERS/COWAN/INDEX.PHP.

12   To some extent this has been accomplished. Papers published on conferences at Notre Dame and Rhodes College, respectively, addressed

I would argue that ACTC's growth since its 1994 inception responds to an intellectual need that institutions and faculty are experiencing. ACTC provides a unique forum for scholars across North America in virtually every field to meet regularly with colleagues in order to share and compare substantive ideas forged in response to common readings of core texts. In such exchanges over core texts, the members of ACTC reflect upon, re-animate, and further develop for students and institutions the vast resources of liberal arts ideas and inventions that have been used by humanity to address its problems and its future. This exchange has grown into nationally-funded ACTC projects in multi-institutional, core text and curricula program and faculty development. Such projects have much potential for the future of extending cross-disciplinary liberal-arted intellectual inquiry.

Of course core text programs die, too, but it is almost certain that the *Trends* project rightly challenged the gloomy picture prevalent in the 1990's of core text and core curriculum programs headed into extinction. There is simply no question that the traditions of core text liberal arts education are a variegated intellectual resource to which faculty of institutions of all sizes and affiliations persistently return to discover their institutional identities and to offer a sound liberal arts education to their students.[13] Properly structured and supported, these same traditions and programs can be centers of intellectual life attached to faculty recognition and advancement.

At the end of Plato's *Republic*, the soul of Odysseus looks carefully for a new life. He selects a very private life because his love of

---

"The Research University and the Liberal Arts College, 2013, and "Religious and Secular Cores," 2014. Also, ACTC has published two volumes on Qualitative Narrative Assessment (for core text programs) edited by Kathleen Burk and David Dimattio.

13   Further, liberal arts education with core texts may have a bright international future, too, since for some years after delivery of this paper, ACTC worked with Chinese institutions and a group of European institutions to help establish programs and hold core text conferences in Europe.

honor had left him through all the sufferings he faced. The lesson of the story is two-part: in an ideal universe, choose a private life that is just, but search for that life through examining all the possible lives one might don. For those in this world who seek a more social life, the lives possible in institutions with sound core text traditions are many and various. They are lives that will profoundly affect not only their bearers, but the institution and colleagues who share a lifetime love of the liberal arts. I suspect that the Columbia lecturers in this audience who devised this conference and who are seeking new positions elsewhere have already learned well the lessons of Odysseus. Still, I suggest that if chance offers you the opportunity, examine as many institutions' programs as you can, consider the entire life you have led, and then choose well.

(Rev. Delivered at the Columbia University Core Conference, March 23, 2007.)

CHAPTER 9

Aeneas' Shield and Arts of the Future

During the mid-90's when Stanford was reviewing its Area One requirements in its general education curriculum and changing its Western Culture course first to CIV: Culture, Ideas and Values, and, then, to IHUM: Introduction to the Humanities, a public document summarizing the effort noted that "at Stanford as elsewhere liberal arts curricula have recently been under attack. Critics both inside and outside of the academy have come to question the relevance of a liberal arts education. The very word 'liberal'--not to mention 'arts' --now has pejorative connotations."[1] What strikes me about the document is the relative absence of art in its rhetoric of justification. True, the word "art" appears 12 times in the summary, associated most frequently with specific titles of courses, but this is less than twice as often as the word "culture," and "culture" is clearly the master term: "[The new IHUM course] aims to make students aware of cultural differences in ancient and contemporary times and to inculcate in students an appreciation of the past's influence on the present." Admittedly, the effort to accommodate the multi-disciplinary nature of humanistic inquiry will and should include cultural concerns. Still one wonders what would have been the considerations in a summary by the faculty of a course with a different title, 'Introduction to the Liberal Arts,' wherein the justification

---

1   Harry J. Elam, Jr. and Cheri Ross. "Reframing the Area One Program: A New Approach to Teaching in the Humanities at Stanford," www.stanford.edu/group/areaone/reference/Reframing_AOP.html.

was targeted toward widening the notion of "liberal arts" through a requirement that at least one work of art be part of the readings. The case, I suspect, is more general than just at Stanford. Even if common core courses are oriented toward Western cultures, our rhetorical justifications of such programs rarely explicitly aim at development of awareness of the arts and reasons why they are essential to a liberal arts education. Were I to engage in a discussion about an "Introduction to the Liberal Arts," I might think seriously about including Virgil's *Aeneid* in such a course, for not only would the work make me reflect on the past's influence on the present, and the similarity of modern American cultural assumptions to Rome's, but I would have to reflect on just what the role of art is in education, especially for a practical, often imperial people of a busy democratic nation.

Aeneas, at his first appearance in the *Aeneid*, facing the sea-storm of Juno-sent Aeolus, feels the fear that saps action so completely that his "limbs fall slack with chill."[2] Shortly after, his care for his decimated party belies his false confidence in boosting their spirits, and his grief over lost comrades leaves him in melancholy silence. By the end of the *Aeneid*, as his eye catches the belt of his dead comrade in arms, Pallas, on the shoulder of his defeated, pleading nemesis, Turnus, Aeneas' "grief" turns to "rage" and he slays Turnus, "whose limbs fall slack with chill."[3] How has Aeneas changed over the course of this epic, and what role did art play in this complete reversal of fortune?

That the belt of Pallas should provide the epic's final reversal is not simply a convenience for the author to provide an excuse for Aeneas' final act of rage. Throughout the *Aeneid* art figures essentially in the work's structural advancement; conversely, Pallas' belt exemplifies art's importance in the epic. Defeated at the end, Turnus calls upon Aeneas to consider the grief a father has for a lost son. Alas, the belt functions as a "memorial" of Pallas' death

---

2   Virgil. *The Aeneid*. Translator, Allen Mandelbaum. University of California Press, 1982. I. 131, p. 4. Lines cited are Mandelbaum's translations.

3   XII, 1270, p. 348.

at Turnus' hands, as well as the "sign" that Turnus not only did not offer similar consideration to one hardly past boyhood but that Turnus gloried in killing the son of a king who leagued with Aeneas. The belt calls upon Aeneas' devotion and sense of responsibility to "my / dear comrade[s]," living or dead; it brings out Aeneas' judgment that there is a causal link between the dead and the living—"it is Pallas who strikes…who takes this payment from your shameless blood"—enacted in a sense of justice over time.[4] The belt itself is not merely a piece of war equipment, anymore than is Aeneas' shield, for the belt depicts the mythic history of the murder of Aegyptus's 50 sons by Danaus's daughters, a brutally thwarted expectation of marriage that permitted the daughters of Danaus to merge with and produce the Danaans—that is, the Greeks—instead of Libyan Egyptians. So, perhaps, Turnus "revel[ed] and glorie[d] in taking of the plunder" from Pallas, for he could wear the belt as a sign of his attempt to refute such a story. The belt had a meaning *to him* for his and his people's future.[5] This artistic evocation of a struggle to unite peoples not only is background to the concluding act of the epic. "Possession of the arts" in the broadest and most multivalent senses of this phrase, stands central not only to the fortune of Aeneas, his family, and tribe, but to the troubling imperial ethos that, as a prediction of the future, seems to characterize Rome:

> …other people will, [no] doubt,
> still cast their bronze to breathe with softer features,
> or draw out of marble living lines,
> plead causes better, trace the ways of heaven
> with wands and tell the rising constellations,
> but yours will be the rulership of nations,
> remember, Roman, these will be your arts:
> to teach the ways of peace to those you conquer,
> to spare defeated peoples, to tame the proud.[6]

---

4   Ibid. 1265-1268.

5   XII, 1254-1270; X, 683-689, p. 269.

6   VI 1130-1137, pp. 166-167.

If the arts are used by the epic's end to tame the proud through rage, is this Virgil's final sense of the usefulness of arts, of the peace of Rome? In order to answer we might pose another question: if arts are deeply involved in the epic change of Aeneas from a man whose limbs go slack with fear to one whose relentless sword thrust founds an empire, how did Aeneas come to this change? The answer, broadly, appears to be that much of the story of the *Aeneid* is Aeneas' education to lead, and that the spectrum of arts provided by Virgil not only measure his growth, but they are absolutely essential for his education to develop him not only as a hero, but as an intelligent participant in an enterprise of future consequence far vaster than his personal, familial or tribal fortunes and far greater than his ability to know its complete development.

From early in the epic Aeneas possesses most of the passions and habits necessary to "wage tremendous war in Italy / and crush ferocious nations and establish / a way of life and walls for his own people."[7] As he spies the cowering Helen near some altars, "Anger spurs [him] to avenge / [his] falling land."[8] Shortly before this moment, as he witnesses the slaying of Priam, he imagines his own father, wife, and son and their fate in the burning city. Later, as he carries his father, whom he instructs to carry the household gods, through the flames of the city, we see he is pious in both the dutiful and reverent sense. And, though he can be discouraged by severe losses, and though he thinks the gods, particularly his mother Venus, to be deceitful, he is a man who does not give up his responsibilities to his clan at its lowest moments, nor does he close his mind to divine or human counsel. His passions and loyalties are clear in war, while he habitually takes steps to build cities during times of peace—at Aenaedae, Pergamum, and Carthage. In many ways, he is "resourceful Aeneas."

Yet, he is not prepared to found a civilization or to lead his Teucrians into war, despite their belief in him as a leader. He is, in fact, in need of an education to become a hero. Certainly, part

---

7   I. 367-369, p. 10.

8   II. 775, p. 48.

of that education happens when Aeneas hastily retreats from Carthage not because he is, as Jupiter would have it, "paying ... attention to the cities / the Fates have given him," but because Jupiter's messenger, Mercury, puts such terror of the "command of the gods" into Aeneas' heart that his hairs stand on his head.[9] Yet the education begins much earlier than this command and must work on this man who is not a "*tabula rasa.*" We may glimpse the education's beginning—and why he is not ready to found a civilization—in Aeneas's memory of the fall of Troy which is almost literally seared into him. Perhaps, the beginning of his education is the moment that, sword poised, "carried off by [his] mad mind," he is about to strike down Helen. This impulse is reversed when his mother asks him, "My son, what bitterness has kindled this fanatic anger? Why this madness?" and then reminds him of what his imagination told him only a moment ago; he should seek out his family.[10]

Calling him to mind is a beginning but not enough. His passion is so full, the moment so critical that her tutelage must leave no "doubt" in him "to carry out [her] commands." So, Venus decides to "tear away each cloud that .... clogs [his] human seeing" and abruptly, shockingly makes him understand that human revenge is no punishment upon those who caused Troy's destruction. Directing his attention away from Helen toward "those to blame," Venus discovers to him that it is Neptune, Juno, Minerva, and Jupiter that are at the battlements, on the side of the Greeks, as Troy burns.[11] Such shocks are typical of Aeneas' education and their appearance alongside the guidance he receives constitutes a reason why he does not perform as perfectly as we might expect of an epic hero. *In extremis*, he follows his mother's commands with regard to his family and clan's safety, but in doing so, loses his wife, who as a shade just after the moment of her death, informs him that without her he "will reach / Hesperia, where Lydian Tiber

---

9   IV, 301-302 and 374-377, pp. 90, 92.

10   II, 802-807, p. 49.

11   Ibid., 813-836.

flows."[12] There is little wonder that this hint of Jupiter's plans simply doesn't register, nor that after being storm-tossed, he treats any god's appearance, even his mother's, with a great deal of skepticism. Such skepticism can only be furthered by the loss of his father, for, though he dutifully consults innumerable divine messengers, none of them warns him that he is to lose his father too. Given his experience, though he is told explicitly by his household gods in a dream the specific destination of his journey and though Apollo reveals through Helenus that he should give due honors to Juno, it is not surprising that he should disastrously neglect to pledge such vows to the one of four divine enemies of Troy who craves "anyone [who] will adore / [her] majesty."[13] Thus he throws his entire quest off course, nearly bringing destruction to the people he is leading, and then forgets all divine guidance in his misguided love affair with Dido.[14]

If we ask why is Aeneas in Carthage and why he remains, we find that most of the motives Aeneas has for attending to Carthage, rather than Ausonia, are invoked by art and require art for their fulfillment. If Aeneas' habits and memory provide him incentives for a pious skepticism, art shapes his passions for a homeland with equal strength. It directs them to cares and comforts left to him by experience and renews his faith in values he and his companions held before Troy's fall. As soon as Aeneas sees Carthage, he "marvels / at the enormous buildings." All the craftsmanship of a busy city leads him to exclaim: "how fortunate are those / whose walls already rise." In the city's heart at Juno's sanctuary he "studied everything [including] the handiwork of rival artists" who set

---

12   II, 1053-1054, p. 55.

13   I, 72, p. 3.

14   That an agent might go awry in actions that should accord with divine instructions or signs is found in other epics and, in effect, sets up a challenge to readers to think what each agent perceives from his or her own point of view. See, for instance, D. T. Niane's translation of the African, *Sundiata: An Epic of Old Mali* a work used in the 1990's Intellectual Heritage program at Temple University in place of any of the Greek or Roman epics.

out the "wars of Troy" on a wall. Such attention has serious effects upon Aeneas. The art of Juno's sanctuary "stilled Aeneas' fears; / here he first dared to hope he had found shelter." While his grief is stirred by the fresco of Troy's fall, so also is an important solace he, Achates, and the Carthaginians seem to share: "here, too, the honorable find its due / and there are tears for passing things; here, too, things mortal touch the mind. Forget your fears; this fame will bring you some deliverance."[15] Not only does the art of the wall give evidence for the regard in which his band and Troy are held, but the very construction of the city promises a brighter future than anything either the displaced Trojans or the Tyrians within Carthage have experienced to this point. The magnificence of Carthaginian building activities is the artistic answer to loss, deception, tyranny, murder and fear which Aeneas, as well as Dido, has faced.

Nor in Dido's city does the power of art to capture a tribe's ethos and history, as well as personal memories, affect only Aeneas. Venus does not simply create a love-forlorn Dido out of nothing; she must work upon someone who is pre-disposed to love's ferment. Before Venus intervenes, Dido herself says to Aeneas "My destiny, like yours, has willed that I, / a veteran of hardships, halt at last in this country. Not ignorant of trials, / I now can learn to help the miserable."[16] The superb, vivid art of Aeneas' own story-telling opens, narrates, and closes the story of Troy's fall and his journeys in a misery that Dido knows too well, particularly in his loss of Creusa. By the story's end, it is clear that Aeneas is much worse off than he appeared to be when he first began to speak, for the story makes clear that the loss of city, wife, and father has left him "alone," driven by a god upon the Carthaginian shore. So, it seems that in Carthage the very narration of the story—art's likenesses

---

15 Another sign of his longing is that he says this, despite the wall narrative's placement within Juno's sanctuary being a sign of her implacable hatred. I, 598-599, 619-620, 645-646, 647, 639-640, 654-657, pp. 16-17.

16 I, 879-882, p. 22.

of personal and cultural histories—powerfully inclines humans to rework the miseries of history through their own personal passions.

It may be a mystery to Jupiter, who can foresee the future, what Aeneas hopes for in staying with Dido to build a city there, but the reader might suspect that it is not a mystery to Aeneas, his art of poetry making it all too clear to himself and his hearers. The inclination to rectify the past through building a better life in the present seems partially to be in accord with what Jupiter plans, and so we might hardly fault Aeneas' desire to build in Carthage. Further, in the face of Aeneas' experience, we might probe the adequacy of the instructions from the gods that he receives before arriving in Carthage. These consist largely of instructions, for example by Helenus, that tell him where to go and where dangers lie; they are concerned with efficiencies. Rarely is he told anything about the underlying import or consequences of these future actions. The limitations of these instructions can be seen very clearly. Not only is Aeneas told by Helenus that the Fates refuse to reveal very much to him, and that he will have to defer any answers about the larger consequences of wars in Italy until he reaches the Sibyl, but when Jupiter sends Mercury with a shock to Aeneas' soul, Mercury fails to convey any sense of the motives that inspired Jupiter's command: "his lovely mother did not promise such a son to us; she did not save him twice from Grecian arms for this—but to be master of Italy, a land that teems with empire and seethes with war; to father a race from Teucer's high blood, to place all the earth beneath his laws."[17] Mercury, instead of this, delivers the alternative message—Aeneas ought to, at least, have his own posterity in mind, which is a much more limited if touching vision.[18]

Indeed, the most extreme form of limitation in instruction is its near total absence for Dido. Left without any sense of larger purposes, Dido must craft them for herself, under pressures and experiences similar to those of Aeneas'. Dido, unlike Aeneas, has

---

17   III, 493; 599-601; IV, 304-309, pp. 69, 72, 90.

18   IV, 353-369, p. 92.

already built her city and brought safety to herself and her comrades.[19] Surrounded by hostile nations, she is ready to unite Tyrians and Trojans should the latter so choose. Murderously deprived of a patrician husband, declared leader by those fleeing and hating tyranny, caught between "love's pain and press," yet restrained by cultural norms that make shameful a second marriage, she is left to decide for herself what to do to both feed her soul and to secure her city. Instead of Jupiter, Dido has Anna, her sister for counsel and advice: "'For I am sure it was the work of the gods / and Juno … If you marry Aeneas, what a city / and what a kingdom, sister, you will see'." This line of argument is enough that in Dido, "hope burned away her doubt, destroyed her shame."[20] Like a medicine taken without proper prescription, love's poison works its way into the contests between woman and man, matriarchy and patriarchy, and destinies in union or duty toward the ends of one or more nations.

Upon Aeneas' breaking off an agreement he "never entered into," Dido's dreams crystallize the terrible fear she faces at the unleashing of these contests; Aeneas has become her furies, driving her, as they did Orestes, to a bitter exile. "She always finds herself alone, abandoned, / and wandering without companions on / an endless journey, seeking out her people, her Tyrians in a deserted land." The affair has unleashed the scorn of the many, closed her off from leading her people in Carthage or "back again upon the sea," and exposed her land to hungry enemies.[21] Because she loved, trusted, and shared her kingdom, experience, and body, she can only see further humiliation, further isolation, further mockery such as she believes she has received from Aeneas. Compare these two lovers, one driven by fear of humiliation, the other by fear of divine punishment, and we can see in art what the blindness of mortals brings *when the mind is not tuned to a wider vision*

---

19   I, 793-794, p. 20.

20   IV, 1-2, 23-24, 33, 63-65, 75, pp. 83-85.

21   IV, 457-459, 641-645, 756 pp. 94, 99, 101

than personal safety, honor, or more immediate concerns.[22] If in flight
Aeneas has shrunk to a man of fear responding almost like a private in the face of an angry general, in death, Dido has shrunk to
an artist of death. The building and art of her city shrinks from
a construction promising a new beginning and a wall telling the
whole story of a civilization's fall to the form of a funeral pyre.[23]
For Dido in her fallen state art can apparently do little more than
either deceive the Carthaginians of her real intentions or remind
her of her past while deepening her present misery:

> And when she saw the Trojan's clothes
> and her familiar bed, she checked her thought
> and tears a little, lay upon the couch
> and spoke her final words: "O relics,
> dear while fate and god allowed, receive my spirit
> and free me from these cares; for I have lived
> and journeyed through the course assigned by fortune...
> I have built a handsome city,
> have seen my walls rise up, avenged a husband,
> won satisfaction from a hostile brother:
> o fortunate, too fortunate—if only
> the Ships of Troy had never touched our coasts."[24] 895-907

---

22   The poem makes pretty clear that we do not need to conclude that
Dido had to die, nor should we feel her deserts deserved. The point is that
humans that are prepared only by experience without education have
no other resources than personal experience, past histories, and limited
immediate concerns by which to make crucial judgments. Depending
on the 'education' one received and the circumstances faced, perhaps a
common lot for us all.

23   Dido deceives her sister Anna by ordering that "'In secret / build
up a pyre with the inner courtyard / ... and lay upon it / the weapons
of the hero. ... Take all of his apparel and the bridal / bed where I was
undone....' But Anna cannot dream her sister hides / a funeral behind
these novel rites...." IV, 681-692, p. 100.

24   IV, 895-907, p. 105

In this city of art unguided by instructions from Jupiter, simple suicide would be insufficient for it would neither convey to Aeneas the final anguish Dido feels nor culminate, appropriately, Dido's sense of loss. The funeral pyre, an art object composed of art objects, reworks Dido's personal history and misery into a public performance, literally erasing the traces of two actors in that history for no other sake than the injury of one person to another.

Still, if the care, comfort, solace, *eros* and the beautiful constructions, i.e. art of the city had been turning Aeneas toward Carthage and away from the piety of compliance with his Jupiter-appointed task, the fault would seem to lie as much in the divine instructions he has received as in any shortfall of attention on his part. The instructions from the gods, which actually begin with Creusa's admonishment to Aeneas not to give way to sorrow at her loss and to seek the Tiber, have a particular character about them that informs a sense of the difficulty of bringing Aeneas to Ausonia. The gods' instructions come through supernatural and natural signs, shades, art, dreams, priests and priestesses, and appearances of the gods themselves. Almost all of these, whether true or false, malicious or beneficial, are omens or prophecies: forecasts of the future. When we examine more closely Jupiter's prophetic statements, prophecy looks strangely like history to our eyes, but in the eyes of the gods and to a limited extent in the eyes of the epic's characters, it looks like executive decrees of an emperor who possesses resources to realize his decrees in action.

When Venus challenges Jupiter on the question of the punishment her Trojans have received at the hands of Juno, she appeals to him as one who "rules," "commands," and "governs." When he answers her, he not only speaks with his authority, but invokes the authority of reading out-loud his written words: "Your son / (I now speak out ...I unroll the secret scroll of the Fates, awaken its distant pages) / shall wage tremendous war in Italy and establish a way of life and his own walls for his people." At least according to Mandelbaum, Jupiter evidently thinks of such pronouncements as having force of law: "This is what I decree."[25] And the decree is fairly clear in its outline. Yet as with Venus working upon Dido, Jupiter must work in the world where his fellow gods and the institutions, characters, and lives of humans shape his words. The problem of all legislation is precisely that it is prophetic; that is, human means must be found for its accomplishment. Once instruction "by legislation" has failed—that is, prophetic announcements by ministers of the divine emperor in Aeneas' visits to oracles before reaching Carthage have failed—and once the message is made loud and clear to Aeneas, then less blunt, more sophisticated instruments are needed. In fact the instruction becomes decidedly more artful.

In the interests of brevity, we pass by the various supernatural signs and help, guidance by the Sibyl, and mustering of courage that Aeneas undergoes in his journey toward Elysium—all of which build in him a growing trust in Jupiter's instructors and instruction. While in Carthage, Aeneas saw his own and Trojan fame through a narration of images of the past, a history pictured in art on the wall of Juno's sanctuary. In Elysium, on the fields where shades of the past congregate to re-enter the world without memories of an earlier life, he glimpses the future of what his present actions will bring. Anchises' brief narrations of the futures awaiting these souls are clearly not just instructions, "my tongue will now reveal / the fame that is to come from Dardan sons / and what Italian children wait for you...."[26]; these revelations have wider educational import as well. Every soul, save that of Marcellus, represents the very opposite of Trojan souls on the wall of Carthage. These are successful heroes and Aeneas sees in them that Teucrians are not fated to a fame which is tethered to defeat while others, the Greeks, possess the fame of victors. The tide of history does turn. The presentation of such future history has as its object the expulsion of all doubt in Aeneas concerning the coming

---

25   I, 320-321, 361-369, 396, pp. 9-11.

26   VI, 999-1001, p. 163. Compare in Plato's *Republic* where Odysseus looks for a new soul. In Elysium the souls have their identities of the future, possibly before they lose their memories of the past.

wars, but the appeal is successful not simply because it is a string of promised virtues and victories. Aeneas' present task is made to appear possible through a glimpse of the nearly unimaginable:

> Now turn your two eyes here, to look upon
> your Romans, your own people... This,
> this is the man you heard so often promised—
> Augustus Caesar, ... who will...stretch
> his rule beyond the Garamantes and
> the Indians—a land beyond the paths
> of year and sun...
> And do we, then, still hesitate to extend
> our force in acts of courage? Can it be
> that fear forbids our settling in Ausonia? [27]

We see the power of the unimaginable is well understood by Anchises, for after identifying Augustus, Anchises, describing the figure of Marcellus, a contemporary of Virgil and Augustus, declares that "the line of Rome, / o High Ones, would have seemed too powerful for you, if his gifts, too, had been its own." But for the early death of this conqueror of unsurpassed promise, Rome's future would compete with the gods. Anchises having "shown his son each scene and fired his soul / with love of coming glory, / then, ... tells Aeneas of the wars he must still wage."[28] His soul seemingly aligned aright, the instruction, the education, of Aeneas seems complete—except perhaps for the diploma.

That comes in Book VIII when Venus hands the shield of Vulcan to her son. The shield is explicitly identified in the poem as a work of art and it synthesizes the arts of blacksmithing, sculpture, prophecy and Aeneas' education into a future story,—not just a set of figures—of Rome. Presented this shield, "Aeneas cannot have enough; delighted with these gifts of the goddess, his eyes

---

27   VI, 1044-1071, pp. 164-165.

28   VI, 1161-64; 1185-1188, pp. 167-168.

rush on everything, admiring…"[29] His reaction seems much the same as when he faced the wall in Carthage, yet not only are the scenes different, but the art is operating differently upon its viewer. Despite a preview of figures in Elysium, Aeneas does not know the future events nor whom the figures are in those events depicted on the shield. In Carthage, likenesses to personal and cultural histories inclined humans to rework their past defeats through the play on their passions, as when Aeneas stood before the wall, or when his story moved Dido to love. This shield bears no such past likenesses. Near the Tiber, at the end of his education, the play on Aeneas' emotion as his soul looks at art and seeks to interpret the future is quite different, "he is glad for all their images, though he does not know what they mean. Upon his shoulder he lifts up the fame and fate of his son's sons." [30]

His reaction to the art on the shield is not simply based on a change in content. We suspect that if Aeneas stood before the wall in Carthage now, his passion would not be directed, as it was then, toward irrevocable personal losses, nor would he feel hope in a shelter from troubles. Aeneas has spent some time seeking assurances from the gods in all that he does, and he has certainly seen the "future history" of characters such as himself transformed into a dream of confidence over what he faces. But this shield gives no security in future particulars; he sees a mother wolf with twin boys, men carrying off women, theatre "games," two figures at an altar, a man torn apart by out-racing chariots, a kingly figure addressing a crowd, warriors rushing another line of warriors with swords drawn, and so forth, circling round to a truly marvelous, but unknown, clash of ships from the east and west occupying the very center of the shield, with one figure on a ship emblazoned by the sun, another, female, on a different ship pale with intimations of impending death. But who these are, when they are, where they are, why they are—Aeneas knows not. Aeneas has seen enough of future history to know this shield is not simply confined to his

---

29   VIII, 799-802, p. 218.

30   VIII, 953, p. 955.

own personal future and, so, he wonders at the scene not because he wants to know its meaning in any particular sense, but in the larger historical sense of confident openness to a future filled not only with strife and victory, *but with a swelling magnitude he knows he is a part of.* And, so, Aeneas is glad.

Often times, we encourage our students to read works such as the *Aeneid* as a way to understand the culture those works express—be it the ancient one they arose in or the current one which is linked to past cultures in large part by such works. It strikes me that the *Aeneid* is a cautionary tale against that approach and that we do better to balance a reading of such texts as cultural artifacts deeply embedded in history with a reading of them as art leading us into the future. While I wouldn't want to stake my argument on the gate of ivory through which both false dreams and Aeneas leave, I still think the gate may help us to see what the caution is. Aeneas, in the poem's terms, is not a dream. In the poem's terms the swelling future history he has been shown and the promise of more immediate victory are likewise not false. To send Aeneas through the ivory gate is something like the logical problem of the picture which tells you "everything you see in this box is a lie." The words actually do leave the box, for if they didn't you wouldn't understand the words. Similarly, the words and images *Anchises* uses to tell Aeneas his future are a false dream, false stories we all tell ourselves, in which our future is secured by figures of a past. The true dreams are found elsewhere, and that is why the shield is important. Vulcan is to the shield as Virgil is to the *Aeneid*, and Aeneas is to the shield as we and our students are to the *Aeneid*. If the meaning of art is only known by setting off into the future, then the events, figures and even historical rivers of the past that we read of in the *Aeneid,* in its art, are, in Virgil's vision, like the prophecies of Jupiter to Aeneas—they are forecasts of a future we can only know by stepping into it. When we acquire an education, it is to learn the meaning of the future.

The *Aeneid* can lead us to a renewed sense of the importance of the arts to higher education in an age not that distant from the headiest moments of Roman rule and in a country, inclined as

Rome was, to see its liberal arts education of the young directed toward practical education. In Rome, poetry may well have been used to educate souls in the imperial way of life, bolstering and bolstered by patriarchal values and powers. But to read the *Aeneid* as if this were the residual inheritance it left us, would be the same as Aeneas standing before the Carthaginian wall and feeling himself at ease. We who live in a democratic state and particularly aspire to liberal education need not rest with such conclusions, and, therefore, we include the arts in a liberal arts education for very different reasons. There are arts of instruction—prophecy really—that prepare men and women for their future. Some of these arts are like job training or legislation; they predict specific acts and require certain skills, perhaps even an alignment of our character and passions. But the most important arts for the souls and lives of men and women are prophetic, and this is one reason why after the word "liberal" the word "arts" follows. These are the arts that allow young men and women to see that there are human endeavors, enormous in scope and importance, which they may enter, not simply as trained foot soldiers, but as future heroes and heroines. This is not a naive notion. Education, particularly liberal arts education, is full of such people. We should help to insure that our business and professions, our societies and our countries have them too.

(Rev. Originally delivered at the annual ACTC Conference in Vancouver, 4/8/2005 and expanded 2/16/2006.)

SECTION IV

Poetic Coda

CHAPTER 10

The Ultimate Argument for the Liberal Arts

T he core of liberal arts learning, the basis for joy in learning, can be a study of invention. Aristotle's *Poetics* strongly
suggests this claim, and the pursuit of it leads to freedom through liberal arts education. Further, Aristotle's philosophy
addresses a key function of liberal arts education: relating different
arts and sciences to each other via arts of discourse. As we argued
in earlier chapters of this book, we can examine great books or
core texts, the works of human hands and minds, to discover the
invention and growth of arts and sciences. Liberal arts studies are
the study of the great explosions of invention in human history.
They examine the moments of the greatest freedom and imagination that have ever happened. That's not enough. The arts and
sciences inspire in each other inventions and freedoms that would
not be dreamt of without converse *among* them. So, to become as
fully human as is possible we must connect and relate the arts and
sciences through a curriculum that prepares us through conversational argument to see the fullest extent of invention.

But that's not enough. Real freedom is not obtained simply by
studying invention; it has to be directed toward making it. Liberal
arts education is, ultimately, concerned with the connection
between "*technē*" and "*poesis*"—between artistry in its fullest sense
and with production. A curriculum for liberal arts students must
help them to produce their own works—in whatever fields their
minds and hearts are drawn to. The reason for including core texts
or pivotal works of the arts and sciences, then, is that they offer to

students consideration of what is best and what ways are best to produce what they think is best—over and over again. That consideration of such texts, that examination, will inspire moments which reshape and grow our students' humanity and our own, but the students will only know they are free if they use their arts to make what has, up to the moment, not been brought into existence before.

This is the ultimate argument for the liberal arts. Invention in art, including the liberal arts, is not only an inevitable expression of our humanity; it is a maker of our freedom. Liberal arts education is a best hope of meeting the challenges that we face, challenges that will require all the inventiveness we can offer.

The Problem of Liberal Education's Defense and Appeals

Current defenses of liberal education adopt a moral line, often in defense of democracy. There is nothing inherently wrong with this approach; these arguments may be true. Further, claims that liberal education, as a pillar of democracy, speaks to Enduring Human Questions, allow for a moral enthusiasm which rouses academics who are most concerned with perpetuating or extending such education to millions of students who have not experienced its many benefits.[1]

But these defenses don't work with a North American public and I doubt that they are very effective with Europeans.[2] I suspect

---

1   In chapters 1 and 7, I have shown that democratic and spiritual defenses of liberal education emphasize not the liberal arts, but the social conditions of liberal education and the social or spiritual purposes liberal education serves, rather than the artistic ends of liberal *arts* education. As with these earlier chapters, this chapter does not argue that political or spiritual defenses should not be employed, but in addition we might deploy artistic defenses and a real attention to what artistry implies for liberal *arts* education.

2   Defenses of liberal education have a peculiar tendency to work in China where there is a hunger for some forms of free thought. There is

the reasons are two. Partially, to gain importance for liberal education, these defenses make it something done not for its own sake,
but as an instrument serving democracy in lands of already free
citizens.[3] Also, the defenses habitually assume that the Enduring
Human Questions are moral or political; at best, art or science are
cast as ethical and political problems in a moral education for a
student body that has far wider interests. Ultimately these political
defenses do little to address public perceptions of the uselessness
of liberal education, and they are inadequate to the available
resources within the liberal arts core text tradition for exploiting
its own attractions.

More broadly, we face a larger persuasive problem because if
we argue from career, utility, or skills,—appeals often used with the
public—we simply become secondary in other ways, often seeming to argue that liberal education finds value as a means to future
earnings.[4] Instead, we can and must find better grounds of argument in our own traditions that not only appeal to those outside
liberal education but represent our own distinctive aspirations and
competence. This chapter concerns the grounds of those appeals,
concentrating on the *art* of 'liberal *arts* education.'

We need a fuller ecology of argument, one where democratic
or moral arguments find partners in the defense of liberal arts education. Any reasonable survey of education programs using core
texts shows that they draw on faculty and texts from across the arts
and sciences. Some sort of model of education that systematically
relates the arts and sciences in their own terms rather than just in a

---

a reason complementary to but not identical with democratic yearnings:
namely, a yearning for innovation and creativity. These latter yearnings
are aligned with some of the discussions of this paper.

3   Similarly, religious defenses make liberal education an instrument
serving a Deity for, mostly, congregants who already believe. Ethical
defenses fall on deaf ears: who does not believe that their upbringing
provides ethical guidance?

4   On the inadequacy of earnings and 'career' arguments, see the
Introduction and Appendix 1, "Turning Ourselves Towards the Public
for the Sake of Liberal Education."

moral/political relation might offer a more varied, nuanced, and in many cases, promising exploration of what liberal arts education has to offer.

At the same time, I do not think we can give up appeals to freedom as an end which organizes liberal education. I want to suggest that Aristotle's *Poetics* offers an alternative way by which to explore the pluralistic freedom appropriate to a core text liberal arts education. That work is still the foremost examination of art we possess and is essential to any discussion of artistic activity, including 'liberal *arts* education.' More broadly, I want to suggest that Aristotle's philosophy addresses a key function of liberal arts education: relating different arts and sciences to each other via arts of discourse. A word of caution: Aristotle only infrequently uses the term 'freedom' or 'liberty'– *eleutheria*—and that in contrast to political opposites such as tyranny and slavery. But in his approach to poetics we can see the freedom of art and poetry operating; so, we hereby adopt the following principle: if there is implication, then we can explicate.

Re-examining Aristotle's *Poetics* for a Defense of Liberal Arts Education

Aristotle was a philosopher who aimed to explain differences.[5] To

---

5   This is quite different from Aristotle's teacher, Plato, who built a philosophy to explain sameness. One editor of the work that this chapter originally appeared in (Emma Cohen de Lara), after reading the manuscript, remarked in correspondence that "Aristotle's ontology is different from Plato's metaphysical ontology. For Plato, a thing is a thing only to the extent that it participates in the Idea of the thing. For Aristotle, a thing is a thing because it generates itself." Her remark carries the thrust of the distinction made here between the efforts of the two philosophies. Plato's principles are comprehensive, Aristotle's reflexive. The difference in the thrust of their philosophic effort means that the discussion of imitation or art is by no means identical or, even, very close. For a thorough distinction between the two philosophers' uses of 'imitation,' see. Richard P. McKeon, "The Concept of Imitation in Antiquity," in Critics and

Aristotle the difference between Nature (*phusis*) and Art (*technē* and *poesis*) was crucial because, while both taken together were origins of almost everything in the universe, Nature moved itself, brought itself into being, while art, separated in various degrees from its maker, was moved, was brought into being, by humans.[6]

Yet, for Aristotle, art imitates nature; it is like nature. For example, a tragic play reminds us of human life; the artist imitates "men doing or experiencing something (*prattontas*)" (Poetics 2, 1148a2-3).[7] But despite likenesses to nature, imitation was distinct because, for Aristotle, "imitation" also means completing something that nature cannot. Nature works through stages: puppies are born, suckle, grow, and turn into dogs. But some processes nature starts but cannot complete. Nature grows wood, but it does not grow tables. It takes human making, art, to bring to completion the table, and thus artistic—not natural—completion is the chief difference of imitation from nature (Physics II, 8, 199a15-18). Consequently the distinguishing feature of art, artistry, making, or imitation is that they are concerned with "something [that] *may* come into being" or "something that *may* either exist or not," all in accord with a huge variety of ends (my emphasis). Art's concern is with variable processes; in art, we are not in the realm of 'necessity' but the possible (NE. VI, 4, 1140a1-14; I, 1, 1094a1-10). Therefore, the distinction between nature and art also raises two important related questions for which the *Poetics* sets out to

---

Criticism, R. S. Crane, ed. University of Chicago, 1952, esp., pp. 160-169.

6 Both were origins of things coming into being. While, for Aristotle, art and science shared a concern with knowledge of causes of the origin of things, all of our modern concerns with power to shape and transform anything in the world were, properly, artistic, that is *technē*, questions. And this is important from the very outset of re-considering liberal arts education.

7 I have quoted from various translations, depending on which translation seems close to the original Greek. Sometimes familiar translations (e.g., Bywater's) will do; other times less familiar translations seem better (e.g., Telford) because of the English closeness to key terms (e.g., 'imitation' for mimesis, not 'representation').

develop answers: if art isn't necessary, then why did it arise at all? And, if art is marked by imitation, which is not born of necessity, how do you *systematically* locate the causes of arts?

As a systematic way to study the liberal arts, one might contemplate the way the *Poetics* proceeds to study imitation and art. To begin the study of "poetic art and its species and powers" Aristotle positions the analysis between "beginning with nature, first things first," and a collective body of arts—tragedy, comedy, dithyrambs, epics, and flute and lyre playing—which "happen to be imitations" and "happen to use" the same materials—language or voice, harmonics, and rhythms—simultaneously, singly, or in combinations (Poetics 1447a11-23). Why begin the analysis half-way between nature and art? Or what is the same question, why not begin with other art materials—*e.g.*, color and figure? Aristotle has chosen means of imitation that are so natural to us as to be nearly inseparable from humans, though in fact they are used in these arts which are often quite separated from their authors or composers. In short, Aristotle has apparently chosen the most human, the most commonly shared, and, thus, the most imitative of artistic means to begin his analysis. If, then, it is humanity that is essential to any liberal education, it should not surprise us that in liberal arts education the exploration of voice, harmonics, and rhythms through various arts would be a good beginning.[8]

The chapters that lead up to the definition of tragedy increasingly rely on the humanity of art to explain its origins, and not surprisingly in that reliance this analysis of art readily fits the goal of most liberal education—for its participants to become more

---

8   There is a sense in which Aristotle has chosen 'the most difficult case' for imitation and art. If these means are so close to human conventional or natural use, and, yet, if we can distinguish through these means (matter, object, manner, and ends) various arts, then the case for artistic imitation as a quintessentially human-yet-separate function provides a window on humanity, outlined later in this paper, not achievable in any other way. As a curricular matter, linguistics (or grammar), including phonetics and prosody, and musical 'theory' as evidenced in art objects would be a way to begin a liberal arts, humanistic, education.

human. Indeed, Chapter 2's first sentence that the imitator imitates human "actings" is confirmation that Aristotle has chosen to pursue an analysis of art that is as human as can be, though he concentrates on the human differences in agents and acting that distinguish one from another—the serious or virtuous agent-acting from the worthless or vicious—and, thus, one art from another.[9]

The object of imitation introduces the political concerns of modern as well as ancient liberal education. However, this seeming ethical distinction that most liberal education wants in some way to center upon, is, in one sense where Aristotle's analysis of liberal education in the *Politics* and much of our modern undergraduate, core text education stops. Governed by the city-state, a liberal education employing harmony and singing or, in more modern versions, ideological and exhortative argument, imitates the characteristic passions of the state with which citizens ought to be acquainted and habituated (VIII, 5. 1340a14-1340b4 and 6. 1340b35-1341a16). But in the *Poetics*, the inquiry takes steps well beyond the *Politics* through its developing history of artistic causes. The defenses of liberal arts that are tied to politics or economic gain, therefore, are acknowledged by Aristotle's *Politics*, but the *Poetics* shows these defenses to be limited. In doing so, it opens a different prospect for liberal arts education, as well.[10]

---

9   That he is not discussing objects of imitation such as grapes, fish, or mountains—common enough in Greece—is a negative confirmation of his intentions, as well.

10   In the *Politics*, Aristotle chides educational programs which emphasize 'professional contests [in which students] seek to acquire those fantastic marvels of execution which are now in fashion,' largely because this form of education aims at vulgar pleasures, whereas the aim in education of children as free persons is that musical, artistic instruction contribute to a mind engaged in leisure of judging and enjoying *noble acts* embodied in the arts—*not the arts themselves*. But in the *Poetics*, learning from the arts results in becoming a good judge of comedy and tragedy, epic and mock epic, or other arts as appropriate. Further, where the *Poetics* speaks from Chapter 4 to Chapter 5 of historical developments in the arts, no such chiding about vulgar pleasures exists. Further, whereas the *Politics* certainly distinguishes means, object and manner

That prospect, more fully human, is one of invention which depends on the possibilities inherent, combined, discovered, and made in each art. In *Poetics* 3 to 5 Aristotle begins to elaborate the consequences of the distinctions he has made among arts that are the most imitative, that is, most human, in his day. If language, or more properly voice, imitates human agents acting, it follows that artists face questions about the use or manner of voice. Poets can adopt a voice that is their own, or they can adapt their voice's harmonics and rhythms to imitate one or more other agents' voices, further differentiated by the possibilities of intertwining these two sets of voices. Since rhythms imply imitations not only by voice but movement, the poet can move his or her hands, body, and feet in accompaniment to the speaking—varying and typifying the movements according to who is speaking. The next step, using other bodies—actors—instead of the poet's own gestures, is an extension of the potentials of combining the matter and objects of imitation which leads through lyrics, epics, and rhapsodes to dramas put on by players.[11]

Notice that what is going on here is a multiplication of possibilities through combinatorics of the means and objects of imitation. Today we speak of indirect discourse, direct discourse,

---

(singing vs. instrumental playing) in music, as well as a generalized discussion of three ends (or melodic modes) of musical arts, the only history of technical development that Aristotle engages in surrounds playing the flute or lyre. The *Poetics* not only develops technical histories of art, but, then, technically analyses the function of two (perhaps, originally four) arts.

11   A similar but not identical development would follow from selecting color or figure as means of imitation. In the *Politics* Aristotle argues that colors are signs, not imitations, of *character* in portraits but they can clearly imitate physical features of humans and action. Alberti's argument in *On Painting* about the incidence of light and use of black and white on color concerns bringing out in greatest "relief" the outlined figures and surfaces of the moment of action in an *historia*. In short, all four aid the completion of the imitation. (Op. cit., pp. 64-64, 73-74, 82-83.) Also, depending on the object of imitation, then, etching, painting, and sculpting may happen to be *manners* of imitation (not means).

narration and dramatization. Clearly, if we were to add a later means of imitation, photography, we would have the manner of 'stills' or 'motion pictures,' i.e., 'kinemation' for the latter. Each manner of imitation would reveal aspects of humanity that others leave aside or less fully touch.[12] Thus by the end of Chapter 3 of the *Poetics* we see a kind of algorithm emerging from the analysis leading to tragedy and comedy, and the same would be true for education: for every selection of differences in imitation that limits or excludes one mode of imitation over against another, new possibilities of making and humanity open up through combination.

At this point, we can begin to draw questions and inferences for today's liberal education. How might the basis of various imitations or inventions be incorporated? What questions should students face about the use or manner of voice? Since the analysis is moving toward kinds of performance—writing and acting—it would indicate an education which would imply, first in Chapter 1, the study of language, harmonics, and rhythms, and, then in Chapter 3, the performance of these means, whether in narratives, dramas, cinemas, orchestras, choirs, conversations in multiple languages, and even, in debates.[13] Two different features of education

---

12   For example, the soliloquy of drama only points out the capacity of novels, poems, and epics to enter the minds of characters directly, while the enactments of drama render in one moment of staging what the novelist or epic poet labors sometimes for pages with far less vivacity to convey. For a powerful exploration of the implications of the kinematic film along humanistic, yet technical, lines of manner see Erwin Panofsky, "Style and Medium in the Motion Pictures," *Three Essays on Style*, MIT, 1995, especially pp. 94, 96, 98, and 101.

13   An illustration of what might be possible is currently provided on Netflix in its serialized show *The Kominsky Method*. Sandy Kominsky runs an acting studio. Students select passages out of plays to perform and listen to critical commentary by their fellow students. The enactment of these passages are often—inadvertently one suspects—the best performances in the entire series. Though apparently 'professional,' the performances are, after all, those of arts which are readily accessible to everyone: director, performers, students, and the audience of the series. Unlike Kominsky, we are not concerned with improved acting, but with

are at stake here. (1) This is the arena in which skills and techniques are developed so that students can actually demonstrate capacities acquired in their education.[14] (2) The manner of education here is a doing or activity. As the next two chapters of the Poetics reveal, the use of these means implies a coming to know of their potentials which cannot be achieved simply through the non-practical study of such means.[15]

The *Poetics'* fourth and fifth chapters elaborate a history of arts as artists of different temperament are drawn to new imitations: first to encomia and invective, then to epic and mock epic, finally to tragedy and comedy. During this history dramatic artists increase the number of performers, the importance of speeches, and the magnitude and number of episodes. They naturalize the diction, and attain tragedy's and comedy's "natural form." In chapters 3 through 5, Aristotle employs a cluster of terms to explore the origins of arts. In English translation, these include 'originated,' 'improvements,' 'improvisations,' 'produced,' 'came to light,'

---

learning the potentials of language for artistic uses. See chapter 1.

14   Whereas in the *Politics* an educational mean short of professional performance, more involved than mere listening, and partaking of the leisure to both cultivate and judge character is sought, in the *Poetics* anything like a mean would, certainly, have to partake of the ends arts offer as a matter of invention. This paper approaches that question in the consideration of the limits the *Poetics* sets itself, below. The question of doing is explicit in the chapter; see the discussion of the geographical origins based on the words *dran* and *prattein*.

15   Practically, curricular or extracurricular development should not be difficult or any more demanding than, say, the vogue for 'internships' or 'civic engagement.' Indeed, many arts would easily satisfy such degree requirements, and there is nothing to prevent colleges from requiring artistic performance or creation through organized clubs or societies. Sometimes, in general education, institutions require the study or practice of fine arts; both could be required. St. John's College devotes two entire years to music tutorials, centering around choral performance, but exploring the monumental works of Western music. Other colleges have similar musical and artistic interests, without becoming professional schools.

'changed' (often translated as 'evolved' or 'developed'), 'chance,' 'art' in his understanding of bringing into being something that might or might not exist, and 'imitation' in the sense of bringing to completion. It is common for translators (*e.g.*, Butcher and Bywater) to insert words like 'new,' 'create,' 'discover' and 'invention' when there is little or no textual warrant. Their reason would appear to be our modern desire for terms to express changes in imitation which involve the appearance of heretofore non-existent arts or developments within arts. If we want to use such terms, less to translate the text than to characterize what is being discussed in it, it is important to see that the discussion of changes in the arts is taking place within two important parameters.

The first of these we have discussed: the additive combinations, the possibilities, that become available as means and matter of imitation are further differentiated through manners of imitation. An analogous but different set of possibilities rests on Aristotle's discussion of the place of learning in imitation or, what is the same, the appearance of the final cause of both tragedy and comedy. For Aristotle, not only are humans the most imitative of animals, and not only do we delight to learn about things external to imitation by mimicking them, but *we also delight to learn about imitation itself through contemplating likenesses by means of differences within the imitation* (1448b15-20).

> The reason we enjoy seeing likenesses is that, as we look, we learn and infer what each [i.e., likeness] is, for instance that 'that is so and so.' (Fyfe translation, my inserted clarification.) [16]

---

16   He also remarks at 1460b 13-23 that in a poet it is a greater failure to produce an unrecognizable imitation than to produce an imitation that by some other standard of correctness than poetic, would be an error—e.g., a hind with no horns. Telford, possibly the most literal English translator, renders: "for men delight in seeing likenesses because in contemplating them it happens that they are learning and reasoning out what each thing is, e.g. that this man [in the painting] is that [sort of man]..." Telford's insertions.

More than any other cause, this delight in learning makes art most human.[17] Aristotle also remarks that if in contemplating a picture, one fails to recognize the imitation, the most one can enjoy in the picture is coloring or execution. In other words, we learn about imitation by thinking about, recognizing, and enjoying the imitation as an imitation, art as art, and each specific art as such. Quite a bit is at stake in the learning origins of imitation.

First, the history of imitation based in learning means that the significance of artistic developments is not necessarily in the intentions of the artists. Though intentions might be important in any given case, artistic significance rests in the *recognition* by all including the artist(s) who gaze upon imitations that there are potentials for and realizations of exploration in the arts. In this sense while I think 'invention' is being discussed in this history of art, it is not necessarily because the intentions of artists are primary to developing a final cause of purgation of pity and fear or a generalizing of satire toward the ludicrous. It is because artists come to recognize the possibilities of making the pitiable, fearful, or ludicrous in art and learn to take advantage of them.[18]

Second, the ultimate answer to why arts arose is that *humans learned through imitative making both what the world of nature is and what the world of art could be.*[19] In virtue of our humanity we are unavoidably impelled toward 'artistic education.'[20]

---

17   Such learning is, ultimately, natural to humans; "All men by nature desire to know." In this passage in the *Poetics*, seeing, gazing at, contemplating by sight occupies the same primary position in learning as the analogous proof Aristotle offers, based in sight, of the human naturalness of learning, which heads toward the contemplation of the arts and sciences. (Meta. I, 1, 980, 21.)

18   In other words, this is why form, relation of parts to whole, and function *are* important.

19   Both how to use nature and how to use art are implied from the very beginning of the analysis, but *what* each is or could be orders what use can be made of each.

20   The issue is not <u>whether</u> we learn by art, but <u>what</u> we get out of learning. In this sense, the first five chapters exemplify a systematic way

Third, throughout Aristotle's development of the possibilities inherent in manners, ends, and inventions of arts, we find that some developments are communal, some arts call into being human associations, and therefore the learning attendant on those arts grows out of artistic potentials for cooperation. Homer seeks a rhapsode; the four great Greek dramatists seek a theatre and a Dionysia. One can imagine Thespis observing, participating in, and thinking about the chorus and choragus as he invents a single actor-character who acts separately from the chorus. What becomes hard to imagine is any sustained development of artistic learning without a body of people and works that share common artistic attributes. Indeed, for Aristotle, it is precisely the appreciation for the potentials of new *communal* arts which draws artists:

> As soon, however, as tragedy and comedy appeared in the field, those naturally drawn to the one line of poetry became writers of comedies instead of iambs, and those naturally drawn to the other, writers of tragedies instead of epics, because the new modes of art were grander and of more esteem than the old. (1449a1-7.)

All three—intentions, artistic invention, and communality of enterprise—affect liberal arts education. If we look to Aristotle's history of the learning of artists, we can begin to see how a curriculum of the liberal arts could operate for students and teachers with respect to formal learning. A curriculum is a made thing, a construction of teacher-artists, itself a work of art. A core text curriculum is a history of human achievement—a work of art containing works separated from their authors. While such a history might have results, there is no reason to think that the works of

---

to explore the potentials of arts increasingly separated from their makers; the sixth through twenty-fourth chapter illustrates what Aristotle learned from tragedy and epic as arts; chapter twenty-six illustrates what one might learn when one is comparing structures of differing arts. Also the first through fifth and the twenty-fifth chapters connect the arts to other areas of inquiry.

that history were intentionally aiming at the curriculum of which they are a part. Further, what is recognized in the works or in the relations of one part of the curriculum to the other, is just as much a matter of the students' as of the teachers' determinations. The curriculum should not assume that students have specific intentions for specific artistic development, but it could readily assume that students will be drawn by temperament in combination with an increasing array of artistic display to move toward a variety of arts and could over time develop artistic intentions in their learning. Such a curriculum should be made so that students may think about it, *recognize in it what they are learning, and take enjoyment in the learning precisely because the curriculum was invented to have students recognize and deepen the joy of learning—for no other reason.*[21] A corollary no less true for the teachers than for students follows: an undergraduate liberal arts curriculum that does not allow for current and future invention, for a joy of discovery and continued learning for teachers, as well as students, is a failure of invention used in this mimetic sense.

From the point of view of liberal education, a whole prospect of learning, which simply is not available in Aristotle's or Plato's political analyses, opens up because of the invention that is possible in art or imitation. This is worth thinking about. It should be possible for an education that was truly interested in a systematic organization of study and practice to make available a variety of relations of arts as a propaedeutic to an expansion into the social and physiobiological sciences. The core of such learning would be a study of invention, complemented by recognition, aka discovery, of what making makes possible. As we will indicate, below, the treatises of Aristotle which are concerned with discourse adumbrate such a course of learning.

The foregoing analysis of the *Poetics* implies that invention is embedded in forms of art and that plots, and also other parts of various arts, *qua constructions,* are the focus of invention aimed at

---

21   We are, here, stipulating the peculiar power of a liberal arts education.

cohesive emotional performance. Aristotle's famous catharsis of pity and fear by pity and fear is the primary case in point, but hardly the only one.[22] We have generalized the *Poetics* to inquire into the construction of liberal arts education or learning through invention, finding a joy in learning for the sake of learning in that kind of education. This is freedom not as a social or political regime, but as an activity of mind. But there's a tension, here, because while a curriculum must provide and a student must perform in a way that is liberal, that is, free, the arts are directed toward making particular outcomes, which might not be characterized as free. Let's first see this tension in an instance examined elsewhere in this book.

Bernard Shaw's *Pygmalion* comes to mind because the play points to two tensions in education between learning and freedom: (1) the education of Liza Doolittle, at least as Henry Higgins conceived and practiced it, may have been generous in its support and may have had certain moments of pride and joy for Liza in learning, but it was shaped by a hard task-master interested in advancing his profession and theories. It is perfectly conceivable for a so-called liberal education to be aimed at disciplinary advancement and to be unfree. (2) Higgins' conception of Liza's education is not Shaw's, and *her conception* of her own education rests upon her discovery of freedom, which while it incorporates

---

22   Aristotle thought that functioning of tragic imitation was largely reliant on the plot; that is, the plot, the chief imitative part, did most of the work by *synthesizing* itself and other parts into a whole. There were six: plot, character, thought, diction, music, and spectacle. Why six? Since a tragedy imitates through actors and musicians on stage [spectacle and music] that's two. Since it uses language [diction], that's one more. Finally, since tragedy imitates actions done by characters who think and feel, that's the final three: plot (or action), character (or traits, purposes, and choices), and thought (argument and feeling). A plot is composed of incidents, any one of which might nor or might be connected to the other. So, the plot not only employed character, thought, etc., but it employed its own incidents to construct a whole. As to the correspondence in liberal arts education to plot, see below.

acquisition of some baccalaureate skills in phonetics, hardly rests upon it.[23]

A liberal arts education cannot just aim at freedom; it has to have the construction that permits the achievement of freedom. Here again the *Poetics* provides in its examination of art three important considerations that could shape our thinking about liberal education: (1) What is the distinctive quality, or function, of works that should be found in it? (2) What are the objections to using such works and what are the answers? How should the works be approached or treated? And (3) what ties such works together and thus leads to freedom?

We may extract the function or distinctive qualities of works in such a curriculum by looking at Chapter 9 of the *Poetics* where Aristotle considers the function of a poet as imitator. Ultimately, the tragic artist aims at pity and fear because in pity our sense of human injury is weighed against our sense of justice.[24] And in fear our sense of injury and justice is cast into the future for someone for whom we come to care deeply about. For Aristotle, this was "philosophical":

> From what we have said it will be seen that the poet's function is to describe, not the thing that has happened, but a kind of thing that might happen, i.e. what is possible as being probable or necessary [within the art]... Hence poetry is something more philosophic and of graver import than history, since its statements are of the nature of [generalities or] universals, whereas those of history are singulars. By a universal statement I mean one as to what such a kind of man will probably or necessarily say or do—which is the aim of poetry... It is evident from the above that the poet must be more the poet of his stories or plots than his verses, inasmuch as he is a poet by virtue of the imitative element in his work,

---

23   See Chapters 4 and 5 for more on this play's insights to modern education.

24   Once tragedy and comedy are recognized as such, it is appropriate to speak of artists aiming at their particular functions.

and it is actions that he imitates. And if he should come to take a subject from actual history, he is nonetheless a poet for that; since some historic occurrences may very well be in the probable and possible order of things; and it is in that aspect of them that he is their poet. (9. 1451b4-6)

Tragedy, indeed all poetry, takes what we know or recognize— whether an old story (or myth) or an historical fact makes no difference—and turns it into something _new_, something _possible_ (9. 1451b27-33), giving to it a probability or necessity appropriate to the artistic perception we experience. Therefore, art was important to Aristotle, not because it "expressed" what the Greeks were to themselves; the Greeks already knew that and had figures like Pericles to tell them if they forgot. _Rather, the importance of artistic invention rested in its making of experience beyond Athens, or—even—the sweep of Greek history. The possible human experience a liberal arts curriculum makes for its students depends on the invention to which it leads._ Aristotle characterizes that invention at the end of his treatise.

Philosophically we come to the real arc and import of the _Poetics_ and its implications for liberal arts education in the treatment of selected works. The discussion of tragedy is framed by an analysis of the origins of poetry in the possibilities of art and in the reaction of critics to the products of artistry. Upon turning to the last part of his treatise, we find that Aristotle wrote the _Poetics_ not only to explain tragedy and comedy, but to protect art from critics—especially specialists—who would limit or bend invention to own their purposes. He writes: "It is to be remembered, too, that there is not the same kind of correctness in poetry as in politics, or indeed in any other art" (25. 1460b13). His rejection of poetry's fidelity to history is only a precursor to a more sweeping vision of the relation between poetry and criticism. The goodness of a work rests not in its subservience to political, religious, or scientific aims, but to its own ends: "Impossibilities … are justifiable, if they serve the end of poetry itself—if … they make the work or some portion of it more astounding" (25. 1460b23-27). An "error" in any art object may be useful, if the poet means to "describe [a thing] in some incorrect way…[so that] it serves the end of poetry itself." Objections by other disciplines about the product or the artistry are of little avail. This is even the case in moral questions, for in the *Poetics* Aristotle's interest in poetry is not whether an action or character conforms to a specific ethical or political system, or models or cultivates a specific character in the audience. Instead, he emphasizes what the "consider[ations]" are in answering whether "something said or done in a poem is morally right or not,"—*i.e.*, "intrinsic qualities of the actual word or deed," and the agent, the purpose, the patient, the means, the time, and the relation of these actions to greater or lesser goods or evils—and all of this is subject to the overriding question of whether they are "necessary and [a] use made of them" in the work. Put differently, in the *Poetics* Aristotle is not resisting ethical or political discussion, but he is resisting such discussion in terms of his own ethics and politics or anyone else's.[25] It is the poet's invention that matters.[26]

---

25   The *Poetics* answer to ethical criticism, thus, stands in sharp contrast to not only Plato's views, which politically subordinate art, but Aristotle's own treatment of art in his ethics and politics where imitation is, simply, an instrument of a regime or an aspect of intellectual virtues which have, at best, secondary importance to happiness.

26   Yet, if we take the *Poetics* seriously as a model for liberal education, then we will not conclude that it is urging attempts at 'marvels of execution' or the production of artists who are 'finished exponent(s)' of artistry as examples of the achievement of wisdom—two characterizations of artistry found in Aristotle's ethical treatises. These are ultimately hollow from a liberal education perspective, that is, from *the learning that may occur through art*. The *Poetics* can be applied to itself: whenever any art's execution, dictums, authority, assessment, or license constrains the freedom of arts and their practitioners—novice or expert—from learning and moving accordingly towards the ends of arts, previously discovered or not, then we have reached the politics or the disciplines of the arts, not the 'poetics' of arts. Ultimately, considered generally, the best means in artistry—liberal or poetic—are aimed at and exemplify poetic freedom. This is why those who would aim core text programs at an end other than the development of possibilities of human achievement are actually aiming at the subservience of the books and liberal education to another

The *Poetics* has served to challenge philosophers and politicians who in their systems and educational plans always tie art to the truth: "If the poet's description be criticized as not true... one may urge perhaps that the object ought to be as described—an answer like that of Sophocles, who said that he drew men as they ought to be ..." (33-35). In a society which had no constitutional concept of rights, the *Poetics was a treatise in defense of freedom*, especially of the emotions and artistic invention. In this the *Poetics* fits core text liberal arts programs—specifically of books and other objects of art separated from their authors and their times—*for these programs are less a study of the truth, than of the possibilities humans have invented and made for themselves.*

Consequences for a Curriculum that Takes a 'Poetic' Approach Seriously

I turn to our most important question: what ties a 'poetic' curriculum together? In other words, what corresponds to 'plot' in a liberal arts education? I have suggested that a liberal arts curriculum is and should be a work of art, composed of and focused upon other works of arts and sciences. Such a curriculum seeks to *differentiate* a wide variety of works precisely because in their completed state they would exemplify the range of freedom available to human beings and in their combinations would expand the possibilities of human freedom. Because core texts tend to be significant human achievements,[27] it is not difficult to work with students and a syllabus to explore the inventions that are constituted by such texts. One begins with "what's new here?", while allowing for innovation to include specific formal, that is, artistic, inventions. None of the other fascinations of these texts need to

---

end than its own development of free thought and making. Enjoyment, the pleasure proper to learning, is very much at stake, here.

27 For criteria for core texts, including that of being a significant human achievement, see Appendix 2, "The Concept of Core Texts: A Synopsis."

be foregone.[28] For example, when I first taught a commonly taken core text curriculum at a university, I approached it thematically as an education in civic and political life. However, after two years I began to recognize that from the beginning liberal arts and the works they examine have been inventive and transformative. So I urged new cohorts of students to examine *the same works I had previously taught* in their political implications *as inventions in the arts and sciences*. Included texts came from rhetoric, history, sacred texts, philosophy, tragedy, autobiography, political science, epics,

---

28   After this chapter was first published as an article, a couple of readers commented that what they missed were the 'plots' or more importantly the probabilities that would cohere texts together into possible curricula. Because I had addressed this issue in earlier publications, I only undertook to outline the more general problems of moving from a 'poetics' to a curriculum including the arts and sciences. The criticism was fair, so in this revised chapter and this volume's appendices I have referred to various curricula. Texts I taught at Temple University and Saint Mary's College of California concerned with inventions and innovations can be seen in chapter 7 and are alluded to, above. Science-and-humanities and liberal arts grants that became faculty seminar and curriculum development projects are also discussed in the Introduction and Chapter 7 and are exemplified in the appendices. Two "Tradition and Innovation" faculty and curriculum development grants (supported by Roosevelt Montás's generous efforts at Columbia, the Bradley and Teagle Foundations, and ACTC's Liberal Arts Institute) were taught by Kathy Eden, Columbia, Norma Thompson, Yale University, and Richard Strier, University of Chicago. Finally, use of trivium texts—ancient to modern—are discussed in the Introduction, Chapter 1, and in the appendix. These seminars were presented as a possible curriculum for any given institution, but none of the institutions involved, including the colleges and universities of the seminar leaders, had these seminars' particular curricula, and all the faculty participants produced curricula which were different than those offered at the seminars. For a different version of the poetics of curricular construction than is contained herein, see, Louise Cowan, "Set It Down with Gold on Lasting Pillars: The Fallacy of Misplaced Concreteness in the Undergraduate Curriculum," in *Tradition and Innovation*: Selected Plenary and Panel Papers from the Third Annual Conference of the Association for Core Texts and Courses." Ed. Scott Lee and Allen Speight. University Press of America, 1999, 17-26.

astronomy, biology, and poetry. As well as Western fare, there were excursions into Muslim and African cultures.[29]

The question "what's new, here?" entails both an examination of the current text and past ones. Correlatively, the texts of such inquiry not only extend into the more recent past as well as across cultural boundaries, but they could also be selected differently. Themes—literary, scientific, philosophic, historical, or political—entail what new constructions achieved. In other words, we are talking about a pluralism of curricula. In any event "likely curricula," analogous to the varying likelihoods of plots, can be developed, but with an important twist. Professors could (and sometimes should) steer students towards specific innovations, but the students themselves can construct what the inventive relations are between texts. They can act as artists of their own education building a capacity to recognize and appreciate innovations in almost any context. Because such innovations affect what we know, as we shall see, shortly, dialectic can be of great aid in this inquiry.

Thus in reply to our three questions above as to what permits the achievement of freedom or a joy in learning for its own sake, we may answer that a liberal arts curriculum which is *in its performance* the free activity of the mind (1) must involve works which provide substantial and multiple possibilities of human experience through the construction of the works themselves; (2) must involve works that are "answerable" to technical and moral questions in

---

29   There are three potential implications of Aristotle's release of art through invention from its immediate historical-political context. The trace of civilizations stems out of language and (mathematical) symbols. Western civilization becomes reinterpreted as an artistic or scientific phenomenon, constantly opening up future possibilities, while organizing communities. And, through recent advances in communication, heretofore 'unthought' future civilizations—intermixtures of present arts and sciences from historically separated cultures—are being constructed, today. None of this negates a political or social concept of civilization, but it would bring into play, dialectically and rhetorically, these different constructs.

their own terms; and (3) must, ultimately, be bound together in a curriculum through a pluralistic exploration of invention per se, with each work seen as an inventive contribution in its own right while yet arguably related to prior and later works, such that students may recognize and appreciate innovations across the arts and sciences, time, and globe.

Readers will have seen that while we have used poetic works to exemplify invention, we have simultaneously expanded the involvement of works to fields well beyond poetry. The end of the *Poetics*, its defense of poetry, is a kind of dialogue between scientific and ethical critics of poetry and Aristotle, who replies as a 'poetic' critic. Those replies are based on poetry as art, poetry on its own terms, without losing the sense that there really are better and worse constructions of artistic works.[30] Would it be possible to approach other works of the arts and sciences in the same spirit as the *Poetics* approaches poetry? And if we include not only mimetic, but historical, political, ethical, and scientific works, how would something like 'artistic' criticism be useful and appropriate for these other works?

The *Poetics'* approach to poetry and criticism suggests looking in Aristotle for other clues on how books—which are art objects whether primarily imitative or not—might be approached in an undergraduate liberal arts program. An immediate parallel is suggested for the sciences by Aristotle's opening to the *Parts of Animals*. Here, instead of imitations and poetry, the works being examined are scientific treatises and the persons doing the examination are of two types: the experts and the 'generally educated person.'[31] The latter is said to engage in criticism. Since the gen-

---

30   See the passages above on "correctness" and justification of "impossibilities."

31   While the word, "paideia" is invoked to describe the generally educated person, unlike the student in Aristotle's *Politics*, this person is not learning to judge noble actions, but is capable of judging argument. Chris Nelson, in the same conference as this paper was delivered at, invoked this passage and illustrated his judgment as a student concerning a paper by Einstein, Poldosky, and Rosen as suspiciously 'circular': "Curiosity and

erally educated person, while knowledgeable, does not have the epistemic motive or knowledge to subject a scientific treatise to an examination for truth, what kind of criticism is open to such a person?

> Every systematic science...seems to admit of two distinct kinds of proficiency; one of which may be properly called scientific knowledge of the subject, while the other is a kind of educational acquaintance with it. For the educated man should be able to able to judge correctly as to the goodness or badness of the method used by a professor in his exposition. To be educated is in fact to be able to do this...It is plain...that [for one] that inquires into nature there must be certain canons by reference to which a hearer shall be able to criticize the method of exposition quite independently of the question whether the statements made be true or false. Ought we, for instance, ...to begin by discussing each separate species ... taking each kind independently of the rest, or ought we rather to deal first with the attributes they have in common in virtue of some common element of their nature, and proceed from this as a basis for the consideration of them separately.[32]

What has happened in this passage is that the tendentious criticism, the criticism objecting to poetry found in the *Poetics*, has been replaced by an inquisitive, structural exploration of scientific

---

Conflict: Liberal Education Today," *in Back to the Core: Rethinking Core Texts in Liberal Arts & Sciences Education in Europe*. Eds. Emma Cohen de Lara and Hanke Drop. Washington DC, Vernon Press, 2017, p. 2

32   I have used "judge correctly" from Forster's translation in the Loeb series for Ogle's translation (639a1-15). In the opening remarks of the *Nicomachean Ethics*, Aristotle notes that the man of *paideia* would be "foolish to accept [persuasive] reasoning from a mathematician or to demand from a rhetorician scientific proofs" (I. iii, 1094b23-1095a). As the texts move from the most theoretical sciences to the most practical artistic works and the form and matter shift, what one looks for and the questions one asks as the generally educated person shift as well.

works. Aristotle still preserves the sense that there are a variety of approaches, but he also argues from the point of view of intelligibility, or exposition, there are better and worse ways to produce scientific inquiries. It must be said that Aristotle directs his criticism toward setting up his own exploration of the parts of animals, but it is equally clear that the same kind of inquiry can be used to explore the basis and developments of other sciences or philosophy or history, much as was done in the *Poetics* at the beginning with the arts.

If a liberal education is to make one free, it must so extend. In an undergraduate structural exploration of scientific works within a liberal arts education, the aim is not expertise. Rather, it is apprehending the ways in which scientific discoveries open our minds to ordered ways of thinking unachievable without such inquiries. This apprehension takes in more than books, though it begins with them. Publication of scientific inquiry (from Lucretius to Watson and Crick) is an essential part of both ancient and modern science, and examination of such works would bring observation, experiment, mathematics, and discovery into any liberal education, just as to examine poetry would bring with it language, performance and invention.

By increasing the variety of works we attend to in a liberal arts curriculum, we have increased the range of possible freedom and a joy in learning, but a liberal arts education could still face a choice between two kinds of freedom. One is the degraded sort of freedom in two varieties: (1) (a) the curriculum is a menu, a hodge-podge of courses which faculty and students 'choose' to offer and take, or, related to this (b) the curriculum is ordered to a variety of ('measurable') goals (or 'competencies'), which 'categorize' courses, often from many different disciplines within any given category, but which are, collectively, simply an unrelated 'heap.' Freedom here not only employs the sort of choice found in (a), but ostensibly adds a kind of 'freedom' of future usefulness for the non-academic world.[33] We are, thereby, back to making liberal

---

33   Often, particularly in areas serviced by the humanities but elsewhere

education secondary for the sake of other ends. (2) The other kind of freedom sees a curriculum as a work of art using the works of arts and sciences. This alternative seeks to find a cohesion among the arts and sciences which could *join their works in combinations* reminiscent of the development of artistic matter, objects, and manner we saw in the *Poetics*.

We have touched upon the prologue to cohesion—the dialogue of criticism of different kinds of work; now, enter the liberal arts of dialectic and rhetoric to tie disparate works together. Here, again, Aristotle's use of these arts is instructive for outlining a 'poetic' model of liberal arts education which would actually be free. Dialectic, as Aristotle conceived it and as we have seen illustrated in the *Poetics* and *Parts of Animals,* is a methodical way to inquire when, as any student in a liberal education finds, there is no one art, science, or single 'paradigm' to guide thought. In essence, this is what an array of works of the arts and sciences, ancient to modern, produces—a situation where students (and faculty) have to relate, pluralistically, disparate arts and sciences to each other.[34] Aristotle's enumeration of dialectic's uses in the *Topics* indicates generally four thrusts for reading in a core text program, all of which bring coherence and essentially characterize freedom, not as a political end, but as an *epistemic* end of learning:

> [1] The possession of a plan of inquiry will enable us more easily to argue about the subject proposed. [2] For purpose of casual encounters, it is useful because when we have counted

---

as well, these goals or competencies are rendered as 'skill sets' with only the vaguest of ties to the scope and potentials of the arts and sciences from which they were ultimately derived.

34   Reinhard Hütter's "University Education, the Unity of Knowledge—and (Natural) Theology: John Henry Newman's Provocative Vision," in *Nova et Vetera* 11, 4, 2014 and E. O. Wilson's *Consilience: The Unity of Knowledge,* First Vintage Edition, 1998, illustrate monisms of relating the arts and sciences, mostly by making their respective fields dominant, with implications for curricula conventionally thought to be well beyond their fields of expertise.

up the opinions held by most people, we shall meet them on their own ground... [3] For the study of the philosophical sciences it is useful... to detect more easily the truth and error ... [4] it has a further use in relation to the ultimate bases of the principles used in the several sciences... For dialectic is a process of criticism wherein lies the path to the principles of all inquiries. (Topics, I. 2. 100a 29-101b 4; my enumeration.)

The question of beginnings and origins is ever-present in Aristotle and often represents a 'transition' point between one set of problems and another and, thus, one portion of education and another. Aristotle begins the *Poetics* in a transition point between poetry and science, as well as art and nature. Rhythm and harmonics, in the form of meter, lead to a confusion between who is an imitator and who is a scientist, the former being exemplified by Homer, the latter by Empedocles, though both wrote in verse. Note that what is being studied are the texts of each. Rhythm and harmonics could become the object of study both physically and mathematically, the former in counting and arithmetic, the latter in proportions, where their use, again as means, in science might be made more explicit. They may, just as easily, be explored in their mutual relations: *e.g.* in Scott Buchanan's *Poetry and Mathematics*.[35]

A curriculum where the faculty and students are formally encouraged to explore these relations by developing a conversation employing dialectic in this fashion *is what freedom is in the liberal arts.* Such freedom is not freedom in terms of the state or of morality, *but of our institutions that are dedicated to learning to be free.* In other words, they educate students to argue well about

---

35   A recent dissertation at the University of Chicago used the *Poetics* as part of the dissertation's "larger project" of relating "our problems of and with teleology ... to various modes of numeracy..." in *The Science of Poetics and the Poetics of Science: Recovering Aristotle's Empirical Science in the Context of our Loss of Teleological Significances.* December 2018, p. 1. See also Chapter 7 on *The Education of Henry Adams* for a liberal arts approach to re-examining a discipline.

almost any subject, to understand others' points of views, to detect truth and error, but, ultimately, *to probe the very bases of what we claim to know.* Adjusted to core text programs, this *artful* idea of a conversation (or, really, multiple conversations) within a constructed curriculum is the way in which encounters across a broad spectrum of texts are achieved in a 'poetic' liberal arts program.[36] Further, there is nothing about such a procedure that would preclude discussion about inquiries with science faculty concerning scientific treatises and findings, or exclude experiments in the lab performed by students directly.[37]

36　The interdisciplinary seminar is often the way to engage in the habits (rarely, arts) of dialectical conversations that 'cohere' a curriculum. But these are frequently consigned to one side or the other of the art or sciences ledger. Two alternative models where these realms are 'bridged' can be found in R. P. McKeon, *On Knowing: The Natural Sciences*, University of Chicago Press, (cited in Chapter 7) and ACTC's "Bridging the Gap Between the Humanities and Sciences" project (of which the syllabi are in this book's appendix). Other means are clearly possible; for example, Wabash College once had a two-semester freshman sequence of core texts; the college also required a senior thesis defended against one faculty member from a student's department and one faculty member representing the college (or non-departmental-disciplinary views.) Students would go back and study their notes from the freshman sequence as the only feasible way to prepare for the 'college-wide' examiner. (Notes from interviews on campus during the research project on "Assessing Trends in the Liberal Arts Core" (cited in Chapter 7 and available through RESPONDEOBOOKS.COM.)) It is to be devoutly wished that dialectic as an art were taught in colleges to all students.

37　Thomas Kuhn's work on "Historical Structure of Scientific Discovery," cited in Chapter 3 is one of numerous discussable examples. Scientists interviewed during the "Assessing Trends in the Liberal Arts Core" project repeatedly stated "…that scientists teaching general education wanted to teach '<u>how</u> scientists think' and the 'problem solving method'." Statistically, this translated into a growth in the lab requirements in general education at institutions across the country between 1978 and 1998. The "Bridging the Gap Between the Humanities and Sciences," project took those statements by scientists seriously and had a number of experiments reaching into the 20th Century (see appendix). In terms of faculty cooperation between scientists and humanists, the

Criticism and dialectic allow for a learning about works and knowledge which may have serious implications for student intentions, but really are not 'about' them, except in the important sense that a liberal arts education would involve all students in invention and knowledge. But curricula do not just cohere materially or as reading programs; they have to join to student lives. Another liberal art, rhetoric, offers numerous opportunities for intentional, purposive and valuable inventive dialogues of various sorts: set speeches, debates, practice in writing communicative and clear prose, or attractive websites devoted to a given concern, probably with attendant social media. These kinds of rhetorical products go beyond simple formal acquisition of academic prose style. Within the context of a liberal arts education, they begin to teach students how to bring a liberal arts education to the public—for themselves and for the public.

To be human means to be free, to have acquired the means and accomplishments of *invention*—especially in the performative arts where cooperation with our fellow humans is a must and in the arts of discourse where reason and clarity are musts. Consequently, beyond those products mentioned above, the proper productions by students from an artful point of view are 1) conversation with fellow students and teachers, 2) the essay, 3) video and audio productions, 4) mathematical inquiries or demonstrations, 5) novel (but not necessarily cutting-edge) experiments, 6) 'field' descriptions of natural phenomena on earth or in 'heaven,' 7) pictorial,

---

discussions of both fields and the lab experiments in "Bridging the Gap" were integral to understanding. Moreover, the syllabi and experiments of the project were devised by a historian of science and philosopher from Notre Dame and St. John's College, respectively. Then the experiments were performed by the scientists from teams in the project, with humanists participating in the labs of the campuses on which seminar took place each year. In short, because it has been done, it is possible to have "liberal-arted" educational conversations about the relations to the sciences and humanities with labs. Chapter 7 discusses these projects' impact on general, liberal education in U.S. institutions See Chapter 3, where Hutchins describes uses of labs as leading to a 'great intellectual heritage.'.

sculpted, and model architectural constructions, 8) musical performance, 10) dance, 11) stage performance, 12) oral interpretations,
13) debates before an audience, 14) original translations, 15) poems,
16) stories, and 17) conversational defenses or explanations of one's
productions, and so forth.[38] Scholarly training is productive as well,
but the inventions listed above must have an audience other than
the teacher. If possible, they should be built into a curriculum of
exhibition and performance with discussion afterwards.

Aristotle defines rhetoric as an artful capacity to discover the
possible (or variable) means of persuasion on any given topic (I.
2. 1355b 26.) Rhetoric is a cultural art through which students
can be encouraged to discover the range of human possibilities
out of which particular student efforts might come to fruition. In
other words, the inventions suggested above are not about getting
a job, but *about the human enterprises* which students may embark
upon. Student production is the means by which students learn
the possibilities of where each of them 'fits.' At the same time
rhetoric provides teachers a means of relating student productions
to much wider human enterprises. Artistically, liberal arts faculty
have the responsibility to have a dialogue of discovery and invention amongst themselves and with their students, not about "how
students will get a job," but what realms of human endeavor, of
human enterprise, a student might enter once she or he leaves the
college. The purpose of such a dialogue, proximate to a course of
study, is that students may not only have the widest range possible
to judge from, but to *judge that they have a future* as individuals in
the vast common enterprises of humanity.[39]

---

38   This list is centered around the most imitative arts as they relate
to the *Poetics*, but as with experiments or field descriptions, so with the
extension to other arts and sciences. In an interview in "Assessing Trends
in the Liberal Arts Core," a professor spoke of once asking a student to
write a paper on what mathematics would be like if there were no imaginary numbers. Imagine the student explaining that paper in a public
address.

39   Failing to have this dialogue as a systematic concern of liberal education leaves defenders of liberal arts virtually inarticulate in public and

Thus, a liberal arts dialogue would synthesize three functions aimed at freedom or the joy of learning: meeting and *making* arguments or imitations on their own grounds, conducting inquiries into the relations and foundations of what we know, and forming judgments for the future, all of which would be in the service of learning the joys of human invention.[40]

Implications of Invention, Change, and Books upon the Argument on behalf of Liberal Arts Education

Criticism as well as defenses of liberal arts education and core text programs would do well to think about the *Poetics'* defenses of poetry in terms of the possibilities humans have made for themselves. Far too often, people have tried to defend liberal education and core texts by invoking political, economic or business, and social ends or advantages for them. Such arguments have been unsuccessful in part because they are not aimed at the liberal arts as its practitioners experience them. Political, economic, or business matters can obviously be taken up in a liberal curriculum, but they aren't its end. Those who speak to the humanity of liberal education are certainly on the right track, but through the *Poetics* and more wide-ranging discussions of arts and sciences, 'what it is to be human' takes on a much richer significance than we have indicated in our defenses of recent years. The joy in learning of the possibilities of invention are more central, often unexplored, and authentic reasons why people study and love the liberal arts.

To be engaged in the practice of arts and sciences is to explore the range and depth of humanity, not only in some Enduring

---

decidedly monochromatic in the vocation (calling) they model to students. In short, the absence of such a dialogue results in a liberal arts education that is less free.

40   Meeting imitations or disciplinary works on their own grounds *is* interdisciplinarity or transdisciplinarity when two or more works not of the same form or not of the same arts or sciences are considered at one time.

Questions to which all the arts attend, nor simply in the range of differences (real or imagined) in human beings, but in the growth and sensitivity of our perception, appreciation and emotion. We become more human precisely because we learn what the great adventure of humanity has accomplished and what its promises and possibilities, as well as dangers and horrors, are. We learn, in our conversation with others about the arts and sciences, what to fear, what to laugh at, what to pity, and how to hope. There is much joy, joy in learning, in all this.

Every art and science can be a source of joy in learning. Science, social science, the humanities, and fine arts disciplines all may involve a joy of learning. Joy in learning can be had in the lab, in programming, in survey research, in mathematical or economic modeling, in diversity studies, as well as in liberal arts core text programs. Additionally, most of these disciplines involves technologies, arts really, of invention for the sake of a future in any given endeavor. Yet only a liberal arts core text program which takes as its sweep the achievements of humanity *promises* as a condition of its education a technology of relating the arts and sciences, cultures and civilizations, and past and present to the future. That 'technology' is comprised of the arts of criticism, dialectic, rhetoric and, ultimately, invention. This book has explored what painting can accomplish as a liberal art. It has examined modern sciences' origins in the liberal arts and left plenty of room for experiment in the liberal arts. It has urged educational performance in many areas of human endeavor. All of these are inventions. Yet that said, the technology of invention is exemplified best, although not exclusively, by a culture of great books or core texts—that is, works of significant magnitude in achievement in all fields, eras, and cultures conjoined to the performative arts of discourse and imitation which make these works come alive. Is it any wonder, really, that liberal arts education's ultimate argument is that inventive freedom and joy in learning are one?

Books—whether of papyri, printed matter, electronic storage and transmission or holographic projection—are a technology of change—of innovation and discovery in knowledge, society, cultural productions and the personal lives of individuals. The book is both the way to examine the history of change and, in the form of a student work, performance, or project to make room for change in the future. Practitioners of liberal arts should extoll the book as a primary agent of change, for books are the best, most continuous, varied and wide-spread pattern of invention that we possess as the human species. When students add to that technology of change through their own inventions, they learn what it is to help make the adventure of humanity their own.

A program that traces invention back to its roots and yields a freedom of mind can extend far more widely than the limited consideration of the *Poetics,* and it doesn't have to be built on Aristotle's philosophy, but in an age where we are no longer persuasive to the public about the value of a liberal arts education and are perplexed as to why our enthusiasms are not shared by the public or prospective students, we would do well to think about the Aristotelian argument for freedom and invention that spans the arts and sciences. Thinking about imitation and art, we might discover that the appeal of liberal arts education is for a loving joy in inventive learning for its own sake, shared by a community which takes that as its greatest good.

APPENDICES

Turning Ourselves Towards the Public for the Sake of Liberal Arts Education

The following paper was delivered at the 2ⁿᵈ Peking-University of Wisconsin Workshop on Higher Education. It was entitled, "Reply to Daniel Kleinman's 'Sticking Up for Liberal Arts and Humanities Education: Governance, Leadership and Fiscal Crisis',"[1] which was a research policy paper in defense of humanities and liberal education in public education. I was asked to respond to this perfectly honorable and respectable paper.

I want to thank Adam Nelson and Shen Wenqin for inviting me to this distinguished international gathering of higher education administrators and scholars on the topic, "Liberal Education in Asia and America: Purposes, Practices, and Policies." Wang Chen, Nicholas Strohl, John Rudolph, and Daniel Kleinman have stressed in their papers that historical and current public discourse affects the perception and construction of liberal education. I think liberal education can be wonderful for women and men of this country, our institutions, and for citizens around the world. But I share Dean Kleinman's sense of crisis, and I have come to worry about and be critical of how our liberal education institutions relate to the public—the very source of both

---

1   Published in *A New Deal for the Humanities*, Eds. Gordon Hutner and Feisal D. Mohamed. Rutgers University Press, 2015, pp. 86-100.

their being and support. That worry is particularly focused on the humanities, which, while not the sole supplier of liberal education, still bear the weight of its traditions and the plurality of its provision. Between my research, review work, and association functions, I have developed into a kind of executive producer of liberal arts projects, and this affects my views of how to persuade the public that humanistic, liberal arts education is worth the candle.

In my response to Dr. Kleinman's well-argued paper, I will focus, first, on several problems in current defenses of liberal education, including the climate of persuasion for liberal education. Next, I'll propose some possible solutions to those problems which are designed to enrich the ecology of persuasion we possess and to bring humanistic, liberal arts education back into contact with the public. My remarks are confined to the North American continent, though I believe they might be salient elsewhere.

Let's begin with what we are asking for in public defenses of liberal education. Professor Kleinman means by the term 'liberal arts education' "a broad integrated education that includes coursework in the humanities, social sciences, and sciences."[2] While integration might take many forms, the most obvious is a bachelor-of-sciences or bachelor-of-arts degree; that is, if you achieve one of these degrees in a state university, then you will have taken courses in the three fields laid out in Dean Kleinman's defense, perhaps also including the fine arts.

The courses for the degrees we are talking about are overwhelmingly offered by departments which represent individual disciplines. The almost universal value within universities placed upon expertise and research insures that hiring and retention through tenure is along lines of specialization through peer-reviewed publication, not teaching. So, first and foremost, what Dr. Kleinman is asking for is a public defense of departments and disciplines as they are found in the modern university, which deliver most of the courses that undergraduate students of liberal education will take.

---

2   Ibid., note 1, p. 97.

In the current structure of universities, the integrated part of education, the possible home of a liberal arts education, is a function of the departmental, disciplinary framework. Broadly, we can say there are three standard sites for liberal arts education: general education, special programs, and electives. Francis Oakley, in Community of Learning: The American College and the Liberal Arts Tradition, cites a 1960's survey study in which professors from a wide range of departments and disciplines averred that a liberal arts education could be had simply by taking the major in their department.[3] I know of no historical arrangement of higher education that would have justified this idea. General education is the site of most undergraduate cross-disciplinary/cross-departmental integrative student work. There has been movement toward inter- and trans-disciplinary and inter- and trans-departmental course work in the past and now—Dean Kleinman's professorial title and publications, as well as the long-standing and famous Integrated Liberal Studies (ILS) program, here, at the University of Wisconsin testify to this movement. The actual number of available electives free to student choice outside the major or general education has probably shrunk since the 1960's in the bachelor's degree.[4]

What, then, is the terrain in general education for liberal education integration? Notwithstanding recent inventions within general education designed to satisfy missions, capacities, and goals of institutions through categories of course-taking that cross disciplinary and departmental lines, as Futao Huang has indicated, the basic structure of a distribution system dominates.[5]

---

3   Francis Oakley, The Community of Learning; The American College and the Liberal Arts Tradition. New York, Oxford Press, 1992, p. 62.

4   *Assessing Trends in the Liberal Arts Core: A Vision for the Future.* Director, George Lucas and Principal Investigator, J. Scott Lee DOE/FIPSE final report, 2002. Published on RESPONDEOBOOKS.COM.

5   "Transfers of the Liberal and General Education from the USA to East Asia: Case Studies of Japan, China, and Hong Kong. Available from the author upon request, Hiroshima University, LATIMES. COM (12/22, 2013) INSIDEHIGHERED.COM/VIEWS/2007/11/13/

Notwithstanding such devices as linked courses and learning communities, student mentors, and close advising—developed in the 1990s at such institutions as Ball State and IUPUI—recent research of a small base of institutional education leaders, particularly at "public colleges and universities," indicates that they think there is room for improvement through "guided pathways and proactive advising strategies. These are efforts to provide students with more structured postsecondary experiences, with more support."[6] When we add to this brew the pervasive use of adjuncts, particularly within state *or* private universities, *liberal arts integration through the bachelor's degree is mostly a student job.* Indeed, the ILS program, here, proves the rule by properly advertising itself as "a coherent program for students [which] offers an alternative to scattered electives." Somehow millions of students are supposed to understand and forge a personal, integrative educational experience out of the combination of diffuse coursework from general education requirements and a major. Regardless of major, it is this system that by-and-large is the 'boots on the ground' impression of integrative liberal education that most of our baccalaureate graduates take away from four years of college.[7]

I grant all the factual arguments Dr. Kleinman brings forward

---

FUTURE-CONTINGENT-FACULTY-MOVEMENT;   WEB.KITSAPSUN.COM/ARCHIVE/1999/04-17/0002_THOMAS_SOWELL__GET_SAVVY_ABOUT_PI.HTML; INSIDEHIGHERED.COM/NEWS/2008/11/06/ADJUNCTS

6   HTTP://WWW.SR.ITHAKA.ORG/PUBLICATIONS/HIGHER-ED-INSIGHTS-RESULTS-OF-THE-FALL-2015-SURVEY/; While we know that public institutions such as the University of Wisconsin, Madison, have six-year graduation rates at or above 82%, we also know that some public universities have graduation rates in the 50% range or less. Meiklejohn's Experimental College, which had a common great books reading syllabus but employed the tutorial system, was, after the 19th Century, perhaps the first of what would today be called a 'learning community.' As noted above, learning communities have had retention success at state schools.

7   I searched for but could find no research on student satisfaction with general education. That most attrition of students happens in the first two years of the baccalaureate is probably an ambiguous indicator of student satisfactions.

about the employability of university liberal education students, and I grant that his defense indirectly addresses cost issues. Still I think this defense is very hard to make. The system being defended as a research effort excels, *but as a liberal education effort the educational system is one which very few can appreciate, even after they have gone through it to graduation.* I am arguing rhetorically; every single proposition I have enunciated is general, common knowledge to those of us who labor in the field of higher education and much of the tuition-paying public has had experience with the instantiations of these propositions. In our appeals for public support, if we are not blinded by our own defenses to the weaknesses of this system as a liberal *education* effort, then I'll simply proceed to note that under this system small, even well-known, private liberal arts colleges are suffering.[8]

I do not wish to argue against Dr. Kleinman's efforts to make liberal education degree holders seem more employable, any more than I wish to argue against those who tie the importance of liberal education to the preservation of democracy.[9] These two kinds of appeal are part of the ecology of defenses of liberal education fully on display at this conference. Yet, I think that ecology of defense is not as robust as it could be, and—when economic or democratic—runs into a host of competing career paths and institutions that offer similar claims of value. But there is even a larger problem in the defenses we currently employ. Our current job is not merely to persuade the public of the efficacy of liberal education, but to persuade the public that persuasion about liberal education matters at all.

---

8   On the shrinkage of colleges, migration of students to liberal education honors programs in universities, and the inhospitality of universities to such programs, see Bruce Kimball, "Revising the Declension Narrative: Liberal Arts Colleges, Universities, and Honors Programs, 1870's-2010's," Harvard Educational Review, 84, 2, 2014.

9   See the discussion of a range of political, civic, or character defenses of liberal education by T. Kronman, P. Deneen, M. Nussbaum and A. Delbanco in Chapter 7 For a brief look at economic defenses, see the Introduction.

To begin to see the problem, let's first keep Dr. Kleinman's argument, whole, intact, and simply do the cutting necessary for public circulation. Next, let's strip out all the citations; we know he's done the work, so let's not quibble about the scholar's need for reference. Next, let's take this piece to a non-academic venue for publishing; it is clearly written and could pass muster for popular publication. It is, after all, a kind of explanation that the public might conceivably read as a defense.

What might be its reception outside of the academic venue we see it in? It is strategic and political as Dr. Kleinman indicates, so its hook is that conservative governors who undercut support for liberal education are not thinking clearly. In contradistinction, liberal education is adduced as instrumental to prominent entertainment and business leaders' success, and data from AAC&U supports the idea of employability and growing income of liberal arts graduates. So, it appeals to the aspirations and utilitarian bent of the public. Maybe the article would be published in a blog or in a cultural magazine, possibly the *New Republic*, or maybe the education section of the *New York Times*; maybe it will have a reduced afterlife as its main arguments make their way to other media outlets. Videoed, it is not likely to go viral, through no fault of Dr. Kleinman, I might add.

So let's moderate our aspirations. By itself, will his or any similar article change any public opinion at all about liberal education? With due respect, I would say, no, again through no fault of the author or argument. To generalize, *any such article* by any such academic will not change public opinion, because even if it is turned toward the public, it would be found to be a voice crying in the wilderness—not exactly alone but with only a small band of similar voices joining in. There is simply no climate for a liberal education defense.

Again, the fault for the muffled sound of Dr. Kleinman's voice is not his, but lies in us—mostly in we humanists who have largely forgotten the audiences and venues in which we had our first origins and were found to be most effective in spreading our form of education. To see the point, let's ask a question that captures in a current way the problem of our own forgetfulness. In the public mind, what, after all, do humanists and liberal artists do? Scientists discover, measure, predict and prescribe. Biologists and geophysicists are concerned with global warming. Chemists produce drugs and petroleum products. Technologists, those artistic inheritors of Bacon's dictum, produce bridges, micro-chips, computers and smart phones. Social scientists, as economists, advise on economic policy and fortunes, or conduct polls or surveys. Even if you share [Wisconsin] Governor Scott's view of anthropologists, as a member of the public you have a vague idea that anthropologists comparatively examine Western and non-modern/non-Western societies, and you know that social workers take care of elderly, the indigent and unfortunate, and the abused. I readily admit that these are popular, though not erroneous, conceptions and do not admit of the sophistication or the extent of research exhibited by scholars at this conference, but they are images that the popular imagination grasps and is right in doing so.

Let's allow that the public thinks liberal artists and humanists 'read and write books' or even 'talk about art and culture,' including questions of identity. Here, because of the differences in career tracking between scientists and humanists, we must begin with baccalaureate graduates. The very versatility of humanities and liberal arts graduates, which Professor Kleinman indicated, works against specific public images of humanists, except for the gross lampoons of humanities professors circulated in the press. Successful business leaders and entertainers are known by their professions, not their undergraduate educations. Public images of humanist liberal education products and activities, unlike the disciplines I indicated above, are scant and not well connected to universities. There are, of course, humanists in the public media, particularly those who write for the arts, politics, and social questions. Such fora are a vastly underused, essential component of a revived respect and admiration for humanistic liberal arts education, but right now media critics have little practical connection to universities or colleges. What's been breaking and broken are the links between what humanists do, our institutions, and the public.

What's been substituted increasingly for a public is *ourselves*; that's who we write and talk to. Unlike our colleagues of other parts of the university, generally speaking, we humanists do not really export our products and so, not surprisingly, few are listening.[10] Moreover, we will certainly teach our students to write and communicate as if they were nascent academics, but more publicly oriented education in writing is not assured.[11]

So, what could the system I outlined above do to change this situation?

When does the public visit universities and college campuses

---

10   Of course, exceptions can always be cited. Note the discussion on philosophical questions and authors that The Stone gets from a wide, public and academic, readership: HTTP://WWW.NYTIMES.COM/ TIMES-INSIDER/2014/07/22/PHILOSOPHY-WITH-A-NEWSIER-EDGE/ But even articles that are noteworthy for the public response they garner are getting between 600 and 1,300 comments, still a small circle of interest.

In February of 2014 Nicolas Kristof got an earful when he bewailed the absence of academics writing for a broad audience. Claire Porter wrote a note to Kristof in CHE, "A Letter from a Public Intellectual" 2/18/2014. She argues not only are there many academics writing blogs for the public, but that 'every time we enter the classroom we engage a broader audience,' that this is especially true at public universities, and that such education is "a contribution to the public good." I agree. However, what is not clear is that there is really any coordinated or pervasive effort, using the resources of social and, even, commercial media to attract the public to the humanities in universities as sources of knowledge, or to develop in the public 'liberal-arted' capacities though which the public could continue to investigate on their own. One consortium of institutions, Imagining America whose focus is largely public issues, seems to have good intentions and broad plans, but inconsistent results.

11   Generally, in my own teaching, I found that when students wrote 'practically,' to write a business report or to write a speech to persuade me to do something, their writing improved markedly. In the former case, they were being asked to learn a series of technical writing products, beginning with how to write a memo. In the latter case, they tended to know the subject, so they could concentrate on crafting an appeal. Sometimes in doing so the they discovered an appeal that they had not thought of previously.

to meet humanists or liberal artists? If there is a controversial ethical or political question, that might draw a crowd. But otherwise, public attendance will be sparse. The question has two dimensions. One is communicative: Right now, the institutional fora which humanities faculty are involved in do not usually support extensive outreach to the public. The other is educational: during those rare moments when the public visits campus for a lecture by a humanist, there will be a train of argument leading to real and interesting insight; that is common enough and has its attractions. But how often does a humanist say, in effect, "we think this way because..."? *This question is crucial* and distinguishes a humanist's answer from the way a scientist will, perforce, answer. The vast majority of the objects of humanistic inquiry are within the range of direct human experience, mediated, usually, by linguistic expressions or direct physical perceptions. I am not indicating that such things as particular languages or cultures do not inform perception. I am saying that much humanistic work is done through linguistic devices and their artistic perceptual equivalents—such as choreography, theatrical staging, church rituals, musical production, and visual arts—that distinguish and make available objects of study found commonly enough in cultures. Consequently, mostly, what humanists are dealing with are those objects which rely on the inventions of language or arts designed to use the body, not the inventions of laboratories or survey workshops. When the public uses a library, tours a museum, listens to a concert, attends a church service, goes to the theatre, attends a political rally or even a sporting event, it is far closer to the objects of humanistic inquiry, in some cases more involved in potential liberal education, than a citizen using a cell phone is to electronic engineering.

There is a persuasive opportunity in this close tie to human experience for anyone interested in humanistic liberal education; the public can learn to be humanists in ways usually unavailable for learning to be a scientist.[12] For the humanities make available to the public the inherited objects of civilizational accomplishment

---

12   There are exceptions to this: most notably math and astronomy.

in the arts and sciences for the purpose of knowing what the world has made possible and the future might offer. The question before all who value liberal arts education is whether we will take the institutional potentials of universities to make that education not only formally available, but publicly accessible.

We are gathered at a meeting on policy and liberal education. The National Alliance for the Humanities and the Federation of State Humanities Councils are taking a turn for the better, I think, in developing a nascent policy of institutional engagement that emphasizes public outreach rather than a straight-up legislative lobbying effort. Next November (2016), they will hold the first of three planned conferences on "how...the humanities can achieve broader public impact and showcase the fundamental role the humanities play in addressing both local and global challenges." This call is a step in the right direction, for the conference is set to consider such practical questions as:

- How can scholars, at all stages of their career, engage with public-facing institutions to enhance their scholarship and their public engagement?
- How can humanities organizations connect with organizations and individuals outside of the humanities community—including civic actors and public or private institutions—to strengthen the impact of their work?
- What does the scholarship of public engagement look like today?

Let's briefly think about one public instance of why these questions are so necessary. I am intrigued by programs that have cropped up in institutions of my core text association which are clearly reaching out to teachers in an effort to shape their practices and to students in an effort to recruit the children of parents. These programs, which are newly developed, show promising contact with a public that was simply, heretofore, divorced from university life prior to this. There is such an outreach program here at Wisconsin.

Building public-facing institutions is becoming part of a

conscientious effort by universities to change the tide of public opinion. And, of course, what these programs are about is teaching the wider public how to think like a humanist. The University of Chicago stands as an example of how institutional links to the public are being built. The University used to tout itself as a theoretical institution. This continued well beyond Hutchins tenure into the 1980's. Then, beginning in the late nineties up through the present, the University began to build institutions, largely self-supporting through revenue streams or contributions, which explicitly reach out to the public. The Francis Kinahan theatre was the first; former Presidential advisor, David Axelrod's, Institute of Politics, which streams its guest speakers, the second; and the "The Logan Center [which] presents concerts, exhibitions, performances, programs... from world class, emerging, local, and student artists" was the third.[13] This last institution intrigues me the most because it represents possible integrations of disciplines and fields of knowledge and productions. As a Chicago musicologist recently said to me, "The question of whether this will work is open," but, then, do we who are devoted to liberal arts, humanistic education really have any choice but to build such institutions—well-endowed or not?

Ultimately, there is one inexpensive way to reach the public and the Alliance for the Humanities is beginning to recognize this—public scholarship. Let's be very blunt about this: unless departments and disciplines will reward faculty members with tenure for public scholarship, there will be no influence by the humanities and liberal educators upon the public.[14] The presidents of universities who are willing to speak up for the humanities are simply way too insufficient in their numbers and, besides, they

---

13 HTTPS://ARTS.UCHICAGO.EDU/EXPLORE/
REVA-AND-DAVID-LOGAN-CENTER-ARTS

14 Legions of specialized publication, at least in literature, has failed to do so. Marc Bauerlein documents an increase from 1,139 to 4,686 scholar journals *in literary studies alone* recognized by the MLA (the universe is, therefore, larger) in a 50+ year span from 1959 to 2012. Literary Research: Costs and Impacts. P. 3. It is very doubtful that public literary production increased anywhere near as much.

have to speak up for dentistry & medicine, technology development, entrepreneurial studies, and so forth. No, the only ones who can change the public perception and conversation about liberal education are liberal educators themselves.

There are examples of public scholarship which can be studied diligently by aspiring graduate students and assistant professors so long as these studies are rewarded by departments and disciplines. A study it really is. A program in Stony Brook University's College of Arts and Sciences has "developed a program that [is] part of a growing movement to train academics of all stripes to speak to a broader constituency without any 'dumbing down' of their arguments."[15] At a recent Columbia University meeting, whose general subject was about conveying the substance and ideals of liberal education to the public, a law professor who has come to deal with public explanations of Columbia's education remarked, "you spend years developing all these distinctions and sub-arguments and your job is to capture in a short article for the public, in a sentence, the very essence of years of thought and research—that's really hard."

A relatively recent example of public scholarship is a 2014 article in the *New Republic* by Helen Vendler.[16] She argues that the recent digitalization of Emily Dickenson manuscripts has revealed that "perhaps, for Dickinson, the principal unit of thought in poetic composition was sometimes not the stanza, not even the line, but the individual word." She makes clear the intellectual, emotive and formal advantages, and the increased precision in vocabulary and perception of such an education in artistic making. Could our students learn from this and produce something similar?

Advertised performance before a public composed of parents,

---

15   Chronicle of Higher Education, February 17, 2016. "Should Academics Talk to Katie Couric?"

16   Helen Vendler, "Vision and Revision: How Emily Dickinson Actually Wrote Her Poems." New Republic, March 24, 2014, p. 48. For a skeptical view on the value of the digital collection, see Angie Mlinko, "Infamy or Urn?" The Nation, Jan. 27, 2014, 31-32. For a fuller discussion of Vendler and two other authors doing public scholarship, see Chapter 1.

citizens, and employers matters. The proper production by students from the humanistic, liberal education point of view is conversation with fellow students and teachers, public performances and public conversational defenses or explanations of one's work.[17] The conversations with students is the collegial "run-up" to production; performances or exhibits are the work itself; and explaining it to a public outside the university is power. Such performances are the liberal arts equivalent of mounting an experiment in the lab or field, or designing a survey questionnaire and the survey's implementation, as well. Just as important: undergraduate students—whose career advancement does not depend on doing research in one small area of a discipline—are more likely to employ their sense of an 'integrated liberal education' if they are given a chance. They are more likely to speak well about their education, research and experience across arts, sciences, and disciplines than most professors who feel, for good reasons, that they should speak to a public only on a topic within their expertise.

In this view, liberal arts education, then, becomes something akin to the open university—by, of, and for the public. We humanistic liberal artists have to reconstruct our rewards. This means in tenure reviews crediting publication for the public as much, perhaps more, than publication in a professional journal or a narrowly specialized book. We have to serve the public, not by simply relying on expertise which will always inform what we do, but by a persuasion that will encourage others to join us in the inquiries of liberal education, on campus, in public venues, or in our homes. We should ask students to join us in this endeavor. They will be very willing. We need a flood of public scholarship, and if we get it, Dean Kleinman's article will be heard because the public will hear the chorus amplifying his voice and begin to care about the fate of liberal education. Let us hope and urge that as we turn

---

17   One wonders when liberal arts institutions will coalesce to offer a "College Facebook or YouTube" of thousands of searchable, selected public performances and explanations of work by their enrolled and graduated students. Colleges clearly have the rights to such performances as they can be found on YouTube, now, but are simply drops in the bucket of billions of videos.

to persuading the public with the support of academic consortia, foundations, and public agencies, we also spend time in our public addresses to indicate how and why arts liberal education might be practiced as an intellectual, public pursuit so that our citizens will feel free to roam over poetry and mathematics, being and becoming, over history and current affairs with eagerness, grace and a sense of the interrelatedness of the world.

(Rev. Delivered at the 2nd Peking-University of Wisconsin Workshop on Higher Education, 5/2016.)

APPENDIX 2

The Concept of Core Texts

A Synopsis

The concepts of "core texts" and "core text liberal education" are theoretical developments of the North American phenomena of "great books" and "great books liberal education" popularized by Mortimer Adler, Robert Maynard Hutchins, Scott Buchanan and others in the middle of the 20th Century. On the one hand, "core" concepts are strongly related to works extending into the foundations of Western Civilization and the textual foundations of other major civilizations, as well. On the other hand, they connect local institutions' educational character to specific traditions and the wider intellectual, historical and artistic traditions on which undergraduate education is, often, based. Users of these terms vary in what is termed "core" relative to texts, education, and curricula, but for the most part they center their concerns on undergraduate liberal arts education as it has been institutionally practiced in the North America and is spreading to other parts of the world. This essay begins with a genealogy that explains the rise and educational focus of core text, liberal arts education. It, then, turns to what faculties and institutions might agree would be a "core text," if the qualities of such texts are accepted. Having established those qualities, the article moves, briefly, to practical implementations of core text, liberal education curricula in colleges and universities around the world.

The idea of "core texts" has its genealogy in three sources. The first is a tradition of written works or, even, artifacts which, having once been produced or published, descend from ancient to modern times, recognized as significant human achievements.

A second tradition stems from the fact that in the long run readers determine what texts are significant human achievements. In modernity, various publishers' lists of such works are sustained by a market readership seeking, presumably, the richness of experience that significant achievements provide. Traditionally, the widest readership—conceived not as a market but as those literate in the language of such texts—begins in ancient readers of Greek and Latin, as well as Hebrew and Aramaic. Later, vernacular texts of European languages derived from Greek and Latin both provided further texts for readers but also provided the languages into which Greek and Latin were translated. In the widest sense, then, the community of readers which determine significant human achievements is a historical civilization sharing common linguistic origins. "Western Civilization" as a linguistic continuation in which there are readers of texts makes sense, whatever political discontinuities may have distinguished the ancients from the early European period or the modern period of the "New" and "Old World" from the early European period. In this literary sense, not in a sense of imperialisms of various sorts, it seems very strange to say that Western readers could determine the significant achievements of Chinese or Indian or Islamic civilizations, or vice versa. On the other hand, the global marketplace is unquestionably making significant human achievements available across civilizational boundaries of readers, and the ancient uniting of Greco-Roman and Hebrew-Aramaic texts into one tradition of reading, as exemplified by Augustine, may prefigure a global reading community.

Equally likely, however, is that a third tradition of core texts, that of educational institutions, may provide a rich pluralism of future canons. Some early canons were matters of seemingly specialized or relatively narrow concern when compared to the apparent complexity of civilization: for example, in the areas of religion and rhetoric. But depending on the influence of the significant achievements of such seemingly narrower concerns upon the broader civilization or culture, 'specialized' canons become cultural exemplification and, therefore, matters of broad education. This appears to have been the case with both the Torah and, later, Christian Bible. It is speculated that Ezra came to Jerusalem and, using a Torah fashioned from four traditions of Jewish texts, read to the Jews this new text as a way to unite the newly liberated Jews.[1] Hundreds of years later, Paul (or more likely his disciple-student) writing to Timothy recognized the texts of the Jewish tradition as central to instruction about, as well as worship of, Christ.[2] And by A.D. 367, acting as a bishop, St. Athanasius and, then, later church councils seem not only to have pronounced authoritatively about the twenty-seven books of the New Testament, but to have captured the spirit of core text canonicity since we have the 4th Century Codex Vaticanus, which incorporated Ezra's reading to Jews and Timothy's commendation of sacred texts into the canon known today as the Bible.

Greek teachers of rhetoric used to collect speeches of orators and distribute them to their students, according to Aristotle, but he cited the distribution of these works as a block to the theoretical development of the art of rhetoric. However, later Cicero and other orators developed Roman rhetorical theory. They illustrated how the authors of Greek and Roman arts could be used to learn to become a consummate orator. While the concept and use of the Ten Attic Orators have been called into question as a canon, no one seems to call into question that a list of authors were employed in instruction by rhetoricians. Quintilian, evidently, used such authors' works within the only schools that existed, as distinct from private tutoring. Such instruction was deeply indebted to literary figures, especially Virgil and Homer.[3]

---

1   *The Oxford Annotated Bible with Apocryphal/Deuterocanonical Books*, edited by Bruce M. Metzger and Roland E. Murphy. New Revised Standard Version, New York, Oxford University Press, OT xxxii.

2   2 Timothy 15-16.

3   Gualtiero Calboli and William J. Dominik, "Introduction to the Roman *Suada*," in *Roman Eloquence: Rhetoric in Society and Literature*. New York, Routledge, 1997, 6-8; Quintilian, *Institutio Oratoria of*

The foregoing hints at the vast diversity in 'canon' that research into subjects and eras reveals. That said, it was probably Matthew Arnold who in the 19th Century expanded the notion of canon, through his senses of criticism and culture, to the civilizational sense of the term. Such an expansion needs a brief explanation.

As late as 532 CE Cassiodorus was recommending specific authors across the trivium and quadrivium and, thus, across pagan and religious literatures for monks and liberal arts schools. Cassiodorus's influence continued on through subsequent centuries.[4] But as (Western) Roman civilization broke apart, many texts were lost to the literary civilization that produced them. Scientific, mathematical, and philosophic works remaining in Eastern/Greek Constantinople migrated with Islamic/Arabic commentaries and translations around the southern Mediterranean into Al-Andulus (the Iberian Peninsula).[5] Latin/Roman literary and rhetorical works descended into private libraries in Western Europe. By 1215 at the University of Paris, while lectures continued across the liberal arts, discussions of grammar were theoretical and exemplary, with little attention to whole literary works, that is, to those significant human achievements.[6] We should bear in mind that readings

---

Quintilian, Tr. H. E. Butler, Cambridge, MA, Harvard University Press, 1953, IV, Book 10, i 76-87. Some scholarship argues that a canon did exist by the 2nd Century CE: A. E. Douglas, "Cicero, Quintilian and the Canon of Ten Attic Orators," *Mnemosyne,* Fourth Series, Vol. 9, Fasc. 1 (1956), 30-40.

4   Bruce A. Kimball. *The Liberal Arts Tradition: A Documentary History.* University Press of America, 2010, 70-75.

5   A useful summary of this transmission is provided by ENCYCLOPEDIA. COM/SCIENCE/ENCYCLOPEDIAS-ALMANACS-TRANSCRIPTS-AND-MAPS/ GREEK-TEXTS-ARE-TRANSLATED-ARABIC.

6   *University Records and Life in the Middle Ages.* Tr. Lynn Thorndyke. "Rules of the University of Paris, 1215," 28. For an example of textual treatment that slightly precedes the University of Paris, see *Medieval Grammar and Rhetoric: Language Arts and Literary Theory, AD 300-1475.* Eds. Rita Copeland and Ineke Sluiter. Oxford University Press, 2009, William of Conches, "From the Second Redaction of His *Commentary*

in any text were largely faculty enunciations of what would have been inaccessible texts for many students, even in the case of philosophical works upon which they concentrated. Still, universities rather quickly replaced direct encounters with original authors by adopting the use of *florilegia*, or textbook compilations of sayings, in instruction.[7] After the discoveries and collection of Roman Latin writers by Petrarch, 15th Century humanists encouraged the reading of whole works. Part of the encouragement was an appeal to ancient literary traditions, eschewing both the rhetorical focus upon judicial questions and the university traditions of concentrations on philosophy.[8, 9] Leonardo Bruni, in encouraging this new humanistic liberal education was not disposed toward learning much of the traditional sciences, and the introduction of modern science into curricula was opposed by church and university authorities well into the 17th Century. In consequence, new human achievements of great significance—Galileo's *Dialogues Concerning Two New Sciences* or Newton's *Principia*—simply were not core to 18th Century university institutional education, nor were works of art in vernacular languages widely read. Only between 1800 and 1813 did one of Great Britain's elite institutions, Oxford, begin to shape a degree to match some of the parts of the Western cultural inheritance, the *Literae Humaniores* or 'Greats' bachelor-of-arts degree, which combined math and physics with studies of ancient authors and rhetoric—all in Greek and Latin. Not until the end of

---

on Priscian's Institutiones: *Prologue and Beginning of the Commentary.*"

7   *A History of Reading in the West.* Edited by Guglielmo Cavallo and Roger Chartier. University of Massachusetts Press, Amherst, 2003, Jacqueline Hamesse, "The Scholastic Model of Reading," 111-113.

8   For example, see, HTTP://BRBL-ARCHIVE.LIBRARY.YALE.EDU/EXHIBITIONS/PETRARCH/ABOUT.HTML.

9   See, for example, Leonardo Bruni, "The Study of Literature" in *Humanist Educational Treatises.* Tr. Craig W. Kallendorf. Harvard University Press, 2008, esp. 53-55. The audience changed, as well, from young male student scholars to women or boys seeking private tutoring or elementary education.

the 19[10] Century did Shakespeare enter undergraduate education in Great Britain or the United States.[10]

Arnold—as a social critic writing from the home of an empire on which the sun never set, deeply conscious that the Greco-Roman and Hebraic-Christian traditions were at odds, yet, to his mind, compatible—opposed the mechanizing of life, the acquisition of power by the state, the 'dissidence of dissent,' the idea that industrialization was culture, and many political movements of his time. Arnold's philosophical stance, leaning on Bishop Wilson, was that culture was a "pursuit of perfection" that existed "to make reason and the will of God prevail'" as an "inward condition of the mind and spirit." He conceived of "culture [as] seeking ... *all* the voices of human experience which have been heard...of art, science, poetry, philosophy, history, as well as religion." [Arnold's italics.] In his social criticism, Arnold often referenced contemporary European authors and argued that culture involved "getting to know...the best that has been thought and said in the world." Yet, Arnold spoke as a product of an entire educational system which did not reflect its civilization's *collective* significant human achievements. Moreover, given that tutors and lecturers set the reading agenda at Oxford, the educational situation, at least at elite universities, was more akin to the flux of texts characterizing ancient Bibles or rhetorical studies than what were to become the Greats' curricular successors in America.

The literature on education widely credits World War I and

---

10   Comically, W. S. Gilbert portrays a view, shared by many theatrical critics of the time, that Shakespeare was rarely read and underappreciated because performance of drastically cut (and re-arranged) scripts were the only way the English public had come to any appreciation of him at all: "Unappreciated Shakespeare" at HTTP://WWW.GSARCHIVE.NET/GILBERT/SHORT_STORIES/SHAKESPEARE.HTM. Remarkably, in an otherwise comprehensive volume on *Shakespeare and the 19th Century*, edited by Gail Marshall (a professor at University of Leicester), Cambridge University Press, 2012, a discussion of Shakespeare's influence in Great Britain, America and Europe touches every art and cultural theme imaginable including criticism, but does not speak to Shakespeare and higher education.

the "war courses" at Columbia University for returning American academics to a re-consideration of a more unified undergraduate experience.[11] But the evidence suggests, in the figures of George Edward Woodbury, James Gutmann and John Erskine, that a dissatisfaction with the neglected role of the intellect within Anglo-American literature, religious controversies, and British Empire military disasters led these university professors to seek renewed liberal education before the war.[12] In other words, Erskine was following the path of social criticism through literature. But unlike Arnold, Erskine as a professor in conjunction with other colleagues was attempting to revive in translation, ultimately for all students at Columbia University, the older, literary tradition of a cultural education across the reach of history towards contemporaneity.

Mortimer Adler and Richard McKeon from Columbia, Robert Maynard Hutchins from Yale, Stringfellow Barr from the University of Virginia, and Scott Buchanan from Harvard coalesced, briefly, at the University of Chicago in 1936. By 1937, the latter two had moved to St. John's College where the first "Great Books" curriculum of required courses was founded. Eventually, Hutchins and, particularly, Adler became the shapers of the *Great Books of the Western World,* while McKeon remained at the University of Chicago and helped to fashion, particularly, the Humanities section of the General Education program of the University towards a liberal arts orientation. After moving to Annapolis, Barr remarked, "Where the Columbia and Chicago book lists leaned overwhelmingly toward the humanities, the St. John's freshmen read their Euclid, their Nicomachus, their Archimedes along with their Homer..."[13] And, in defending the

---

11　For example, see, Michael Nelson, ed., *Celebrating the Humanities: A Half-Century of the Search Course at Rhodes College.* Vanderbilt University Press, 1996, 5-6.

12　John Erskine, "The Moral Obligation To Be Intelligent." HTTP:// KEEVER.US/ERSKINE.HTML

13　The statement is true, but it appears to limit the reach of liberal arts

program against attacks for including the readings of Marx and Freud, Barr noted "...surely both St. Thomas and Freud are part of the intellectual tradition of the Occident."[14] In other words, the St. John's curriculum attempted to span the arts and sciences from the ancients to modernity.

While these three institutions were central to the development of great books and core text curricula, they were part of a larger cultural discussion in North America about liberal, general education, extending from the 30's to the mid-60's. Within that discussion, programs with a core text orientation arose independent of direct influence by Columbia, Chicago, or St. John's. Yale's Directed Studies, a track within a more diffuse general education program, and the University of Dallas' disciplinary Core Curriculum, arising out of the work of Louise and Donald Cowan, exemplify the range of invention of programs during this and later periods.[15]

The *Great Books* collection was prefaced by a volume entitled, *The Great Conversation: The Substance of a Liberal Education.* Hutchins opened the preface noting that "masterpieces of the tradition...were the books that had endured" but that "it is the task of every generation to reassess the tradition in which it lives, to discard what it cannot use, and to bring into context with the distant and intermediate past the most recent contributions to the

---

humanities courses within general education which treat scientific texts as epistemic subjects or problems. See Richard P. McKeon, *On Knowing: The Natural Sciences,* University of Chicago Press, 1994. This is a transcript of one quarter of a three quarter sequence treating one problem of knowledge in the sciences, social sciences, and humanities: motion. Large selections from Plato, Aristotle, Galileo, Newton, and Maxwell were used in the course. A similar course at the University of Chicago treated sequences of problems successively (e.g, being or existence), not subjects.

14   David W. Dunlap, "Stringfellow Barr, Educator, Dies: Pressed Study of 100 Great Books." *New York Times*, February 5, 1982.

15   For discussion of other institutions, see Chapter. 7

Great Conversation." [16] However, that admitted, Hutchins argued for the exclusion of 19th Century American authors who were not "indispensable to the comprehension of" the Great Conversation, as well as authors whose corpus of work, rather than an individual work, made a contribution to the conversation.

In 1994-1995, amidst the so-called "culture wars," the Association for Core Texts and Courses (ACTC) was formed by faculty and administrators who taught in various "great books," "great ideas," "intellectual heritage," and similarly named programs. The institutions mentioned above were invited to join the organizing conference, at Temple University, along with 20 other institutions. Mindful of the criticisms of earlier mid-twentieth century programs that they included only "dead white males" (itself a racist locution) and that many attendees' programs included texts from female, African-American, Native American, South American, and, occasionally, Islamic, Indian, and Chinese authors, the organizers drafted a statement of mission which involved a brief phrase describing 'core texts' and the role of faculty cooperation in determining these for any given institution: ACTC "brings together colleges and universities that promote the integrated and common study of world classics and other texts of major cultural significance. Members of ACTC advocate the growth of such programs in order to strengthen undergraduate education in the United States and Canada... ACTC is committed to the education of free citizens, equipped to conduct their public and private lives informed by the best that has been thought and expressed in Western and other traditions."[17] In sum, the organizers thought that it was the collective responsibility of faculty working in cooperation with each other to determine what were the core texts for their *institution's* students, and they aligned such programs with the idea of freedom. Centrally, the organizers of ACTC recognized

---

16   *The Great Books of the Western World.* Robert Maynard Hutchins, editor in chief. I. The Great Conversation: The Substance of a Liberal Education. Chicago: Encyclopedia Britannica, 1952, Preface, p. ix.

17   WWW.CORETEXTS.ORG/MISSION-AND-ORGANIZATION-STATEMENT

that conversations within and across institutions concerning what texts were core texts within cultural and institutional contexts were essential to the vibrancy of discussions about the arts and sciences, as well as the moral foundations of such programs.

The argument that the great books tradition could extend beyond Western civilization was accepted by Hutchins, except he thought that, at the time of publishing the original collection, there was insufficient expertise to warrant such an extension. At least nine academics, including Hutchins, Adler, Barr, Buchanan, and Erskine, made the selection of works, and 37 academic indexers warranted that there was something to talk about in the selected books in so far as they created the Syntopicon to locate discussable ideas.[18] In other words, when in 1952 Hutchins argued that there was insufficient expertise at the time to make a world collection of great books, he was speaking as the president of one of the world's premier research universities and was working with faculty educated by and working in more than a half-dozen colleges and universities.

Still, Wm. Theodore de Bary, at Columbia University, began to work in 1949 before the *Great Books* collection was published to expand the world classics read at Columbia. Subsequently, de Bary published source books on Asian classics—conceived as stretching from the Middle East to Japan—with some of the circle that Hutchins and Adler were working with, including Jacques Barzun and Mark Van Doren. Later, St. John's College Santa Fe faculty constructed their own masters program in Indian and Chinese classics. All of this was in place before the culture wars arose, and the response to the culture wars by the experience of faculty with Western and other major civilizations' works had effects upon the institutional programs and individual members of ACTC.

The conversations carried on at ACTC and in institutions

---

18   In addition to the "Preface" to and opening pages of the "Synopticon" of the *Great Books of the Western World*, see Tim Lacy, *The Dream of a Democratic Culture: Mortimer J. Adler and the Great Books Idea*. New York, Palgrave MacMillan, 2013, 50-51.

seem to have involved seven characteristics that mark the edu-cative function of core texts and, therefore, the courses in which they are read. It is possible to order the characteristics as a kind of "color wheel" of faculty and institutional emphasis. As one emphasizes the first four characteristics, one approaches core texts in their canonistic sense. As one emphasizes the latter three, one approaches the conversational and institutional sense of core texts. Using all seven approaches the emerging global sense of 'core texts as great books,' differentially instituted in colleges and universi-ties. It helps in illustrating these characteristics to use two texts from two different civilizational traditions, Plato's *Phaedrus* and Confucius' *Analects*:

1. Core texts are primary, original, and fundamental in the sense that they are the backbone of all subsequent scholarly pro-duction, often in many disciplines, or they represent a nearly complete re-orientation, a new opening of a field or a literature. The *Phaedrus* and the *Analects* are original, fundamental, and primary. As authors, Augustine, Shakespeare, Galileo, Newton, Descartes and, possibly, Freud, Virginia Woolf, and Toni Morrison would represent new openings or re-orientations in the West. Augustine and Chu Hsi both illustrate a new orientation of a tra-dition and how thoughtful conversation about earlier authors is essential to core text education. These conversations can be quite lengthy—the entire history of a civilization, perhaps constituting civilization through its art and science, and, thus, the texts tend to be time-tested. In approaching more modern texts, professors often think about which ones might be future classics to include in course reading.

2. Core texts as world classics address the intellect. In liberal education courses, they are directed toward neither immediate practical application nor the inexhaustible fecundity of the world. Such texts often have social, specialized, or artful application, and the Eastern tradition is very concerned with the relation of text to practice. However, core texts and particularly core text educa-tion involve the growth of the mind through the apprehension

of thought.[19] That is, core texts teach as much through what they require of minds, as they do in the content, concepts, or understandings we find in them. Ancient rhetoric's instrumentalism, in Plato's view, did have application; he just thought it could be turned to improve the minds of students through a kind of speculation. Confucius knew we should consider the *dao* and *li*, but he created questions and leaps of thought to enlarge our minds to see what *dao* and *li* involved.

Literature, history, religion, politics and science all make their own demands upon the human soul and expand its capacities even further. Aristotle remarks in his *Poetics* that poetry is more philosophic than history because poetry deals in the possible. The remark is apt to core text programs, as well. Collectively, core texts are an enormous intellectual resource for thinking about the possibilities that humans have made and can make for themselves. In this sense, core text programs do not rest in transmission of traditions, but aim the students, instead, toward the future. (In this volume, the argument has been made that core text programs most completely aim at the future when students are encouraged to produce works appropriate to a liberal arts education.)

3. Core texts are complete, not in the sense that they finish a subject, but in the sense that they present concepts and problems that become a focus of permanent disciplinary interests or cultural pre-occupations. "Education" in the *Phaedrus* and *Analects* is both a professional and cultural pre-occupation. Education is a permanent problem in human affairs; there never is one answer to what and how we should teach humans to learn or study. There are obviously other such concerns: What is it to be human? What is love or honor? What is science or art? What are discovery and invention? What is nature? What is divinity? What is the good life or the way to live? What are good human institutions or systems of

---

19   The idea of an address primarily to the intellect is well-discussed in Eva Brann's *Paradoxes of Education in a Republic*, 143. Aside from illustration by both the *Phaedrus* and the *Analects*, a core text's address to a student, as opposed to either subject or experts, is particularly well outlined, for the case of music, in Aristotle's *Politics*.

organizing society? What is knowledge? To have undertaken some educated thought on these questions is to match in studying and life the completeness offered by these texts.

4. From such questions it follows that core texts are accessible or inviting. A world classic is a text that can be read with intellectual and, possibly, moral improvement by anyone who has had an education equivalent to an entry student at a university. In its inventive capacity, a core text might well be said to inspire young students to greater things. One does not require special training or special talents to engage in the reading of core texts. In this sense, core texts are eminently democratic. This does not imply the words of a teacher are not valuable. Rather, a reasonably intelligent reader can begin thinking about these texts on his or her own.[20]

5. Core texts lead to the remote, but they are not remote. Obviously to go back in time or across seas to another epoch of human life through reading core texts is to be led to the remote. But for undergraduates most journeys start at home. For example, everyone knows that there are studying and learning, teachers and students, but professors or our students may never have thought

---

20   This doctrine had various formulations in the first of core text courses in the mold discussed in this paper: the Columbia University Contemporary Civilization (CC) and Literature/Humanities (Lit/Hum) courses. While detailed faculty scrutiny of the readings was the rule for establishing the texts of CC, the nature of the texts in relation to student and faculty were the focus of the extended development of Lit/Hum. Originally, in predecessor courses, the selected texts were thought to be appropriate to select students (effectively an honors reading list.) But by the time of the full adoption of the Lit/Hum sequence into the Core Curriculum of Columbia in 1937, the course was being offered to "unselected, and, so to speak, unprepared freshmen" "with books that a man must at some time read for the first time." Lit/Hum took its founding pedagogy from John Erskine's General Honors course: "In Erskine's plan, students would read and discuss each book rather than being introduced to it in lectures and through secondary sources." The reliance on discussions, not lectures, was a trademark of the CC course, at inception. Timothy P. Cross, *An Oasis of Order: The Core Curriculum at Columbia College,* University Publications, Columbia University, 1995, 13-17, 28-29; 32-33; 25; 13.

about education the way that either Plato or Confucius think about it. Moeover, the familiar invites an institution's faculty to bring very local circumstances into the wider considerations surrounding programs and textual selections. Secular and religious traditions of given institutions do inform faculty selections of core texts. The Aga Khan Humanities Program of the late 1990's was conscientiously aware that the geographic location of Silk Road implied that Central Asia was a crossroads of Eastern and Western cultures and its choice of texts reflected that intersection. The Chinese University of Hong Kong is conscientiously aware of what the *shuyan* means to it as an institution and to the concept of learning with core texts that this institution developed.[21] In 2016, Sacred Heart University instituted a core text program named The Catholic Intellectual Tradition.

6. A core text is a work that promotes institutional unity and identity among faculty and students. As part of a curriculum, particularly as part of a course that is offered to all, most, or many students of an institution in general education, core texts bridge the gaps between disciplines for they bring those inside and outside a discipline together to think about common human concerns that have preoccupied humanity since the mists of the past began to clear. Working together on common, core text curricula, faculty may break down disciplinary silos.

7. Finally, if a core text is taught commonly by an institution's faculty to all, or most, or many students, a core text is a text for students. A core text is there for the sake of students—not the subjects, disciplines, or professors—first and foremost. A use of Plato or Confucius precludes any notion that a core text for students cannot be difficult; in fact, they usually are. However, while these core texts certainly range toward theory (as speculation) or toward *dao*, Plato's *Phaedrus* begins in speeches about

---

21 "Tang Junyi and the Philosophy of 'General Education'." Wm. Theodore de Bary. *Confucian Tradition & Global Education.* The Chinese University Press, Hong Kong, and Columbia University Press, New York, 2007, 59.

love and Confucius' *Analects* begins with questions about pleasure and studying. Students know something about these. A core text's value is to invite the exercise of conversation *by students to students* on what the texts mean in relation to the world. Ultimately, they invite the friendship of teachers to encourage students to think through for themselves what the texts imply.[22]

The ultimate context for core texts is cooperating teachers. Core texts, however great the learning contained in them or imparted by them, cannot be part of formal education if places in the curriculum of institutions are not made for them. What makes core text curricula possible is the cooperative, good spirited work of collaboration and inquiry that professors from all disciplines bring to these programs. The question all faculty face is: "Can we work together on core text courses in each of our institutions to produce core text educations that cross from discipline to discipline, era to era, culture to culture, civilization to civilization out to the world of the 21ˢᵗ Century?" That is the educational choice that core texts, world classics, present institutions around the world.

Apparently, in China and Europe that question is being taken quite seriously. The Chinese Association for Suzhi Education meets annually, and in its inquiries into theoretical and programmatic development of *Suzhi*, General, and Liberal Education in China core texts and their curricula are a regular topic of discussion. Boya College at Sun Yat-sen University offers a degree composed of courses half of which come from Chinese traditions and half of which come from Western traditions. Recently, the first Conference on "Liberal Arts and Sciences Education and Core Texts in the European Context" convened at Amsterdam University College in 2015 with 120 participants from Europe and the U.S.[23] A second conference is scheduled at Winchester

---

22   Readers may wish to consult the list of questions by Hutchins to the editors of the *Great Books* about texts to be included. See Lacy, 50.

23   A carefully edited volume of proceedings has been published: *Back to the Core: Rethinking Core Texts in Liberal Arts and Sciences Education in*

University in 2017. Attendees from Europe, Asia, the Middle East, South and North America regularly attend ACTC annual conferences and populate many of ACTC's curriculum development workshops.

The concepts of 'core texts' and 'core text education' have had a theoretical and curricular development stretching back over two thousand years, grounded in the aspirations of liberal education. That development has proven to be both an insightful epistemic and educational corrective in colleges and universities to the fragmentation of knowledge and exclusive devotion to specialization. Its further advantage is that it encourages undergraduate students to think freely about what is at stake in arts, sciences and civilizations, as well as to imagine a future for local and global communities. Finally, it yields an appreciation of what individual human beings can achieve through thoughtful productions of books and other works of culture.

(Rev. Originally published, 2017 in the (online) European Encyclopedia of Educational Philosophy and Theory)

Europe. Eds. Emma Cohen de Lara and Hanke Drop. Vernon Press, 2017.

Syllabus for ACTC Summer Seminar

"Rejuvenating and Reinventing the Liberal Arts,"
July 8—July 19, 2019 at Carthage College

Benjamin DeSmidt, Professor Classics and Great Ideas, Carthage College and Joshua Parens, Dean of the Braniff Graduate School and Professor of Political Science, University of Dallas leading two sections of the seminar.

Kathleen Burk, Executive Director of the Association for Core Texts and Courses, project director.

J. Scott Lee, former Executive Director of the Association for Core Texts and Courses, writer of the grant, seminar organizer, and participant observer.

The seminar will be conducted in classrooms using seminar tables.

1. *Monday, July 8, Morning, 10:00–12:00*

Art and the Liberal Arts: the nature, scope and ground of arts:

> Plato, *Gorgias*, 447a-466a. *Republic*. VII.

Afternoon, 2:00–4:00

> Aristotle, *Physics* Bk. II, Chap. 1, 2, 8. *Nicomachean Ethics* Bk. VI, Chap. 1, 3-7. *Topics* Bk. 1 Chap. 1-2. *Rhetoric* I, 1-5 to 1360b17; II, 1-4, 12, 20; III. 13, 17, 19. *Poetics* 1. 1447b5-11.

2. Tuesday, July 9, Morning, 10:00-12:00

Building the *technē* of a liberal art: Rhetoric

> Cicero. *De Inventione*. Bk I i-iv. 1-20.

Afternoon, 2:00-4:00

Applying the *technē* of a liberal art to everyday life: the value and history of practical rhetoric and how the elements of the trivium work together to form a process of thought and expression.

> Cicero, *Pro Archia*
> Seneca, *Prefaces of Controversiae*. From, Books 1, 2, 3, 4, 7, 9, 10.

3. Wednesday, July 10, Morning 10:00-12:00

The identity and difference of arts and sciences: Logic

> Aristotle, *Categories* Chap. 1-5; Posterior Analytics I. 1-6; II. 1-2, 8 -11.
> Porphyry *Isagoge* (Porphyry: Introduction [whole = ca. 21pp.], Barnes ed., Clarendon Press, 2006).
> Boethius, *On Division* (In Cambridge Translations of Medieval Philosophical Texts, vol. 1, Kretzmann and Stump, eds., pp. 11-38).

Afternoon, 2:00-4:00

Distinctions in language: Grammar

> Plato. *Cratylus* 383a-399d, 423c-440e.
> Terentius Mauris. *De Litteras* (From *Medieval Grammar and Rhetoric: Language Arts and Literary Theory*: 300-1475, Rita Copeland and Ineke Sluiter eds. p. 73-75.)
> Aelius Donatus. *Ars Minor* and *Ars Major* (From *Medieval Grammar and Rhetoric*. p. 83-98.)
> Priscian. *Institutiones Grammaticae* and *Institutione De Nomine Promine Verbo* (From *Medieval Grammar and Rhetoric*. p. 167-189.)

4. Thursday, July 11, Morning 10:00-12:00

Extending the implications and boundaries of the liberal arts.

> Robert Kilwardby, "On the Nature of Logic" (From *Readings in Medieval Philosophy* [Oxford, 1996], pp. 694-706.)
> Alfarabi. *Introductory Letter* and *Five Aphorisms*. Translated by Terence Kleven Central College, Iowa. (unpublished manuscript).
> William Ockham. "Modal Consequences" (In *Cambridge Translations of Medieval Philosophical Texts*, vol. 1, Kretzmann and Stump, eds., pp. 312-336)

Afternoon: 2:00-4:00

Relating the liberal arts in a comprehensive education

> Hugh of St. Victor. *Didascalicon*. Preface, 1 Chap 1-4, 9, 11; II 1-2, 20, 28-30; III 3-5, 8-9 (Columbia, 1991).

5. Friday, July 12, Morning, 10:00-12:00

Expanding the world of thought: argument, practices, and reception

> Christine de Pizan. *The Book of the City of Ladies*. Rev. ed. Jeffrey Richarcs, trans. Chap 1-4 Persea Books, 1998.
> Leonardo Bruni. "The Student of Literature To Lady Battista Malatesta of Montefeltro," in *Humanist Educational Treatises*, trans. Craig W. Kallendorf (Cambridge, MA: Harvard University Press, 2008), 47-63.
> Martin Luther. "On Christian Liberty."

Afternoon: 1:00-4:30

Discussions by participants of their plans to use the seminar in course and curriculum development. Exploration of possible addition of seminar texts to core text courses. Five-minute presentations by individuals or teams.

— WEEKEND BREAK —

6. *Monday, July 15, Morning, 10:00-12:00*

Thinking anew about the limits of the Liberal Arts

> Leon Batista Alberti. *On Painting*. Penguin Books, 2004. (Whole and complete).
>
> Isadore of Seville. *Etymologie*. Book 2, xviii. In Copeland and Sluiter.
>
> Quintilian. *De Institutio Oratoria*. X.2, XI.10. Loeb, Harvard U. P.
>
> Botticelli. Five pictures of the *Adoration of the Magi*, concentrating on the del Lama ("Uffizi") commissioned altarpiece.

Afternoon, 2:00-4:00

A new tradition of constant innovation in the arts

> Francis Bacon. *The Advancement of Learning* II. 5-9. (Paul Dry Press, 2001).
>
> _____. *The Great Instauration* (From New Atlantis and the Great Instauration, Weinberger ed. [Croft Classics, 1980, 1989], pp. 1-32).
>
> _____. *New Organon, or True Directions Concerning the Interpretation of Nature*. Preface, I, aphorisms 1-74, 95-107, 109-110. Bk II 1-3. (Cambridge, 2000).

7. *Tuesday, July 16, Morning, 10:00-12:00*

Which are primary, liberal or mechanical arts?

> Rene Descartes. In *Philosophical Writings of Descartes*, vol. 1. "Rules for the Direction of the Mind (or "…Our Native Intelligence)." Rules 1-7, 10-12 (Cambridge, 1985), pp. 9-28, 34-51.
>
> _____. *Discourse on Method*. Parts 1-3. Kennington trans. (Focus, 2007), pp. 15-32.
>
> _____. *Geometry*. Opening pages.

Afternoon, 2:00–4:00

Traditions of liberal arts, revival and rejuvenation:

> John Quincy Adams. *Lectures on Rhetoric and Oratory.*
> Selections from vol 1. And 2. Cambridge, 1810.
> Thucydides, *Peloponnesian War,* Pericles' "Funeral Oration."
> Abraham Lincoln, "Gettysburg Address."
> W. E. B. Dubois, *The Souls of Black Folk.* Chapters IV, "Of the
> Meaning of Progress," and Chapter V, "Of the Wings of
> Atalanta."

8.   *Wednesday, July 17, Morning, 10:00–12:00*

Traditions of the liberal arts: revival and rejuvenation, continued:

> Emily Dickenson. [Selected poems.]
> Vendler, Helen. 2014. "Vision and Revision: How Emily
> Dickinson Actually Wrote Her Poems." *New Republic.* An
> emphasis on the 'word' as the basic unit of Dickenson's
> compositions.
> Virginia Woolf. "Letter to a Young Poet" and "A Room of
> One's Own."
> Martin Luther King. "Letter from Birmingham Jail."

Afternoon: 2:00–4:00

Language re-envisioned:

> Ferdinand Saussure. *General Course in Linguistics.* Chap. 1-4.

9.   *July 18, Thursday Morning, 10:00–12:00*

Extending the liberal arts in the 20th Century:

> Kenneth Burke. In *The Rhetorical Tradition.* Patricia Bizzell
> and Bruce Herzberg, eds. Selections from *A Grammar of
> Motives,* and *A Rhetoric of Motives.*
> Marshall McLuhan. *Media: The Extensions of Man.* Second
> edition. Part I. Introduction to Second Edition, Introduction,
> Chapters 1, 2, 3, 7. Part II, Chapters 8, 9, 11, 18, 24, 29, 31, 33.

Afternoon, 2:00–4:00

To bring or not to bring the liberal arts back into universities and colleges:

> Henry Adams. *The Education of Henry Adams.* Selected chapters relating HA's youthful stay in London to a decision to revamp the discipline of history through the use of the arts and grammar, in particular. Chapters: iv, x, xiii, xiv, xix, xxii, xxv, xxvii, xxviii, xxix, xxxi, xxxiii, xxxiv, xxxv
> Robert Maynard Hutchins. *The Higher Learning in America,* Chapters 2 & 3.
> Harry D. Gideonese. *The Higher Learning in a Democracy.*

Friday, July 19, Morning 10:00–12:00

To rejuvenate and reinvent the liberal arts in the university and college:

First hour:
> José Ortega y Gasset. *Mission of the University,* pp. 22-33, 60-66, 78-81

Second hour and afternoon 1:00–4:30 PM

Discussions by participants of their plans to use the seminar in course and curriculum development. Exploration of possible addition of seminar texts to core text courses. Ten-minute presentations by individuals or teams.

> Kathleen Burk: Brief presentation on ACTC's Qualitative Narrative Assessment project.

End Seminar

NEH/ACTC Seminar

"Bridging the Gap Between the Humanities and Sciences"

Year One

St. Johns College, Annapolis

"Motion and Natural Law in a Philosophical
and Political World"

Day 1: "Science, Wholeness, and Beauty: the Classical Mathematical Cosmos."

This session will introduce participants to the idea of the liberal arts, the ordering of knowledge, and the tensions between a purely rational analysis of the cosmos and the demands of observation. This section also brings to the fore the importance of aesthetic criteria in scientific understanding.

> **Morning:** Platonic Cosmology: Selection from Plato, *Republic*, Books VII 524a to 530 e. (Any edition is fine, Bloom's preferable; Plato on the ordering of the Liberal Arts); Plato, *Timaeus*, Kalkavage translation 27a-47e2; 53c-56e; 86b1-92c9.

> **Afternoon:** Mathematics as a Way to Truth: Euclid, *Elements*, Greenlion edition: Book I, Definitions, Common Notions, Propositions 1,4,5. Book V,

Definitions 1-13; enunciations of Props. 1-2; Book VI, Definitions, Prop. 1, 2, Book VII, Defs 1-5, 20 only.

Laboratory, 7:30 PM: A laboratory visit to a planetarium at St. John's will demonstrate the observed motions of the planets and the heavens.

Day 2: *"Saving the Phenomena": Making Rational Explanation Account for Appearances*

This session brings to the fore the problem of experience and its analysis. We open with Aristotle's opposition to the Platonic mode of treating experience in order to illustrate the way in which nature can also be approached through a qualitative "physical" analysis that gives primacy to sensory experience. The second session then illustrates the way Ptolemy's Hellenistic astronomical treatise represents a synthesis of the approaches of Plato, Euclid, and Aristotle to create an exact predictive mathematical model of the heavens. We see Ptolemy's attempt to take into account the claims of experience, Aristotle's physical assumptions about motion and rest, and the idealizing mathematical treatment of phenomena of Plato and Euclid.

> **Morning:** The Aristotelian approach to nature: Readings, all in McKeon edition: Aristotle, *Physics*, Book II. chps. 3-4 (194b16-196b 10); chp. 7, 8 (198a12-199b33); *De Caelo*, Book I, chps. 1-2 (268a 1-269b.18); Book II, chps. 13-14 (293a15-298a20); Book III chp. 2; (300a 20-301b35); Book IV, chp. 1 (307b 30-310a 15); *Metaphysics*, Book 12, chps. 7-9, (1072a20-1075a5).

> **Afternoon:** Integration: Ptolemy's system of the World: Readings, Ptolemy *Almagest*, opening discourse and Book I (as found in Crowe, 42-65); Selections from Book III, iii. We will work through the geometrical demonstration of the equivalence of the eccentric and epicycle-deferent systems to allow participants to see exactly how Ptolemy is using Euclid to generate a system

in which the exact observational "phenomena" can be saved.

Laboratory 8:30 PM: Leave St. John's for laboratory on naked eye astronomy in the evening. Back by 10:00. The crescent moon; Jupiter, the zodiac.

Utterly optional laboratory at 4:30 AM. This naked-eye observation may allow us to see Mercury precede Venus into the morning sky before sunrise. Mars also will be visible.

Day 3: "Cosmology, Theology and Poetry: Dante's Cosmos"
This day will be entirely devoted to Dante's *Divine Comedy* as a work of literature, theology, and scientific cosmology displaying the integration of these elements in the great epic of the high middle ages, illustrating how the cosmology of Aristotle, with some aspects of Ptolemaic astronomy, are used as a framework for developing this great medieval epic.

> **Morning:** *Inferno* Cantos 1-2, 34; *Purgatorio* Canto 1; *Paradiso* Cantos 1-6 (Allen Mandelbaum trans.)
>
> **Afternoon:** *Paradiso* Cantos 10, 13, 18-20, 21, 27, 30-33.

Day 4: "Transforming Natural Philosophy I: Reordering the Heavens"
This section focuses on the conceptual restructuring of the heavens by Copernicanism and the wider implications of these changes for literary thought and theology.

> **Morning:** readings in Copernicus, *On the Revolutions of the Heavenly Spheres*; read all as found in Crowe anthology: 100-133. Possible supplementary reading: Book III, Chapter 15: Copernicus' equivalency proofs.
>
> **Afternoon:** Readings of selections from Galileo, *Starry Messenger* (as found in Crowe anthology) and *Dialogues on the Two Chief World Systems* (Short handout to be

distributed at seminar); Galileo "Letter to Castelli" (a short version of Letter to the Grand Duchess on science and theology, to be handed out at the seminar).

Day 5: "Transforming Natural Philosophy II: Ratio and the New Science of Motion."

This unit will analyze Galileo's novel ways of relating demonstrative mathematics and natural phenomena in his final work. It will also be intended to show the complexity of his new "experimental" discourse. At issue will be the following questions: "What does it mean for nature to be lawful?" "What does it mean for experiment to be necessarily approximate but nevertheless to 'prove' a law of nature?" "What is the exact relationship between rational construct and natural phenomena?"

> **Morning:** Galileo, Two New Sciences: from the introduction, pp. xvii-xxi; pp. 5-8, "Letter to the Reader" and "Letter of the Publisher," First Day, pp. 61-69; 79-88; Opening discussion from "Third Day."

> **Afternoon:** Galileo, Two New Sciences; Third Day, "On Local Motion"; "Opening Discussion" and Definitions and Axioms. Read just enunciation of Propostions 1-6 on "Uniform Motion" and the section on "On Naturally Accelerated Motion," through Proposition II, Theorem II (pp. 153-67); Fourth Day, just pp. 232-34.

Laboratory 4:00 PM: A laboratory on the Inclined Plane and Pendulum will be used to illustrate the complex ways in which rational construct and experience interact in this simple experiment from physics. (This accompanies the reading of Galileo).

Day 6: *"Transforming Natural Philosophy III: The World as a Rationally Mastered Machine"*

This Session is devoted to the larger conceptual revisions of natural philosophy taking place in the early modern period that attempt to synthesize the piecemeal transformations in cosmology, mechanics, and philosophy. In this we will see the explicit development of modern notions of "laws of nature" as distinguished from the Stoic-Medieval conception of "natural law." The session will also explore the new ways of conceiving the relation of the world to divine action. This session will again raise in a new way the complex interaction of rational constructs and empirical experience.

> **Morning:** read Descartes, *Discourse on Method* (Cottingham edition) (pp. 109-151); selections from *The World* (*Le Monde*) (pp. 81-98)

> **Afternoon:** Descartes, "Author's Letter" to the *Principles of Philosophy* and selections from Part II (pp. 223-247), IV (pp. 267-292) of the *Principles*; Selection from *Treatise on Man* (pp.99-108).

Day 7: *Mastering the Political World*

This session explores the ways the new science of Galileo and Descartes provides a framework for a reconceptualization of a new "science of politics" in the work of Thomas Hobbes.

> **Morning:** read Hobbes, selections from Man and Citizen (Hackett Publishing), "Author's Preface,"; "Liberty" chps. 1-3; "Dominion" chp. 7, 12; "Religion" chp. 15 (illustrating connection of the natural philosophy and political theory).

> **Afternoon:** Reading: "Newton's Philosophy of Nature":

This session introduces, selectively, the powerful synthesis by Isaac Newton of the various strands of natural philosophy previously encountered in readings from Copernicus, Galileo, and Descartes into a comprehensive solution to the issues of celestial mechanics. With this, we will have reached the culmination of the first great break in scientific thought away from classical scientific reasoning. This session will also be concerned to illustrate the ways in which this Newtonian synthesis can be developed in practical ways into current or to-be-developed curricula of our participating institutions.

> **Readings:** Newton, (In Cohen and Westfall, Norton Anthology) excerpts from *Principia* pp. 221-238 (preface, definitions, laws of motion)

> **Laboratory 9:00 PM:** Telescopic Observations: St. John's observatory and additional provided telescopes.

Day 8:

> **Morning:** Readings: Newton, excerpts from *Principia* Book I, Book III (Rules, Phaenomena,, Moon proof. Law of Universal Gravitation. (in Cohen and Westfall, pp. 238-246; 257-273). We might use Sloan's commentary (emailed) on this material along with this.

> **Afternoon:** Newton, General Scholium. (pp. 339-341) Queries to the Opticks (pp. 184-190). Literary reactions to the Scientific Revolution: Donne, "Anatomie of the World," in First Anniversary, (website printout); Selections from Crowe Anthology: Pascal, *Pensées*; Milton, *Paradise Lost*; Addison, "Ode," and Young, "Night Thoughts."

Days 9-10   (Later dispersed to Day 5 and Day 10)

Review of curricula of schools in light of curriculum discussed, here. Discussions and suggestions by all participants will focus on two issues: (1) means of integrating the texts discussed into current courses, (2) suggestions from participating institutions for developing new humanistic curricula that utilize the insights gained from the experience with these primary texts.

NEH/ACTC Workshop

"Bridging the Gap Between the Humanities and Sciences"

Year Two

The University of Notre Dame

"Life: Origins, Purposiveness, and Transformations"

May 30, 2004-June 11, 2004
Opening Reception: Sunday, May 30

Day 1: Monday, May 31

This session looks at some great questions about the origins of the living state. It opens the workshop with a set of questions that will be followed through the various sections.

Morning: The Question of Origins

Readings:

>Plato, *Timaeus*, esp. 39e-48e; 72e-92c (Kalkavage edition)
>Genesis I, 1-11, NRSV.
>Empedocles, *On Nature*, trans. Freeman (Reader)

Afternoon: What is Life? Classical Reflections

Readings:

>Aristotle, *Parts of Animals* I.v, 644b25-646a (McKeon pp. 656-58)
>_____. *On the Soul*, Book II, chps 1-4 412a1-416b30 (McKeon pp. pp. 554-64)
>_____. *On Respiration* 470b1-475b10; 479b17-480b30.

(Reader) Galen, On the Natural Faculties, Selection from Book I, (Reader)

Evening: Lecture, Peter Kalkavage, "On the Timaeus"

Day 2: Tuesday, June 1:
The Ancient Debate: Are Organisms by Design or Chance?

Morning: Reflections on Chance and Design

Readings:

> Lucretius, *On the Nature of Things* Book I, Book V.
> Galen, *On the Usefulness of the Parts*, trans. M.T. May, Book VI. (Reader)

Afternoon: The Heart

Readings:

> Galen, *On the Usefulness of the Parts* Book VI, (Reader)
> Galen, *On the Natural Faculties Selection* from Book III (Reader) Vesalius, Selection from *Epitome on Anatomy* trans. L.R. Lind (Reader)

Laboratory: Dissection of the Heart, Lung and Trachea according to Galen.

Day 3: Wednesday, June 2:
"Life as a Mechanism"

Morning: Harvey on the Circulation of the Blood

Readings:

> Harvey, *On the Manner and Order of Acquiring Knowledge* (Reader) Harvey, *On the Motion of the Heart and the Blood,* trans. Willis. (Reader) Film: *William Harvey and the Circulation of the Blood* (Welcome Institute)

Afternoon:

Readings:

Descartes, *Discourse on Method*, Part V, *The Philosophical Writings of Descartes* Vol. 1 (Cambridge UP) pp. 131-41.

Descartes, *Selection from Treatise on Man.* pp. 99-108 (Cambridge ed) Lavoisier, Antoine "Experiments on Respiration (1777)" (Reader) Lavoisier and LaPlace, selection from "Memoir on Heat" (1780) (Reader).

Evening: Begin showing of film series *The Voyage of Charles Darwin* (7 parts) Parts 1-2-3.

Day 4: Thursday, June 3:
Nature as a Work in Progress

This session will be devoted to the issues of form, function and transformation. It will begin with readings and a laboratory on morphology and then move into the reading of the *Origin* in the afternoon.

Morning: "Form, Function and Transformism"

Readings:
> Selection from Aristotle, *Parts of Animals* I. chps i-iv (McKeon pp. 643-56.) Lamarck, selection from the *Zoological Philosophy* Part I (Reader)
> Cuvier, Selection from "Lectures on Comparative Anatomy" (1800) and "Natural History of Fishes" (1828). (Reader)
> Dissection Laboratory on the Squid and Fish

Afternoon: The Darwinian Transformation and Darwinian Transformism

Reading:
> Darwin, *On the Origin of Species* 1st ed. (Harvard U Press 1964), chps. 1-4.

Evening: Darwin Film Series Parts 4-5-6-7.

Day 5: Friday, June 4:
Darwinian Transformism continued
Morning:

Reading:
> Darwin, *Origin of Species*, chps. 9, 13, 14

Afternoon: Teams meet to discuss integration of what they have read and discussed to this point.

— WEEKEND BREAK —

Day 6: Monday June 7:
Humanity in an Evolutionary Universe
Morning:

Readings:
> Darwin, *Descent of Man*, 2nd ed. (1874), chps. 3,4,6,8, General Conclusion.

Afternoon: Evolution and Literature: Contrasting Views"

Readings:
> Tennyson, "In Memoriam." (1858). (Norton Critical Edition)
> Hardy, Poems "Hap" 1866, "Convergence on the Twain" and "In Tenebris" (Reader)

Day 7: Tuesday, June 8:
The Question of Inheritance Classical Mendelism
Morning:

Readings:
> Mendel, "Experiments on Plant Hybridization" (St. Johns College Edition) DeVries, Hugo, "The Law of the Segregation of Hybrids" (1900) (Reader)

Afternoon: Difficulties in Mendelism and the Theory of Chromosomes

Readings:

> Morgan, T. H. "Sex-linked Inheritance in Drosophila" (1910) (Reader)
>
> Sturtevant, "Linear Arrangement of Six Sex-Linked Factors in Drosophila" (Reader) Laboratory on Fruit-fly inheritance and Mendelian ratios.

Day 8: Wednesday, June 9:
Mechanism, Reductionism and Purpose:
The Contemporary Debate

The point of this final day of actual course work will be to return us to the issues of the first sessions and the "big questions" of form, function, and teleology.

Morning: Modern reductionism and the question of purpose:

Readings:

> Jacques Loeb, "The Mechanistic Conception of Life" (1912). (Reader).
>
> Roux, W. "Contributions to the Developmental Mechanics of the Embryo" (1885) (Reader) Driesch, H. "The Potency of the First Two Cleavage Cells" (1891) (Reader)
>
> Driesch, H. Selections from *The Science and Philosophy of the Organism* "introduction", "Elementary Morphogenesis," "Analytic Theory of Morphogenesis", "The Problem of Morphogenetic Localization" (Reader).

Afternoon: The Molecular Option:

Readings:

> Schrödinger, *What is Life?* (1945) (Cambridge U Press edition)
>
> Dorothy Wrinch, "On the Molecular Structure of the Chromosomes" (1936) (Reader)

Evening: Full Length BBC Film Life Story. This dramatizes the work of Watson, Crick, and Rosalind Franklin. It raises methodological and scientific issues, and it also develops in a complex and nuanced way the contribution of men and women to this development.

Day 9: Thursday, June 10:
The Double Helix and Beyond Morning:
Readings:

> Watson and Crick, the short 1953 papers. (Reader)
> Marjorie Grene, "Biology and the Problem of Levels of
>   Reality" (Reader) Kay, Lily "Life as Technology" (Reader)

Afternoon: Group Meetings and Assessment

Evening: Party & optional reading of selections of Jonathan Tolins' "eugenics" play, The Twilight of the Golds.

Day 10; Friday June 11:
Presentations about Past and Future
Curricula Developments

Overview of Next Year's Seminar.

2:30 PM. End Seminar.

NEH-ACTC

"Bridging the Gap Between the Humanities and Sciences"

Year Three

Location: Saint Mary's College of California "Technology, Art, Values, and the Problems of Technoscience"

The workshop this year will explore the connection between science and the humanities through the themes of nature and art, beauty and power, the good and the useful, and the goals and problems of a technological society.

Pre-Reading: Leon Kass, "Introduction" and Chap. 1 "The Problem of Technology and Liberal Democracy" in *Life, Liberty and the Defense of Dignity: The Challenge for Bioethics* (Encounter Books, 2004). This is to raise a set of general issues for this workshop.

— FIRST WEEK —

Day 1 (Monday):
Nature, Cause, Art as Know-How, and the Human Good

Morning:

Reading:
   Plato, *Gorgias*, (Nichols ed.)

Afternoon:

Readings:
   Aristotle, *Physics*, Book 2 (chapters 1-3, 8); *Nicomachean Ethics*, Book 1 (chapters 1-7), Book 6 (chapters 3-8); *Poetics*, chaps. 1-14, 25 (McKeon edition)

Evening: Lecture "Technology as Liberal Art," Phillip Sloan

Day 2 (Tuesday):
Invention, Beauty, and Divine Limits on Making
Morning:

Reading:
> Plato, *Timaeus*, 27c-29D; 35a-36B (Kalkavage edition)
> Laboratory on the monochord

Afternoon:

Readings:
> Cicero, "On Invention" Books 1-5 (p. 3–17), 7-9 (pp. 19-25),
> 11-14 (pp. 31-41) (Loeb Classical: also available as e-text)
> Dante, *Divine Comedy*, "Inferno," Cantos 1, 2, 5, 26, 34;
> "Purgatorio," Cantos 1, 10, 11, 12 (Mandelbaum –Bantam
> edition)
> Reynolds, *Discourses on Art*, "Discourse 7"

Day 3 (Wednesday):
Expanding *Technē*: The State as a Work of Art
Morning:

Reading:
> Machiavelli, *The Prince* (Mansfield Edition)

Afternoon

Reading:
> Shakespeare, *The Tempest* (Penguin)

Evening: Robert Weiner "Leonardo Da Vinci" (one-man act)

Day 4 (Thursday):
The Mastery of Nature

Morning:

Reading:
> Bacon, "The Great Instauration" and *New Organon*, Bk. I

Afternoon:

Reading:
> Bacon, *New Organon*, Bk. II, Aphs 1-21; *New Atlantis* (Hackett edition)

Day 5 (Friday):

Morning: Institutional Developments in Last Year and Planning for Next.

Afternoon: Laboratory on Genetic Mapping in Bacteria (Waring Blender Experiment)

Readings:
> Laboratory Outline in *St. Johns Manual: Evolution and Genetics*, pp. 187-201 plus separate laboratory writeup.
> First Reading of Jacob and Monod "Genetic Regulatory Mechanisms in the Synthesis of Proteins" St. John's Evolution and Genetics pp. 129-43.

— SECOND WEEK —

Day 6 (Monday):
The Critique of Mastery

Morning:

Readings:
> Jonathan Swift, *Gulliver's Travels* (opening Letter, "A Voyage to Laputa"); (St. Martins)
> Rousseau, *Discourse on the Arts and Sciences* (Hackett)

Afternoon:

Reading:
    Huxley, *Brave New World* (Perennial Classics edition)

Day 7 (Tuesday):
Making Scientific Facts

Morning:

Readings:
    Latour and Woolgar, *Laboratory Life*, chps 1-3 (Princeton)
    François Jacob and Jacques Monod, In *St. John's Manual*
    with Sloan detailed outline. Second detailed reading.

Afternoon: Laboratory on Results of Blender Experiment

Day 8 (Wednesday):
Science, Morality and Politics

Morning:

Readings:
    Franz Kafka, "In the Penal Colony" (Barnes and Noble)
    Hawthorne, "The Birthmark" and "The Artist of the
    Beautiful" (Dover)

Afternoon: Jonas, *The Imperative of Responsibility*, chps. 1-3

Evening: M. Frayn *Copenhagen*. (Group reading of the Play)

Day 9 (Thursday):
Technology and the Human Good

Morning:

Readings:
    Jonas, *The Imperative of Responsibility*, chps. 5-6
    Kass, Life, *Liberty and Pursuit*, chps. 3, 4, 5

Philip Kitcher, Science, *Truth and Democracy*, chps. 13–14 ("The Luddites Laments" and "Research in an Imperfect World")

Day 10 (Friday):

Review: Institutional Planning for use of Year 3 materials Discussion of all three years: Possibilities for future seminars.

End of Seminar

(Reports on progress were filed by all participating institutions and the results of these appear on- line at RESPONDEOBOOKS.COM, as "Report to the National Endowment for the Humanities on "Bridging the Gap Between the Humanities and Sciences: An Exemplary Education Project.")

PARTICIPATING INSTITUTIONS IN ACTC LIBERAL ARTS PROJECTS: 2002-2019

Trends in the Liberal Arts Core, Phase 2, ACTC cohort, 2002-2005

Aurora University

Averett University

Benedictine University

Brigham Young University

Drury University

Fresno Pacific University

Gonzaga University

Indiana Purdue University of Kokomo

James Madison University

Kentucky State University

Loyola College in Maryland

National University

St. Bonaventure University

St. Mary's College of California

St. Olaf College

Bridging the Gap Between the Humanities and Sciences Seminars, 2004-2006

Benedictine University

Mercer University

Norfolk State University

St. Bonaventure University

Saint Mary's College of California

St. Olaf College

Samford University

Seton Hall University

Truckee Meadows Community College

University of Dallas

Seminar leaders from:
St. John's College, Annapolis
University of Notre Dame

Tradition and Innovation Seminars, 2014 and 2016

Beijing Institute of Technology

Boston University

Chinese University of Hong Kong

College of Charleston

East London Science School

Hostos Community College/ CUNY

Leuphana Universitaet Lueneburg

Lewis & Clark College

Manhattan Christian College

Memorial University, Grenfell Campus

Midwestern State University

Morehead State University

Oxford College at Emory

Sacred Heart University

Universidad de Navarra

Universitat Internacional de Catalunya

University of British Columbia

University of Mary-Hardin Baylor

University of Dallas

Valparaiso University

Xiamen University

Seminar Leaders from:
Columbia University
University of Chicago
Yale University

Rejuvenating and Reinventing the Liberal Arts Seminar, 2019

Central College

Chinese University of Hong Kong

East London School of Science

Kinder Institute of Political Thought – University of Missouri

Universidad de Navarra

University of Dallas

Seminar Leaders from:
Carthage College
University of Dallas

ACKNOWLEDGEMENTS

I gratefully acknowledge the permission to reprint from the following sources:

"Cultural Institutions, Theatre and Humanistic Liberal Education: Reconsidering `Art' in Liberal Arts Education," published in the Journal of Interdisciplinary Studies XXVIII 2016: pp. 151-170. (Revised as Chapter 1 in this volume.)

"Enriching Liberal Education's Defense: Liberal Arts, Invention, and Technē" was first published in the St. Johns Review, Fall, 2014, pp. 14-47. (Revised as Chapter 7 in this volume.)

"Freedom, Arts and Sciences, Criticism in the Liberal Arts: an Aristotelian Perspective," in *Liberal Arts and Sciences and Core Texts in The European Context.* Ed. Emma Cohen de Lara and Hanke Drop. Vernon Press, Malaga, Spain, Wilmington, DE, 2017. (Revised as Chapter 10 in this volume.)

"Core Texts and Liberal Education," *The Encyclopedia of Theory and Practice of Education.* Ed. Michael A. Peters. Springer, 2017; an online encyclopedia. (Revised as Appendix 2 in this volume.)

Portions of Chapter 2, focusing on the poetic but not rhetorical aspects of Botticelli's work, first appeared in *Core Texts, Community, and Culture: working together in liberal education, "Art, Integrating*

Disciplines, and Liberal Education: Imagining the Possible with Botticelli" Eds., Ronald J. Weber et al. (10th Annual Conference of the Association for Core Texts and Courses, April 15-18, 2004. Dallas.), University Press of America, Lanham, MD, 2010, pp. 113-122.

The author, publisher, and editor wish to acknowledge and thank Adam Robinson of Good Book Developers—our book designer, electronic compositor, and proof editor—for his patient, careful, and excellent work.

J. Scott Lee, Ph.D. in the History of Culture, is the co-founder and retired Executive Director of the Association for Core Texts and Courses. He directed numerous national and international curriculum initiatives, founded the ACTC Liberal Arts Institute, researched the development of general and liberal education, and taught core text courses at Temple University and Saint Mary's College of California. This book represents the fruit of his research, organizing, and productive efforts on behalf of liberal arts education. His bachelor-of-arts degree is from St. Olaf College, was shaped by three majors, and included a Global Semester in Africa, India, and the Far East. His graduate degrees were earned at the University of Chicago.

Colophon

This book is set in Adobe Caslon, Carol Twombly's updated
version of the old-style typeface from the British engraver,
William Caslon I (d. 1766). The chapter and section numbers
are set in Trajan, also by Carol Twombly, inspired by writing
in ancient Roman texts.